What are people saying about Kingdom Triangle?

I profited greatly from reading *Kingdom Triangle*. J. P. Moreland is one of the keenest thinkers of our day; in this book he will challenge you and in the surprise ending perhaps provoke you. But if so it will lead to a very healthy discussion that is much needed within the evangelical church. A fine and thoughtful piece of work.

— Chuck Colson, founder, Prison Fellowship

Here's a compelling call for renewing the mind, replenishing the soul, and releasing the Spirit. This is vintage Moreland: passionate, practical, well-reasoned, and ultimately hopeful. It's an important book that must not be ignored.

— Lee Strobel, author, *The Case for the Real Jesus*

J. P. Moreland has a first class mind and a heart to match. I have watched him enter more deeply into the things of God's Kingdom over the past four years. *Kingdom Triangle* is an astute analysis of our culture and its mindset and a profound way forward, within it, for the evangelical church. I highly recommend it.

— Lance Pittluck, senior pastor of the Vineyard Church of Anaheim

J. P. Moreland reveals the hunger in each of us to be part of a grander story and systematically shows how postmodernism and naturalism fail to adequately address this hunger and to offer a coherent way of living. Moreover, he wisely observes that too often followers of Christ live as postmodernists and naturalists, lacking expectancy of God's intervention and the knowledge and spiritual formation necessary for true transformation. A powerful assessment of the Western church and cultural climate with practical, compassionate insights for the Christian journey.

— Ravi Zacharias, author and speaker

Moreland does an outstanding job challenging the believer to pursue happiness — not in the sense that our 21st century defines it, but rather in the classic sense. He takes the reader on a journey to pursue a life that is well lived, consisting of virtue and character, and one that manifests wisdom, kindness, and goodness. He maps out strategies for this journey with the ultimate end not being pleasurable satisfaction but instead, an end containing a deep sense of well-being.

— Ken Smitherman, president, Association of
Christian Schools International

This book is gutsy. As I was reading it, I felt like the proverbial frog in the simmering water getting a wake-up call about my spiritual life. This is a book that is, paradoxically, hard to put down and yet difficult to get through. J. P. points the long, bony finger of truth into the crevices of my mind, heart, and soul. This is a no-holes-barred tome on real spirituality. J. P. lays out an agenda for becoming a holistic Christian, and in so doing, he dons the garb of philosopher, psychologist, and pastor. Passion fills every page. You know that he lives this message! Not everyone will agree with everything that he says, but all will be challenged to think through their views and values. *Kingdom Triangle* is highly recommended. Strap yourself in and get ready for a great ride!

— Daniel B. Wallace, executive director, Center for the Study of New Testament Manuscripts; co-author, *Reinventing Jesus: How Contemporary Skeptics Miss the Real Jesus and Mislead Popular Culture*

This book reminds us to value both our minds and our "hearts," interests sometimes cultivated by different segments of the church. It also offers an essential wake-up call to many parts of the church skeptical of the Spirit's miraculous working today, activity clearly widespread in global Christianity and a major factor in the explosion of the gospel in many regions of today's world.

—Craig Keener, author of *Gift and Giver: The Holy Spirit for Today*

A longtime intellectual leader in the evangelical world, philosopher J. P. Moreland now urges churches to move forward to a fresh appreciation of the supernatural. While revealing the "thinness" of secularism, Moreland makes a persuasive case that a robust conception of biblical truth not only grounds the intellect, but also opens the door for miraculous healing and personal transformation.

—Nancy R. Pearcey, Francis A. Schaeffer Scholar, World Journalism Institute

KINGDOM
TRIANGLE

KINGDOM TRIANGLE

RECOVER THE CHRISTIAN MIND

RENOVATE THE SOUL

RESTORE THE SPIRIT'S POWER

J.P. MORELAND

ZONDERVAN.com/
AUTHORTRACKER
follow your favorite authors

Kingdom Triangle
Copyright © 2007 by J. P. Moreland

Requests for information should be addressed to:

Zondervan, *Grand Rapids, Michigan 49530*

Library of Congress Cataloging-in-Publication Data

Moreland, James Porter, 1948 –
    Kingdom triangle : recover the Christian mind, renovate the soul, restore the Spirit's power
/ J. P. Moreland.
    p. cm.
    Includes bibliographical references and index.
    ISBN-13: 978-0-310-27432-2
    ISBN-10: 0-310-27432-X
    1. Christianity – Philosophy. 2. Apologetics. 3. Philosophy and religion. 4. Naturalism –
Religious aspects – Christianity. 5. Postmodernism – Religious aspects – Christianity. I. Title.
BR100.M67 2007
230 – dc22

                                      2006034757

All Scripture, unless otherwise noted, is taken from the *New American Standard Bible.*
Copyright © 1960, 1962, 1963, 1968, 1971, 1972, 1973, 1975, 1977, 1995 by The Lockman Foundation.
Used by permission.

Internet addresses (websites, blogs, etc.) and telephone numbers printed in this book are offered as
a resource to you. These are not intended in any way to be or imply an endorsement on the part of
Zondervan, nor do we vouch for the content of these sites and numbers for the life of this book.

Interior design by Mark Sheeres

Printed in the United States of America

07 08 09 10 11 12 • 12 11 10 9 8 7 6 5 4 3

To

JIM and JEANIE DUNCAN,
KLAUS and BETH ISSLER,
PAUL and LISA WOLFE

Three couples who live and promote
the Kingdom Triangle

CONTENTS

Foreword by Dallas Willard 8

Acknowledgments 11

Preface 12

PART 1

ASSESSING THE CRISIS OF OUR AGE

1 The Hunger for Drama in a Thin World 17

2 The Naturalist Story 38

3 The Postmodern Story 64

4 From Drama to Deadness in Five Steps 91

PART 2

CHARTING A WAY OUT: THE KINGDOM TRIANGLE

5 The Recovery of Knowledge 111

6 Renovation of the Soul 141

7 Restoration of the Kingdom's Miraculous Power 165

Conclusion: Confronting the Crisis of Our Age 191

Postscript: Making New Friends 200

A Selectively Annotated Bibliography 203

Endnotes 218

Indexes 226

FOREWORD

J. P. Moreland helps us position ourselves for effective action on a number of issues vital to Christian faith in our times. Those issues gather around the one central question of whether or not the follower of Jesus has unique and indispensable knowledge to guide human beings today into life that is "life indeed." This is a book about *Christian knowledge.*

Knowledge has a unique and irreplaceable function in human life. Unlike any other human capacity, it authorizes individuals to act, to direct, and to teach, and the lack thereof disqualifies one in those same respects. This role of knowledge in human life is as ancient as humanity itself and still sustains itself throughout practical life, no matter what views may be aired in circles thought to be sophisticated.

You have *knowledge* of a certain subject matter when you are capable of representing it as it is on an appropriate basis of thought and experience. Providing that basis is the function of study, training, and — so one hopes — of education. Knowledge therefore lays the foundation for confident and successful dealings with reality and, as such, is one of the most precious things one can acquire. People "perish for lack of knowledge," as the Bible tells us, precisely because, without it, disastrous encounters, or lack of encounters, with reality are certain to occur; most importantly, they occur with reference to God, God's Kingdom, and any possibilities for an eternal kind of living.

Through most of Western history those identified with Christianity — in short, "the church" — were thought, and thought themselves, to possess a unique and indispensable *body of knowledge* about human life. This body of knowledge included specific teachings about how to live in God's universe in such a way that one would have a good or "blessed" life and become a truly good person, forever. This body of knowledge was thought accredited not only by special interventions of God into human history, but also, in many respects, by ordinary human thought and experience.

Because of a complicated sequence of processes and events, this position of "the church" as possessing and communicating such a body of *knowledge* about reality and human life was historically negotiated away.

Today you will find few among Christian leaders, even in Christian "higher education," who are prepared to say loudly in their professional contexts that their institutions are in possession of a body of knowledge for life that secular organizations do not have; much less will they teach what they teach *as* knowledge.

The causation back of all this is complicated. For one thing, the development of Christian traditions has managed to bring knowledge into opposition to faith and grace. But the valid contrast to faith is not knowledge, but "sight" or sense perception. In emphasizing that faith comes through grace, we must not make the mistake of thinking faith does not amount to insight into reality or that it has no involvement with "appropriate" thought and experience on the human side. Grace does not eliminate intelligent *effort*, though it does eliminate *earning*.

The "secular" world has, for its part, been busy *redefining* "knowledge" in such a way that knowledge of God and of the spiritual life are impossible. "Not scientific," and so forth! Of course, with that, almost everything of fundamental importance to human existence has also been eliminated from the field of "knowledge." Given what knowledge really is and does, however, *that* could not be tolerated. The "postmodern" reaction is to insist that "scientific" knowledge also is not knowledge in the traditional sense, involving truth and reality. Everything we call knowledge is considered, in that reaction, to be just a human construct for negotiating life within the range of present concerns. So all that is really left is politics and power. Political correctness is the only correctness left, and it is not a matter of being right, but of winning. The "best man" is always the one who wins. There's no other standard. That is pretty much where we stand today, even in many segments of the church.

If you will carefully work your way into what Moreland has to say about knowledge, you will be prepared to profit from his discussions of *spiritual formation into Christlikeness* and of *the life of Kingdom empowerment*, the other two points in his "Kingdom triangle." The knowledge issue comes first, for otherwise practicing Kingdom living will look weird and unapproachable. You have to understand that you are in a domain of reality and trustworthy knowledge, tested by multiplied thousands of pilgrims before you. Otherwise you will not be able sensibly and experimentally to begin to learn simple Kingdom life under the personal direction of Jesus. It is by stepping experientially into the practices of spiritual transformation and into the "with God" life of power beyond yourself that all the truths about

God and his Kingdom become truths about your actual existence. This is how you seek and find the Kingdom of God and his righteousness.

With clear insight and lucid explanations, Moreland puts the thoughtful Christian in a position to understand the issues swirling about us today and to return to a responsible presentation of "the way of Christ" as a way of knowledge, with all the rights and responsibilities accruing thereto. No one is better prepared by thought and experience to do this than Moreland. He writes for the nonspecialist, but the points hold up under the most thorough and critical examination. He knows about knowledge and about knowledge of the way of Christ. It is his life.

DALLAS WILLARD

Acknowledgments

I want to thank my faculty friends at Biola University for teaching me how to love God with my mind. In particular, William Lane Craig has been a constant inspiration to me in this area. I also thank Chris Linamen, Dallas and Jane Willard, along with John Coe and the Biola Institute for Spiritual Formation for guiding me into spiritual formation and the inner life. And I am so deeply grateful to Michael Sullivant, Sam Storms, and the brothers and sisters who make up our congregation at the Anaheim Vineyard Church for showing me that the supernatural power of God's Spirit and Kingdom is very, very real and available today.

Thanks to Stan Jantz for urging me to bring my thoughts together and put them in a book. Working with Katya Covrett at Zondervan has been a special joy. Her excellent and tireless work helped strengthen the book. Thanks also to Carlos Delgado for his editorial work on the manuscript. I also thank Dr. Craig Hazen and the Biola Christian Apologetics program for valuing all three aspects of the Kingdom Triangle. If you are looking for a place to grow in the Kingdom Triangle, sign up for this program! Many thanks to Eidos Christian Center and its members for freeing me up to write this book.

Finally, I am so very grateful to my friend Joe Gorra for proofreading the manuscript, developing the index, and helping with the bibliography and study questions. More than any other single individual, Joe has been a necessary condition for this book to appear. You served me with excellence and joy, my brother, and I thank you for it (and don't go to sleep again on my living room floor!).

PREFACE

The year 1974 was declared the Year of the Evangelical. Apparently no one was listening. The year came and went as our culture continued slouching towards Gomorrah. Fast forward to 2007. Islamic terrorism threatens our borders, our political discourse is shrill and spoken in sound bites, and an epidemic of pornography addiction threatens the very possibility of healthy relationships between men and women. People have to think twice about whether saving aborted babies or snail darters is more important. We can't agree about the sexual makeup of a flourishing family.

Spirituality is in, but no one knows which form to embrace. Indeed, the very idea that one form may be better than another seems arrogant and intolerant. A flat stomach is of greater value than a mature character. The makeup man is more important than the speech writer. People listen, or pretend to listen, to what actors—*actors!*—have to say! Western Civ had to go, and along with it, the possibility of getting a robust university education. Why? Because political correctness so rules our universities that they are now places of secular indoctrination, and one is hard-pressed to find serious classroom interaction from various perspectives on the crucial issues of our day. *The DaVinci Code*—I just can't go there.

What are we to do? In 1974, we Evangelicals were not ready to step into the vacuum and lead our culture to higher ground. And because the 1960s revolution had not been around long enough to do its damage, the culture was still living on the borrowed capital of a Christian worldview and could not sense the urgency to return to the faith once for all delivered to the saints. Today, we stand at a crossroad in the American Evangelical church. Since the mid 1800s, there has never been a greater window of opportunity for us to seize the moment and, by our lives and thought, to show our culture the way forward. Now is the time for us to stop being thirty years behind the times. Now is the time for us to gather our confidence and lead.

Signs indicate we are gaining momentum and may well be ready to manifest our Lord's true character in a way appropriate to the crisis of our age. Our Christian schools are already outperforming our secular counterparts. More and more churches are recovering our rightful role in racial reconciliation, in caring for the poor, and in being a presence of light in a dark place. There is a growing dissatisfaction with playing church. The Intelligent Design movement cannot be stopped. Christians have substantially recaptured lost ground in the discipline of philosophy in universities around our land. Rumors of miracles are starting to trickle out of our churches. We are figuring out that the Holy Spirit didn't die when the apostle John was martyred. Tools for spiritual formation are available as never before in my lifetime.

But the way forward is often murky to us, and in the pages to follow I want to shed light on the crisis of our age and the way out. I hope to provide an understanding of the times that will give you the courage to believe that a return to Jesus and life in his Kingdom is the only solution to this crisis. I also want to give you eyes to see the worldview issues that underlie the news, the entertainment industry, and the chaos and confusion all around us. Finally, I hope to envision for you and your church what I call the Kingdom Triangle—the essential ingredients for the maturation of the Evangelical community and the profundity of its presence in the general culture.

Because it may appear presumptuous for me to speak on these matters, permit me for a moment to speak as if insane (when Paul boasted to defend his right to speak with authority, he said he spoke "as if insane"; cf. 2 Cor. 11:23). I came to Jesus in 1968 in the midst of the sixties but more importantly in the center of the Jesus movement. I served with Campus Crusade for ten years and planted two Crusade ministries, including opening the ministry in the state of Vermont. Educationally, I was honored to study under Howard Hendricks during my Th.M. studies at Dallas Theological Seminary. Subsequently, I studied under Dallas Willard during my Ph.D. work in philosophy at the University of Southern California, and Dallas and Jane Willard have been mentors to my wife, Hope, and me for twenty-five years.

I have been in the ministry for thirty-seven years, I have planted two churches and pastored in two others, and my pastoral duties have ranged from the learning center, to small group leader, to pastor-teacher. I have spoken on around two hundred college campuses and in hundreds of churches in forty or so states, I have participated in twenty-five debates, and I have taught in three different seminaries over the course of twenty-seven years.

I am painfully aware of my inadequacies, and there is a scared little boy in me just as there may be a scared little boy or girl in you. I have been in

Christian therapy for three years and know many of my limitations (one of my limitations is that I don't know all of them!). My thirty-nine years of Christian experiences, study, and passion for God, along with countless hours of discussion with non-Christian thinkers and other Christian leaders, have given me enough of a background that I am starting to have something meaningful to say. Of course, you will be the judge of whether this book is among those meaningful assertions! But I cannot in good conscience before the Lord remain quiet about what I am seeing and thinking regarding the health and future of our community.

While I am at bottom an advocate of mere Christianity and, thus, have much in common with conservative Catholics and Orthodox believers, I am also convinced that Evangelical Protestantism of a supernatural kind is the best expression of Christianity available. Besides, no one listens to me outside that community! So I offer my community my deepest reflections on the crisis of our age and the way forward. I have done my best to be faithful to the message exploding out of me, and I regret that there are many things I have omitted. May God have mercy on me and on all of us!

With this in mind, I challenge you to gather into groups of fellow believers, to read and argue about the ideas that follow, and to find ways to put into practice the ideas you judge true and worthy. I hope that entire churches and parachurch groups will take this manifesto seriously. If you discover a more effective way forward as a result, then to God be the glory. After all, I have been mistaken before. In fact, I once thought I was mistaken about something, but later found out I was wrong. That fact alone guarantees that there is at least one mistake in this book.

I want to foment a revolution of Evangelical life, spirituality, thought, and Spirit-lead power. My purpose is to mobilize, inspire, envision, and instruct an army of men and women for a revolution on behalf of Christ. If this book contributes to that revolution, I will be thankful indeed. Make no mistake about it: The crisis of our age requires nothing less than a revolution of those who live in, proclaim, and seek to advance the Kingdom that was not made with hands.

PART 1

ASSESSING THE CRISIS OF

OUR AGE

CHAPTER 1

THE HUNGER FOR DRAMA IN A THIN WORLD

Helen Roseveare is a physician from Northern Ireland who has served as a medical missionary in Zaire, Africa, and the surrounding region for some time. Here, in her own words, is an eyewitness account about a hot water bottle. I would love to sit down with you and ask your honest, unfiltered reaction to this story. Your response would tell me a lot about you — specifically, whether you believe the naturalist, the postmodernist, or the Christian story. But I'm getting ahead of myself. These vastly different perspectives will be the focus of the next three chapters. For now, here is what Dr. Roseveare heard and saw. It's a bit long, but as you will soon see, it's well worth the time.

> One night, in Central Africa, I had worked hard to help a mother in the labor ward; but in spite of all that we could do, she died leaving us with a tiny, premature baby and a crying, two-year-old daughter.
>
> We would have difficulty keeping the baby alive. We had no incubator. We had no electricity to run an incubator, and no special feeding facilities. Although we lived on the equator, nights were often chilly with treacherous drafts.
>
> A student-midwife went for the box we had for such babies and for the cotton wool that the baby would be wrapped in. Another went to stoke up the fire and fill a hot water bottle. She came back shortly, in distress, to tell me that in filling the bottle, it had burst. Rubber perishes easily in tropical climates. "... and it is our last hot water bottle!" she exclaimed. As in the West, it is no good crying over spilled milk; so, in Central Africa it might be considered no good crying over a burst water bottle. They do not grow on trees, and there are no drugstores down forest pathways. "All right," I said, "Put the baby as near the fire as you safely can; sleep between the baby and the door to keep it free from drafts. Your job is to keep the baby warm."

The following noon, as I did most days, I went to have prayers with many of the orphanage children who chose to gather with me. I gave the youngsters various suggestions of things to pray about and told them about the tiny baby. I explained our problem about keeping the baby warm enough, mentioning the hot water bottle. The baby could so easily die if it got chilled. I also told them about the two-year-old sister, crying because her mother had died. During the prayer time, one ten-year-old girl, Ruth, prayed with the usual blunt consciousness of our African children. "Please, God," she prayed, "send us a water bottle. It'll be no good tomorrow, God, the baby'll be dead; so, please send it this afternoon." While I gasped inwardly at the audacity of the prayer, she added by way of corollary, "and while You are about it, would You please send a dolly for the little girl so she'll know You really love her?"

As often with children's prayers, I was put on the spot. Could I honestly say, "Amen"? I just did not believe that God could do this. Oh, yes, I know that He can do everything: The Bible says so, but there are limits, aren't there? The only way God could answer this particular prayer would be by sending a parcel from the homeland. I had been in Africa for almost four years at that time, and I had never, ever received a parcel from home. Anyway, if anyone did send a parcel, who would put in a hot water bottle? I lived on the equator!

Halfway through the afternoon, while I was teaching in the nurses training school, a message was sent that there was a car at my front door. By the time that I reached home, the car had gone, but there, on the veranda, was a large twenty-two pound parcel! I felt tears pricking my eyes. I could not open the parcel alone; so, I sent for the orphanage children. Together we pulled off the string, carefully undoing each knot. We folded the paper, taking care not to tear it unduly. Excitement was mounting. Some thirty or forty pairs of eyes were focused on the large cardboard box. From the top, I lifted out brightly colored, knitted jerseys. Eyes sparkled as I gave them out. Then, there were the knitted bandages for the leprosy patients, and the children began to look a little bored. Next came a box of mixed raisins and sultanas—that would make a nice batch of buns for the weekend. As I put my hand in again, I felt the … could it really be? I grasped it, and pulled it out. Yes, "A brand-new rubber, hot water bottle!" I cried. I had not asked God to send it; I had not truly believed that He could.

Ruth was in the front row of the children. She rushed forward, crying out, "If God has sent the bottle, He must have sent the dolly, too!"

Rummaging down to the bottom of the box, she pulled out the small, beautifully dressed dolly. Her eyes shone: She had never doubted! Looking up at me, she asked, "Can I go over with you, Mummy, and give this dolly to that little girl, so she'll know that Jesus really loves her?"

That parcel had been on the way for five whole months, packed up by my former Sunday School class, whose leader had heard and obeyed God's prompting to send a hot water bottle, even to the equator. One of the girls had put in a dolly for an African child—five months earlier in answer to the believing prayer of a ten-year-old to bring it "That afternoon!" "And it shall come to pass, that before they call, I will answer; and while they are yet speaking, I will hear." Isaiah 65:24[1]

What do you make of this? Your answer will depend, in part, on your worldview. If you are a *naturalist*, you're likely to think that the story is a fabrication. Dr. Roseveare is either a bald-faced liar or someone with such a desire to promote her religion that she is prone to exaggeration and the selective employment of a self-serving, faulty memory. Or maybe it's just a big coincidence. But a miracle? Nonsense! Such things are unscientific relics of an age gone by.

If you are a *postmodernist*, you may think that this is just wonderful for Dr. Roseveare, Ruth, the baby, and others close to the story. It's great that these people have their truth, but we all have our story that's true for us, and no one has a corner on this market. It would be intolerant and downright bigoted for Dr. Roseveare to force her beliefs on other people. The story may confirm Dr. Roseveare's truth, but there are lots of other truths out there.

If you are a *Christian*, you are either incredibly touched and encouraged at this kind act of God, or you are wearied by it. These things happen to other people, you may reason, especially to those on the mission field. They don't happen to my friends or me, so I can't really relate to the story.

Regardless of your worldview, if you read the story carefully and with feeling, there's something about it that's hard to dismiss—it is filled with *drama*.

WE HUNGER FOR DRAMA

It doesn't really matter who you are or what you believe. You love drama. In fact, you hunger for it. God made you—yes, *you*—to lead a dramatic life. No doubt you've had this experience at the mall: You are walking by the electronics section of a department store when you come upon a crowd of people gathered around a TV set. It's the bottom of the ninth inning, the home team is down by a run, the bases are loaded with two outs, and the team's leading hitter is at the plate. There's drama in the air and people are compelled to stop to see what happens. From romance novels to Harrison Ford movies to athletic events to tense moments on the evening news, people love to experience drama, even if only vicariously.

I got a taste for drama my senior year in high school. In ninth grade, I was the quarterback of the Grandview Junior High School football team that had one game left on the schedule. A victory—and we would have been the first undefeated team in school history. Though we had the best team, we lost the game on one fluke play to a school we hated: Lees Summit. Our senior year was payback time, and we had worked and waited three years for revenge. We always played Lees Summit the week before the last game of the season, and in my senior year, going into the game, we were tied for first place.

Since it was the biggest game of the week in the Kansas City area, the stadium was packed. As if we weren't excited enough, we learned before the game started that several players from the Kansas City Chiefs were in the stands. Talk about drama! In the face of all this excitement, we managed to stick to our game plan, which worked to near perfection. Lees Summit moved to within two points of us in the first play of the fourth quarter, but we tightened our defense, and they managed to run only two more plays the rest of the game—an incomplete pass and an interception. We went on to win 32–18 in, well, dramatic fashion.

Until my junior year in college, I remember longing for that kind of drama again, and I kept the game's memory alive and fed off it. I remember thinking: *If only life were like the Lees Summit game. If only there were a quest, a cause, a war, a real and important theater that commanded all I have and for which the stakes are high! Oh, how I wish life could be like that! Why is life so mundane? Why can't daily life be dramatic?*

My guess is that in your life you have had your own Lees Summit games, and I suspect you have had this same longing for drama, faint though its realization may seem when your life appears boring and you feel trapped. Many of us have seen a good movie, finished a great novel, or left an invigorating sporting event, only to return to a life we may consider drab compared to the supposed drama we have just experienced vicariously. It is precisely this convergence of two factors—a persistent hunger for drama and a feeling of boredom with our own lives — that creates an addiction to dramatic stories, media-driven celebrities, sports, or other vicarious substitutes for our own authentic drama. This tells us two things: We were made for greatness, but there is something about our culture that undermines both its intelligibility and achievement.

While the hunger for drama gives pangs to us all, our culture is unable to satisfy them. To repeat: *The current addiction to the cult of celebrity and professional sports, along with our preoccupation with happiness, tells us something about our true nature and the bankruptcy of our culture.* Allow me to explain.

HAPPINESS, DRAMA, AND THE CRISIS OF WESTERN CULTURE

In 1941, Harvard sociologist Pitirim A. Sorokin wrote a book entitled *The Crisis of Our Age.* Sorokin divided cultures into two major types: *sensate* and *ideational.* A *sensate* culture is one in which people only believe in the reality of the physical universe capable of being experienced with the five senses. A sensate culture is secular, this worldly, and empirical.

By contrast, an *ideational* culture embraces the sensory world, but goes on to accept the notion that an extra-empirical immaterial reality can be known as well, a reality consisting of God, the soul, immaterial beings, values, purposes, and various abstract objects like numbers and propositions. Sorokin noted that a sensate culture eventually disintegrates because it lacks the intellectual resources necessary to sustain a public and private life conducive of corporate and individual human flourishing. After all, if we can't know anything about values, life after death, God, and so forth, how can we receive solid guidance to lead a life of wisdom and character?

As we move through the early portion of the twenty-first century, it is obvious that the West, including the United States, is *sensate.* To see this, consider the following. In 1989, the state of California issued a new Science Framework to provide guidance for the state's public school science classrooms. In that document, advice is given to teachers about how to handle students who approach them with reservations about the theory of evolution:

> At times some students may insist that certain conclusions of science cannot be true because of certain religious or philosophical beliefs they hold.... It is appropriate for the teacher to express in this

regard, "I understand that you may have personal reservations about accepting this scientific evidence, but it is scientific knowledge about which there is no reasonable doubt among scientists in their field, and it is my responsibility to teach it because it is part of our common intellectual heritage."[2]

The importance of this statement lies not in its promotion of evolution over creation, though that is no small matter in its own right. No, the real danger in the Framework's advice resides in the picture of knowledge it presupposes: The only knowledge we can have about reality — and, thus, the only claims that deserve the backing of public institutions — is empirical knowledge gained by the hard sciences.

Nonempirical claims (those that can't be tested with the five senses) lie outside the hard sciences, such as those at the core of ethics, political theory, and religion; they are not items of knowledge but matters of private feeling. Note carefully the words associated with science: *conclusions, evidence, knowledge, no reasonable doubt, intellectual heritage.* These deeply cognitive terms express the view that science and science alone exercises the intellectual right (and responsibility) of defining reality. By contrast, religious claims are described in distinctively noncognitive language: *beliefs, personal reservations.*

In such a culture we now live and move and have our being. Currently, a three-way worldview struggle rages in our culture: between ethical monotheism (especially Christianity), postmodernism, and scientific naturalism. I cannot undertake here a detailed characterization of scientific naturalism — we will examine its nature and impact more thoroughly in chapter 2 — but I want to say a word about its role in shaping the crisis of the West.

Scientific naturalism takes the view that the physical cosmos studied by science is all there is. Scientific naturalism has two central components: a view of reality and a view of how we know things. Regarding the former, scientific naturalism implies that everything that exists is composed of matter or emerges out of matter when it achieves a suitable complexity. There is no spiritual world, no God, no angels or demons, no life after death, no moral absolutes, no objective purpose to life, no such thing as the Kingdom of God. Regarding the latter, scientific naturalism implies that physical science is the only, or at least a vastly superior, way of gaining knowledge. Since competence in life depends on knowledge (you can't be competent at selling insurance if you don't know anything about it!), this implies that there just is no such thing as learning to live life competently in the Kingdom of God. Spiritual competence is a silly idea.

Partly out of a reaction to naturalism, a second worldview — postmodernism — has come on the scene. Like a magnet, it's attracting more and more people, especially those in the arts and the humanities as well as the dilettantes of pop culture, by its mesmerizing power. Postmodernism is so important that we will devote an entire chapter to examining it (chapter 3). The following précis will suffice for now.

Because postmodernism is a loose coalition of diverse thinkers from several different academic disciplines, it is difficult to characterize it in a way that is fair to this diversity. Still, it is possible to provide a fairly accurate characterization of postmodernism in general, since its friends and foes understand it well enough to debate its strengths and weaknesses.[3] From a philosophical standpoint, postmodernism is primarily a reinterpretation of what knowledge is and what counts as knowledge. More broadly, it represents a form of cultural relativism about such things as reality, truth, reason, value, linguistic meaning, and the self.

In a postmodernist view, there is no such thing as objective reality, truth, value, reason, and meaning to life. All these are social constructions, creations of linguistic practices, and as such are relative not to individuals but to social groups that share a narrative. Roughly, a narrative is a perspective (such as Marxism, atheism, or Christianity) that is embedded in the group's social and linguistic practices.

Under the influence of naturalist and postmodern ideas, many people no longer believe that there is any ultimate meaning to life that can be known. These folks — and they are legion — have given up on seeking that meaning and instead are living for happiness. Today, the good life is a life of happiness, and it is the goal most people have set for themselves and their children. A major talk radio host has interviewed hundreds of people over the last few years by asking the question, "What did your parents want most for you — success, wealth, to be a good person, or happiness?" Eighty-five percent said "happiness."

"Happiness" is a good thing, all things being considered. But if it is overemphasized or made the focus of one's life, it leads to depression, a loss of purpose in life, and a deep-seated sense of fragmentation. In short, it ruins your life. Why? For one thing, there are more important things in life than being happy. There is a larger meaning and a bigger purpose that should be our life's aim. Put simply, we are wired for more than happiness. We are made to live for God's honor by learning how to become spiritually competent, mature members of his Kingdom and to make that Kingdom our primary concern. If happiness is what life is all about, then things like discipline, sacrifice, and their kin are intrinsically evil, or at least meaningless.

Tell that to Mother Teresa! Happiness may be a big deal to most people, but living for the cause of God and his Kingdom is bigger still. And such a life is preoccupied with a lot more than trying to be happy.

There's a second reason why happiness should not be the be-all and end-all of the human condition. This reason is what philosophers call the "paradox of hedonism": The contemporary sense of happiness (i.e., pleasurable satisfaction, feeling really good and stoked inside) cannot be found by seeking it. If you have ever tried to be happy, you know this is true. If you spend all your time trying to be happy, you end up focusing all your attention on yourself and how "happy" you are and, as a result, you become a shriveled self who can't live for some larger cause. Your life will center on yourself and your moment-by-moment focus will be on how you feel inside. Your sole criterion of evaluation for seeking a job, making friends, finding a spouse (or staying with a spouse!), and selecting a church will reduce to one overarching concern: How does this particular thing make me feel?

The best way to be happy in the contemporary sense is to forget about it, to try to live a good life for a bigger purpose, especially for the cause of Christ. If you do that, you will not be so worried about periods of unhappiness, and you will end up being happier than you would if you were preoccupied with happiness!

There are some sobering consequences to living within the framework of this pursuit. Parents view children as a means to their own happiness; couples see each other as a way to enhance their own pleasurable experiences; work is satisfying only if it makes me happy; even God himself exists merely as a means to make me happy. In short, the entire universe will revolve around my internal pleasure and me!

A Culture Filled with Empty Selves

My observations about happiness are not ivory-tower ruminations. I speak here with real gravity. For the first time in history a culture — ours — is filled with what psychologists refer to as the "empty self". The empty self (also called "the false self") is so widespread in Western culture that it is sometimes referred to as a cultural plague. According to psychologist Philip Cushman,

> the empty self is filled up with consumer goods, calories, experiences, politicians, romantic partners, and empathetic therapists.... [The empty self] experiences a significant absence of community, tradition, and shared meaning ... a lack of personal conviction and worth, and it embodies the absences as a chronic, undifferentiated emotional hunger.[4]

Most of us would recognize characteristics of the empty self among adolescents, and it would be wonderful if the problem left when teenagers became old enough to vote. Unfortunately, that is not the case. People continue to manifest features of the empty self well into middle age. It does not take a rocket scientist to observe that the features of the empty self simply make spiritual growth impossible. The path of discipleship and the life of an empty self mix like oil and water.

When people live for pleasurable satisfaction, they become empty selves and, because God did not make us to live for "happiness," their lives fall apart. Professor Martin Seligman is the nation's leading researcher on happiness. He has devoted much of the last thirty years of his life studying the topic.[5] Seligman has noted repeatedly that when people live for "happiness," they turn their attention inward and become shriveled selves who are anything but "happy." In 1988, Seligman found that in the span of one single generation—the Baby Boom generation—Americans experienced a tenfold increase in depression compared to earlier generations.[6] This is a stunning cultural shift, and it will be useful to us to find out what caused it.

According to Seligman, this massive shift resulted from the fact that Baby Boomers stopped imitating their ancestors, who tried to live for a cause—God, family, one's country—bigger than they were. Instead, Boomers began to spend all their energy on living for themselves and their own pleasurable satisfaction. The result? They lost any sense of giving themselves daily to the art of becoming a wise, virtuous person of character and living for a cause bigger than themselves. The shift from seeking character and living for a cause to being preoccupied with daily consumption of pleasurable satisfaction (i.e., the contemporary notion of happiness) brought with it a loss of both character and pleasurable satisfaction. Since 1988, study after study shows that things have grown steadily worse.

The lesson is this: Far from delivering pleasure and happiness, this strategy of living for self has brought about discontent and depression.

In other words, the naturalist and postmodern perspectives have undermined the objectivity of meaning to life and, ironically, have brought spoilage to happiness. But that's just one part of the story. Now let's consider what these worldviews have done to drama.

THICK AND THIN WORLDS AND THE REALITY OF DRAMA

Philosophers use a tool called "possible worlds" to aid in their thinking. Before you glaze over on me, there is an easy way to think of a possible world. *A possible world is simply a way things could have been.* Think of a possible world as an entire universe from beginning to end that God could have made. The world that's really here is a special possible world, namely, it's the actual world. But God could have created unicorns instead of goats, you could have gone into a different line of work than your actual occupation, and God could have given your parents a different set of children than the ones he actually gave them. In that case, you would not exist.

In all these cases, we can say there's a possible world with unicorns and no goats, one with you as a lawyer and not a schoolteacher, one where your parents have children that will never actually be born and in which you don't exist. By calling these "possible worlds," we don't mean that there's an actual place out there next to the real world in which unicorns but not goats exist, and if you're lucky you may get to go there someday. We are just using "possible worlds" as a convenient way of talking about how things might have been or, unknown to us, how they might actually be.

That said, it is important to ponder the fact that there are *thin* and *thick* possible worlds.[7] A "thin" world is one with no objective value, purpose, or meaning. It is a world that is just there; it wasn't made for some purpose. There's no real essence to what counts as a proper flourishing human life, and there's no life after death. Atheist Bertrand Russell (1872 – 1970) gives a nice description of a thin world:

> That man is the product of causes which had no prevision of the end they were achieving; that his origin, his growth, his hopes and fears, his loves and his beliefs are but the outcome of accidental collocations of atoms; that no fire, no heroism, no intensity of thought and feeling, can preserve an individual life beyond the grave; that all the labors of

the ages, all the devotion, all the inspiration, all the noonday brightness of human genius, are destined to extinction in the vast death of the solar system, and that the whole temple of man's achievement must inevitably be buried beneath the debris of a universe in ruins—all these things, if not quite beyond dispute, are yet so nearly certain that no philosophy which rejects them can hope to stand. Only within the scaffolding of these truths, only on the firm foundation of unyielding despair, can the soul's habitation henceforth be safely built.[8]

If the world is as thin as Russell claims—if there's no objective meaning or purpose to anything—it's hard to see why Russell thought it important to say so. Indeed, as Russell aged he acted as though he lived in a thick (and not a thin) world, in spite of what he claimed to have believed. That's why an aging Russell appeared on the cover of *Life* magazine as part of a protest movement against nuclear war. Perhaps consistency is the hobgoblin of little minds. In any case, Russell's statement nicely illustrates a thin world.

There are three disastrous implications of a thin world. First, nothing is important enough to rise above the level of a custom. In a fascinating televised interview with cannibalizing serial killer Jeffrey Dahmer just before he was murdered in prison, Dahmer articulately explained the process that lead him to a life of serial murder. Dahmer pointed out that we all have desires—for food, recreation, recognition—and that we will seek their satisfaction unless we have overriding reasons not to. As a teenager, the world became thin for Dahmer. He became an atheist who believed human beings evolved out of slime and that there was no God, no reason why any of us is here, no afterlife, and no judgment for what we have done in this life. Dahmer quite correctly could not find room for objective values in such a thin world and, as he explained, came to see moral rules as mere social conventions on the level of principles of etiquette for proper eating or dressing for different occasions. Social conventions were not weighty enough to constitute overriding reasons to refrain from seeking the satisfaction of his desires, and the rest is history.

Second, absent of objective and ultimate meaning, purpose, and value, there can be no real drama in a thin world. However, people are made in the image of God whether or not they acknowledge it, and the hunger to be part of some dramatic purpose bigger than they are will not go away. As a result, more and more people seek to satisfy the hunger for drama by attaching value to relatively meaningless events (such as the Super Bowl) or by living vicariously through their favorite celebrity (thus, the incredible popularity of *People* magazine and its imitators). Since these substitutes for real drama do not satisfy, like Edmund's ingestion of Turkish delight in *The Lion, the Witch and the Wardrobe*, they become addictive.

𝆑 As a result, society is increasingly populated by passive people whose greatest fear is not suffering but boredom. As Scott Peck noted, neurosis is always a substitute for genuine suffering. In today's "meaningless" milieu, that neurosis is usually incarnated in a desensitized, oversexed culture addicted to promiscuity and pornography that fails to satisfy our God-given longing for drama. Nowhere is this more evident than on the campuses of our anchorless universities. As 2001 Princeton University grad Laura Vanderkam stated in *USA Today*, "Hookups do satisfy biology, but the emotional detachment doesn't satisfy the soul. And that's the real problem—not the promiscuity, but the lack of meaning."[9] It takes discipline and sometimes suffering to avoid or escape addictions, sexual or otherwise. But there can be no real suffering in a thin world since the objective distinction between good and evil collapses and all that's left is the avoidance of boredom.

Third, in a thin world there is no objective difference between Mother Teresa and someone who devotes his life to being the best male prostitute he can be. Indeed, advocates of physician-assisted suicide make use of this fact. Atheist philosopher James Rachels is a leading advocate of active euthanasia and physician-assisted suicide.[10] According to Rachels, what gives us value is not the fact that we are human persons with intrinsic dignity. Rather, we have "value" to the extent that we have biographical lives. A person has a biographical life if and only if he has freely formulated goals, values, and objectives he finds meaningful from his own point of view and can pursue the realization of those goals in a way he finds satisfying.

Rachels applied this notion to the famous "Dax's case" involving Dax Cowart. In his early twenties Cowart suffered burns over 90 percent of his body. While pain management was appropriately administered, in the months following his accident Cowart repeatedly asked his physicians to kill him with a lethal injection. Rachels reasoned that the doctors should have complied because even though he was a human being, Cowart had lost his value because he no longer had a biographical life; that is, he no longer could pursue his freely chosen goals in a way he found satisfying. What were those goals and values? Cowart was a "ladies man" and a rodeo performer. After his accident, Cowart could no longer chase women, ride in rodeos, and go dancing; as a result, he had no moral value that required him to continue to live and doctors to refrain from taking his life.

It follows that if two people equally have biographical lives—if they each have plans, goals, and values that they equally (and arbitrarily) find important, and they can seek them in equally satisfying ways from their own (arbitrary) point of view—they and their life pursuits have equal value. In this thin world, there is no objective difference between the life aims of Mother Teresa and Dax Cowart. As long as you can "do your own thing," who's to judge? No one, if we live in a thin world. It's not hard to see how the absolutization of immediate gratification and desire satisfaction rapidly replaces a life of fidelity to objective truth and value in a thin world.

Now let's consider what a "thick" world is all about. A thick world is one in which there is such a thing as objective value, purpose, and meaning. In a thick world, some things really matter and other things don't. Some things have meaning, others don't. Mother Teresa's goals in life are better than those of Dax Cowart. Some things are right and others are wrong. You can lead a heroic life or waste it. The world in general, and human beings more specifically—and you in particular—were put here for a purpose.

The Muslim world is a thick world. That is, if Islam is true—if God is real, Allah is God, and the Koran is his word—people live in a thick world. Islam provides its followers with meaning and purpose and a cohesive worldview. Recently the president of Iran asserted, for example, "It is possible to prove in a debate which of the two political systems is a better choice for the world nations: the one that is established based on the norms of liberalism and has caused so many dilemmas and plight for the mankind, or the one that is established based on monotheism and justice." This statement reflects a thick worldview. The problem is that Islam is, on the whole, false, and its worldview is deeply flawed, though I cannot argue that point here. However, there is one worldview that is true and therefore superior to all others—thick or thin—and it provides the only hope of living in a thick world. I'm speaking of a Judeo-Christian worldview—more specifically, the worldview of mere Christianity.

When Truth Is Ignored

One burden of this book is to show what happens when the Christian worldview is replaced with naturalism and postmodernism, both of which present us with a thin world. I will also offer a vision for revitalizing the Christian worldview with power, authenticity, and deep reflection. For now, I merely note that because the centers of power in Western culture—the universities, public schools, major news media, movies, television, music, and other forms of contemporary art—are dominated by naturalism and postmodernism, they cannot sustain the drama necessary for their own work to have the meaning they so desperately desire. As a result, the centers of power in Western culture do not have the resources necessary to diagnose and properly solve the serious spiritual, economic, political, and moral problems of our age. Let me tell you a story that illustrates the cruel irony of the situation.

In 2002 I had been invited to a beautiful home in Orange County, California, to hear Daniel Pipes, who is an expert on Islam, deliver a lecture and field questions. A group of about seventy were present. It was a mixed group indeed, with outspoken secularists, conservative Jews, and a modest number of Christians. Pipes has taught at Harvard, the University of Chicago, and the University of Pennsylvania. He appears regularly on network and cable news such as ABC and CNN, and he is regarded as one of two or three of the world's leading experts on Islam, Muslim culture, and the Middle East. At that time, Pipes was a chief advisor to President Bush and was in regular communication with Colin Powell.

Pipes' central thesis was this: The United States in general, and President Bush in particular, must stop seeing our war as one against Muslim terrorists. Rather, it is against an extremist form of Muslim ideology that has to be fought ideologically as much as militarily. The ultimate solution, Pipes argued, is to use argumentation and propaganda to persuade Muslims to adopt the views of Western democracies and, thus, to embrace this form of government.

I was appalled. It wasn't that I rejected most of Pipes' view of the ideological nature of the conflict or his desire to see democracy spread to the Middle East. No, I was appalled at how poorly my fellow Christians grasped the undertow of what Pipes was saying, and I was shocked by what followed. When the question time began, I was the first to raise my hand. I pointed out that according to Yale law professor Stephen Carter, Western democracies are so secular that they tolerate religion as long as commitment to it does not rise above the level of a hobby.[11] Because of that, I argued, neither Pipes nor any other secular experts could bring themselves to say that the problem was Islam itself—a claim that, if true, implies that besides a military response, the ultimate "solution" is a missional one, not one the state is capable of providing.

Thus, Pipes was limited to saying that the problem is Muslim *commitment* to their religion, not the religion itself. The solution, then, is to create liberal *secular* democracies in which commitment to secular democracy should be more important than commitment to Islam. In short, the Muslims need to view their religion as a hobby. They are *too committed* to it for those like Pipes, who limit their discourse to what is judged appropriate if we live in a thin world.

I went on to argue that my observation was not merely of theoretical interest. In fact, two days earlier an editorial appeared in the newspaper comparing Evangelicals who oppose abortion to the Muslim terrorists. The point of comparison was that both groups took their commitment to their religion to be more important than their allegiance to the values of a secularized democracy. I finished by giving my punch line: I told Pipes that his analysis omitted one small thing — truth. What if Islam were true, Allah was the only true God, the Koran was his word, and jihad was mandated by Almighty God against the West? I am against the terrorists because I think Islam is false and their actions are immoral. But if I thought their understanding of Islam were true, I could not find fault with their actions.

It was as though Pipes thought I was from another planet. He never really responded to my punch line. Instead, he reasserted his original thesis in different words. Here was one of the leading thinkers on Islam and the Middle East who has apparently never given serious consideration to the truth claims of Islam. Do you see the implications of this? Regardless of his private religious views, Pipes seemingly has adopted a naturalist worldview and a thin view of the world along with it. In a thin world, religion is not the sort of thing that can be true. Religion is merely a cultural, social phenomenon to be analyzed by sociologists.

So understood, religion is a hobby to be subsumed under the demands of secular democracy, not something to be taken seriously. Assessing the truth claims of any religion — Islam or Christianity included — is beside the point. Some of Pipes' ideas seem right to me, but the implicit framework that underlies his approach (a framework that remained hidden from view even to Christians present) is a naturalistic worldview. But if a thin world is the most plausible implication of naturalism, then Pipes' own sense of drama for his work on behalf of the Bush administration does not really matter at the end of the day.

I am convinced that only if naturalism and postmodernism are rejected in favor of the perspective of the Kingdom of God and the worldview of Jesus of Nazareth and Holy Scripture, only then can we—you and me, Oprah Winfrey, Ted Turner, Barry Bonds, Daniel Pipes, and everyone else—escape the suffocating confines of a thin world and enter the dramatic riches of the only thick world that is true and can be known as such, the Christian "story."

Many people are resistant to this idea—and you may be one of them—because they see Christians as a whole as shallow, intolerant, and hypocritical. I agree that Christians haven't always done a good job of living out their faith with authenticity, love, and—dare I say—drama. However, if there is something wrong with the meat, you don't start by fixing the meat. You make sure the salt put in the meat is actually salty. Thus, the only way we are going to move from our boring lives to lives filled with the drama of the Greatest Story is for those who embrace mere Christianity to set aside the shallowness of their thought and the weakness of their spiritual practices, and corporately to enter afresh into Kingdom forms of life and thought worthy of the name of Christ.

I want to be a part of the solution and not part of the problem. How about you? I want to live a life filled with the kind of drama Helen Roseveare experienced in the heart of Africa. If you share my passion for playing a role in the drama of the Kingdom and its advance in the twenty-first century, then read on. I hope to give you eyes to see things you have not seen before, and I pray that God will give you the wisdom to know what to do about what you are going to see. In chapters 2–4 I will make explicit the current of ideas against which we Christians must swim. But before we can do that, we need to pick up some paddles.

Navigating Our Way through Worldviews

In 2 Corinthians 10:3–5, Paul describes the core of spiritual warfare as a struggle of ideas, a conflict of worldviews: "For though we walk in the flesh, we do not war according to the flesh, for the weapons of our warfare are not of the flesh, but divinely powerful for the destruction of fortresses. We are destroying speculations and every lofty thing raised up against the knowledge of God." Note carefully that we are to destroy fortresses—speculations, theories, patterns of ideas—raised against the *knowledge* of God. Such a task involves reasoning—argumentation of careful, savvy thought—and one of its main focuses is how knowledge itself is being depicted as it bears on knowledge of God. In turn, this requires the ability to think about worldviews.[12]

A person's worldview contains two important features. First, it includes the set of beliefs the person accepts, especially those about important matters such as reality, God, value, knowledge, and so on. But a worldview is more than just a set of beliefs. Consider, for example, this sentence: "The best time to visit Disneyland is in the fall during the week." It is not just a list of thirteen words. Rather, it is a grouping of words whose unity consists in the grammatical structure that occurs among them. Similarly, a worldview includes the rational structure that occurs among the set of beliefs that constitute it. Some beliefs are central and basic, while others are relatively peripheral.

In general, the more central a belief is, the greater would be the change in one's worldview if the belief were abandoned. Central beliefs support and give justification to more peripheral ones. Belief in the reality of God, the faithfulness and reliability of the Bible, and the deity and humanity of Christ are central to a Christian worldview. Less central are beliefs about local church structure, the nature of spiritual gifts, and so on. In understanding a worldview, it is important to grasp the relevant set of ideas along with the various support relations that take place among them.

While a worldview affects what one sees, it is a mistake to compare a worldview with a set of glasses. Here's why. Glasses stand between a person and the external world such that a person's access to reality is mediated *through* the glasses. One does not have direct access to reality itself. But it is wrong to place things between knowing and experiencing subjects and the real world, things like one's cultural, historical location, one's tradition, or one's worldview. One troublesome implication of such a model is that people can never correct their beliefs by comparing them to things themselves. Yet, as we will see later, people, including little children, do this all the time. A better way to describe the role of a worldview in seeing reality is to depict it as a habituated way of directing our attention or inattention, as the case may be.

Let me explain. One day a missionary spoke in the seminary chapel, and without telling us where they were taken, he showed a set of slides from a culture he had visited. He asked us to list on paper everything we saw. After we were finished, he spoke a while, and then put the slides up again and asked us to start with a fresh sheet of paper and list everything we saw this time. Interestingly, people's second list was virtually identical to their first one. Why? Because people tend to look to confirm what they already see and believe rather than adopt a fresh perspective and launch out from scratch. Over time, people fall into ruts and adopt ways of seeing things according to which certain features are noticed and others are neglected.

I'm not claiming this is a good or bad thing. I'm simply noting that it happens. I suggest that a worldview functions as a set of habits, forming background beliefs that direct our acts of noticing or failing to notice various features of reality. Depending on factors, this worldview function may yield accurate or inaccurate experiences and beliefs. It's not that we cannot see reality itself. In fact, through effort we can look at things from a different perspective and further confirm or disconfirm our previous viewpoint. Habit-forming beliefs do not stand between a person and reality as do glasses. Rather, they habitualize ways of seeing and thinking, which, through effort, can be changed or retained, on the basis of comparing them with reality itself.

You and I have lives to live, and we want to live them well. We hunger to find a role in a true, important drama and to play it well. If there is no such drama, I for one, would like to know that. Given these existential concerns as a backdrop, it is important that we do not analyze and evaluate different worldviews merely as an intellectual exercise. Too much is at stake. A person's actual worldview from which he lives and moves and has his being is the most important fact about that person. With this in mind, there are at least five important questions that should be put to any worldview:

What is real?

What are the nature and limits of knowledge?

Who is well-off? What is the good life?

Who is a really good person?

How does one become a really good person?

We are going to look at the worldviews of scientific naturalism and constructive postmodernism, respectively, in the next two chapters. Among other things, we will look at how they answer these five questions. I should warn you of something before we proceed. Chapters 2–4 may be tough sledding for you and, to be honest, I have intentionally written that way. Why? It's not that I have tried to be opaque and "academic" for academic's sake. Quite the contrary. It is part of my thesis that we Christians must grasp more deeply the worldview struggle in our culture and recapture a view of Christian teaching as a source of knowledge, not mere true belief accepted by blind faith.

To be consistent with my own thesis, therefore, I want to stretch you, to give you a treatment of worldview issues in which you can be confident. I want you to stand out among your secular friends and peers in the depth of insight you possess regarding our current crisis. It is precisely as a Christian that I want you to so shine. So prepare yourself for a journey through some deep waters. It will be worth it. Let's begin in earnest, then, and investigate scientific naturalism.

QUESTIONS FOR PERSONAL REFLECTION
OR GROUP DISCUSSION

1. This chapter begins with the dramatic account of Helen Roseveare. What is your honest, unfiltered reaction to this story?

   a. Contrast your initial response with your response after the author considered the account in light of a naturalist, postmodernist, and Christian perspective. Did anything change in your response? If so, how and why?

   b. Have an acquaintance read the story and see how he or she reacts with their worldview. How might a difference in reaction indicate a difference in worldview?

2. The author maintains that "a persistent hunger for drama and a feeling of boredom" creates an addiction to substitutes of authentic drama (pages 20–21). How and why do you think this is true?

   a. How does Pitirim Sorokin's distinction between "sensate" and "ideational" culture help explain this addiction? In what ways do you think that our culture is "sensate"? How does a sensate cultural emphasis privatize religious claims and beliefs?

   b. Observe your daily experience. Do you tend to live your life as if a sensate culture is best or as if an ideational culture is best?

3. A three-way worldview struggle rages in our culture between ethical monotheism (especially Christianity), postmodernism, and scientific naturalism. How do you see postmodernism and scientific naturalism championed in our sensate culture? Why is "happiness" often made the comprehensive focus of one's life in a sensate culture?

4. Making "happiness" the focus of your life is a morally and spiritually inadequate way to live well. What two reasons does the author give for this (pp. 23–24)? In light of these reasons, clarify for yourself what it means to be well-off, or to raise a family, or to grow a church.

   How would you advise a hedonist to see that there are more important things in life than being happy and that the pursuit of pleasurable satisfaction is itself unobtainable?

5. The pursuit of happiness as an end in itself has created an entire cultural plague of "empty selves" attempting to live meaningful lives in a sensate culture (page 25–26). What has been the net result of the proliferation of the empty self? What implication does this have for discipleship, apologetics, and evangelism?

6. Philosophers make a distinction between "thick" and "thin" possible worlds. What is meant by a "thin possible world," especially as atheist Bertrand Russell illustrates this?

   The author affirms that we are to live our lives as they are meant to be lived. Does this entail a thick or a thin world? If we live in a thick world, why do people live their lives as though they lived in a thin world? If we live in a thin world, what would it even mean "to live our lives as they were meant to be lived"?

7. Living in a thin world has at least three disastrous implications (pages 27–28). What is it like to live in a world where these implications are present? What images come to mind? Can you think of any stories, movies, or song lyrics that take any of these implications to be true of reality?

8. Religion has been marginalized in public policy thinking and decision-making. Assess how the author personally interacted with Daniel Pipes (page 30–31). How do you respond to the author's punch line: "I am against the terrorists because I think Islam is false and their actions are immoral. But if I thought their understanding of Islam were true, I could not find fault with their actions."

9. In 2 Corinthians 10:3–5, Paul describes the core of spiritual warfare as a struggle of ideas, a conflict of worldviews (page 32). What does this passage reveal about Paul's perspective of his life and its missional purpose? How does this passage clarify your view of spiritual warfare?

10. The author notes at least five important questions that should be put to any worldview: What is real? What are the nature and limits of knowledge? Who is well-off, or what is the good life? Who is a really good person? How does one become a really good person? (page 34). What are some answers that you or someone else could give to these questions?

CHAPTER 2

THE NATURALIST STORY

It is sometimes said that Western culture is living off the borrowed capital of a Judeo-Christian worldview and the loan is past due. This is a trustworthy saying, and there are at least two reasons why it is critical for Christians to understand why this is so.

First, a person will not look for ways to pay off a debt unless its existence is first acknowledged. We who love King Jesus hunger to penetrate our increasingly secularized culture with his power and majesty. We want to see him honored. We want people to become his disciples. This will not happen if we allow the culture to be dominated by opinions and attitudes that reduce the way of Jesus to a mere privatized hobby for those who need that sort of thing. As the great Evangelical scholar J. Gresham Machen warned nearly one hundred years ago,

> false ideas are the greatest obstacles to the reception of the gospel. We may preach with all the fervor of a reformer and yet succeed only in winning a straggler here and there, if we permit the whole collective thought of the nation or of the world to be controlled by ideas which, by the resistless force of logic, prevent Christianity from being regarded as anything more than a harmless delusion.[1]

We need a Christian community filled with disciples with eyes to see where the ideas of culture are moving, how they impact the cause of the gospel, and how we can bring a Christian worldview to bear on them. A good place to start developing those eyes is getting a vision of the intellectual debt our culture owes to a Christian worldview.

Second, Christians today need a lot more courage and confidence that what they have to offer is true, reasonable, and critical for a wide range of issues at the center of the public square. For too long we have looked for ways to insert a word about Jesus into cultural discourse that is largely secular, and we often lack the courage needed to speak up about our views without coming off as defensive on the one hand and arrogant on the other. One way for employees to develop confidence about their company's product is to learn of its widespread value. Similarly, by understanding just how powerful and pervasive a Christian worldview is, we Christians can gain an attractive sort of confidence needed to bring honor to the Lord we love so much.

To illustrate the need for Christians to learn to think, see, and live in light of their worldview, consider the following incident taken almost at random from daily life. Some time ago, Elizabeth Vargas, who was anchoring the evening news on ABC, did a story on Rick Curry, who was selected Person of the Week. In a deeply moving way, the segment described how Curry had developed a theater for the disabled. Curry regularly directs plays in which the actors are all disabled people who, under ordinary circumstances, would never have the opportunity to do such a thing. Curry's activities have been a huge success for everyone involved, most of all for the disabled people themselves. When asked why these theater performances have been so successful in helping the disabled, Curry noted that it gave them a feeling that they were part of something bigger than themselves. They derived a sense of value and worth from their involvement even if it was only for a short period of time.

You must understand that it is not easy to justify the real, intrinsic value of Curry's activities in light of every worldview available. On a Christian worldview, there is, in fact, a larger framework in which objective meaning in life exists, human persons have intrinsic value, and so on. Given that this worldview is true, Curry's activities make incredible sense and provide a model that people should imitate.

But what if some thin worldview is true — specifically, scientific naturalism? What if there is no meaning in life? What if we are just modified monkeys who have appeared as a result of a blind process of chance and necessity? What if values are just cultural epiphenomena of the mindless processes of evolution? If naturalism is true, then Curry's behavior is like those who continued to play cards while the Titanic sank. Why not select a greedy Wall Street mogul as Person of the Week instead of Curry? In fact, why select a *person* of the week instead of, say, the dog or cat of the week? If the mainstream media are largely secular and naturalistic in orientation, it is a sad irony that stories like Curry's pepper the news produced by people without the worldview resources needed to make ultimate sense of them.

In this chapter, I will explain the dominant worldview of Western culture, scientific naturalism, and unpack some of the implications that most reasonably follow from this thin perspective. By doing so, I hope to give you some tools for understanding the times and for increasing your courage to use them in spreading the Kingdom and living more dramatically on its behalf. My primary purpose is to expose naturalism for what it is, not to provide an apologetic critique of it. But from time to time I will criticize an aspect of naturalism if I think it can be done briefly and helpfully.

The Worldview of Scientific Naturalism

Naturalist philosopher David Papineau boldly proclaims that "nearly everybody nowadays wants to be a 'naturalist.'"[2] What do Papineau and others of his persuasion mean by scientific naturalism? Philosopher John Post provides a helpful answer:

> According to a number of influential philosophers, the sciences cumulatively tell us, in effect, that everything can be accounted for in purely natural terms [the naturalist theory of knowledge]. The ability of the sciences to explain matters within their scope is already very great, and it is increasing all the time [the naturalist creation story]. The worldview this entails, according to many, is *naturalism*: Everything is a collection of entities of the sort the sciences are about, and all truth is determined ultimately by the truths about these basic scientific entities [a physicalist view of reality].[3]

Scientific naturalism (naturalism for short) includes three key elements:

1. a theory of the nature and limits of knowledge
2. the Grand Story, a creation story about how everything came into existence, a story described in natural scientific terms with a central role given to the atomic theory of matter and evolutionary biology
3. a physicalist view of reality, according to which everything that exists is either physical or else it depends necessarily on the physical for its emergence and continued existence

For most naturalists, the ordering of these three ingredients is important. Frequently, the naturalist theory of knowledge serves as justification for the naturalist creation story, which, in turn, helps to justify the naturalist's view of what is real. Regarding the naturalist theory of knowledge, whatever exists should be knowable by third-person scientific means.

Regarding the Grand Story, one should be able to show how anything taken to exist can be accounted for in terms of a naturalist history of the cosmos. That history amounts to a series of events beginning with the Big Bang to the present, governed by natural law in which various physical parts (subatomic particles, atoms, molecules) come together to form aggregate wholes with increasingly complex physical structures.

How does a naturalist decide what exists? There are three constraints for developing a naturalist view of what is and is not real. Before some alleged entity should be taken as actually real:

1. It should be capable of being known within the limits of the naturalist view of knowledge.
2. Its origin should be capable of explanation in terms of the Grand Story.
3. It should be an object that is either fully describable in the language of chemistry and physics or that can be shown to depend necessarily on facts that are fully describable in the language of chemistry and physics.

These claims will become clearer as we examine more fully the three key elements of naturalism.

THE NATURALIST THEORY OF KNOWLEDGE

In the early 1960s, naturalist Wilfred Sellars announced that "in the dimension of describing and explaining the world, science is the measure of all things, of what is that it is, and of what is not that it is not."[4] Naturalism begins with a view about the nature and limits of knowledge known as scientism. Scientism comes in two forms: strong and weak. *Strong* scientism is the view that we can only know things that can be tested scientifically. According to strong scientism, scientific knowledge exhausts what can be known; if some belief (for instance, a theological belief) is not part of a well-established scientific theory, it is not an item of knowledge. *Weak* scientism admits that some claims in fields outside of science (like ethics) are rational and justified. But scientific knowledge is taken to be so vastly superior that its claims always trump the claims made by other disciplines. *The first component of naturalism, then, is the belief that scientific knowledge is either the only kind of knowledge there is or an immeasurably superior kind of knowledge.*

Years ago I was invited to speak at an evangelistic dessert and I was put on notice by one believer that he was bringing his boss, a man who had been a chief engineer for decades, who was finishing a belated Ph.D. in physics from Johns Hopkins University and who went out of his way to attack and ridicule Christians. Upon being introduced to me at the dessert table, he wasted no time launching into me. "I understand you are a philosopher and theologian," he said in an amused manner. Before I had a chance to respond, he said, "I used to be interested in those things when I was a teenager. But I have outgrown those interests. I know now that the only sort of knowledge of reality is that which can and has been quantified and tested in the laboratory. If you can measure it and test it scientifically, you can know it. If not, the topic is nothing but private opinion and idle speculation!" This is what I mean by scientism. It never occurred to the gentleman that his claim was self-refuting since it could not itself be "quantified and tested in the laboratory."

Scientism accords the right to define reality and speak with knowledge and authority to scientists and scientists alone. This posture is, sadly, pervasive throughout our culture. In the June 25, 2001 issue of *Time* magazine, the cover story was entitled, "How the Universe Will End." The universe is winding down, it says, and will eventually go out with a cold, dark whimper. It never occurred to the writer that if something is winding down, it must have been wound up, and if something is wound up, there has to be a winder-upper!

But for those with eyes to see, the article's claim about the fate of the universe is not the main issue of concern. Rather, it's the article's implicit epistemology (theory of knowledge). It claims that for centuries, humans have wanted to know how all this will end, but because they could only use religion and philosophy, solid answers were unavailable. But now that science has moved into this area of inquiry, for the first time in human history, we have firm answers to our questions, answers that will force religion and philosophy to rethink its views.

This is scientism, and *Time* magazine employed the naturalist epistemology without batting an eye or, indeed, without knowing it was doing so. In the same issue, *Time* featured an article defending stem-cell research on human embryos: "These [embryos] are microscopic groupings of a few differentiated cells. There is nothing human about them, except potential—and, if you choose to believe it, a soul."[5] Note the presupposed scientism: We *know* scientific facts about embryos, but nonscientific issues like the reality of the soul are not items of knowledge. When it comes to belief in the soul, you're on your own; there is no evidence one way or another. You must choose arbitrarily or, perhaps, on the basis of private feelings what you believe about the soul. In a scientistic culture, belief in the soul is like belief in ghosts — an issue best left to the pages of the *National Inquirer*.

Remember the Columbine high school massacre on April 20, 1999? For the next week and a half, the entire nation was in search of something: knowledge. We sought answers for why this sort of thing was breaking out among our adolescents. To whom did we turn for answers? Scientists. A few days after the tragedy, the cover of *Newsweek* featured a story in which neurophysiologists offered opinions on the role of brain chemistry in the event. Night after night, Peter Jennings, Tom Brokaw, and Dan Rather interviewed sociologists, psychiatrists, and other scientists, probing them for knowledge.

Ministers were involved in the weeks following the tragedy, but their role was limited to providing comfort to the families and others. To my knowledge, no theologian, no ethicist, no minister was asked to provide insight or knowledge about the cultural matrix surfaced by the massacre. It was as though the ministers were allowed to sing the national anthem before the real game began and were whisked off the field so scientists could warm up for the game itself.

The scientistic epistemology of naturalism is pervasive in the university, the public schools, and the media. As a result, other forms of knowledge are regarded by the average citizen as either nonexistent or vastly inferior to science. This not only gives science incredible authority to define reality for all of us, it also causes believers to wonder if science has in some way discredited their Christian beliefs. Speaking of the negative impact of secularism, of which scientism is a part, Dallas Willard notes that

> the crushing weight of the secular outlook ... permeates or pressures every thought we have today. Sometimes it even forces those who self-identify as Christian teachers to set aside Jesus' plain statements about the reality and total relevance of the Kingdom of God and replace them with philosophical speculations whose only recommendation is their consistency with a "modern" [i.e., contemporary] mindset. The powerful though vague and unsubstantiated presumption is that *something has been found out* that renders a spiritual understanding of reality in the manner of Jesus simply foolish to those who are "in the know."[6]

THE GRAND STORY: THE NATURALIST CREATION ACCOUNT

The scientifically, indeed, the culturally authorized story of how all things came about revolves around the atomic theory of matter and evolutionary theory. As Phillip Johnson observes,

> the materialist story is the foundation of all education in all the departments in all the secular universities, but they do not spell it out. It is,

> In the beginning were the particles and the impersonal laws of physics.
> And the particles somehow became complex living stuff;
> And the stuff imagined God;
> But then discovered evolution.[7]

According to the atomic theory of matter, all chemical change is the result of the rearrangement of tiny parts—protons, neutrons, and electrons. According to evolutionary theory, random mutations are largely responsible for providing an organism with a change in characteristics; some of those changes provide the organism with a survival advantage over other members of its species; as a result, the organism's new traits eventually become ubiquitous throughout the species.

This story is deterministic in two ways. First, the state of the universe (and everything in it, including you) at a particular time and the laws of nature are sufficient to determine or fix the chances of the next successive state. This is temporal determinism. Second, the features and behavior of ordinary-sized objects like glaciers, rocks, human beings, and animals are fixed by the states of their atomic and subatomic parts. This is bottom-up or parts-to-whole determinism.

It is important to note the relationship between the naturalist theory of knowledge and its creation story: Most naturalists believe that the physical cosmos is all there is, was, or ever will be because their creation story is allegedly the only one that claims the backing of science.

This relationship explains the widespread anger and loathing for Intelligent Design (ID) theory. I think the evidence for naturalistic evolutionary theory is meager. However, even if we grant (for the sake of argument) that there is a decent amount of evidence for evolution, the degree of certainty claimed on its behalf and the widespread negative attitude toward Intelligent Design are beyond what is warranted by the evidence alone. Regularly, opponents of Intelligent Design resort to name calling ("Intelligent Design is merely a tool of the Religious Right to force their social agenda on the rest of us"), silly slogans ("Intelligent Design is just old-fashioned creationism dressed up in a tuxedo"), and "arguments" repeated in mantra-like fashion that indicate that they have not really read ID literature ("There's no scientific evidence for or against God because religion and science are two completely different things that should be kept separate"). What is going on here? Why are these dialog-stagnating red herrings dragged before us with monotonous regularity when those dragging the bait should know better?

The answer lies in the scientism that underlies the debate. The widely accepted intellectual authority of science, coupled with the belief that ID theory is religion (rather than science), means that evolution is the only view of the origin of life that can claim the backing of reason.

If two scientific theories are competing for allegiance, then most intellectuals, at least in principle, should be open to all evidence relevant to the issue. But what happens if one of two rival theories is considered scientific and the other is not? If we abandon the scientific theory in favor of the nonscientific one, given the sole intellectual authority of science, this is tantamount to abandoning reason itself. Because many think that ID theory is religion masquerading as science, the ID/naturalistic evolution debate turns into a controversy that pits reason against pure subjective belief and opinion. In the infamous creation–science trial in Little Rock, Arkansas, in December 1981, creation science was ruled out of public schools, not because of the weak evidence for it, but because it was judged religion and not science. Today, in the state of California, you cannot discuss ID theories in science class for the same reason.

As I write this, the media are focusing great attention on the debate about Intelligent Design. In fact, when I picked up this morning's paper, I found a two-paged feature story entitled "Intelligent Design Debate Heats Up."[8] The article cites lay Catholic theologian at Georgetown University, John F. Haught, as opposing ID theory as bad science and bad theology. According to Haught, just as different explanations can be proffered for why water is boiling (the kinetic energy of water molecules are responding to heat, and as evidence someone wants tea), so evolution can be seen as both the result of natural selection and part of God's purposes.

I disagree with Haught about the scientific and theological merits of ID theory, but he is entitled to his opinion. If ID theory is bad theology and bad science, then so be it. What troubles me, however, is that Haught and others who opt for theistic evolution seem to do so with little appreciation for the emergence of scientism in our culture and its impact on people's perception of the availability of theological, ethical, and political knowledge. Theistic evolution is intellectual pacifism that lulls people to sleep while the barbarians are at the gates. In my experience, theistic evolutionists are usually trying to create a safe truce with science so Christians can be ~~left alone~~ to practice their privatized religion while retaining the respect of the dominant intellectual culture.

I am not interested in that posture. ~~I don't want to play not to lose; I want to play to win.~~ I want to win people to Christ and to "demolish strongholds" (NIV) that undermine knowledge of God (2 Cor. 10:3–5), to penetrate culture with a Christian worldview, and to undermine that culture's plausibility structure, which, as things stand now, does not include objective theological claims. While there are exceptions, many theistic evolutionists simply fail to provide a convincing response to the question of why one should adopt a theological layer of explanation for the origin and development of life in the first place. Given scientism, theistic evolution greases the skids toward placing nonscientific claims in a privatized, make-believe realm in which their factual, cognitive status is undermined. Thus, inadvertently, Haught and those of his persuasion contribute to the marginalization of a Christian worldview.

The Naturalist View of Reality

The picture of reality that results from this creation story (which is, in turn, the only story alleged to have the support of scientific ways of knowing) is physicalism: The physical, material cosmos is all there is, was, or ever will be. Everything that exists is either physical or can be shown to emerge of necessity from the physical when it is in a suitably complex arrangement. The naturalist view of reality is either reductionist or eliminativist: What you cannot reduce to (identify with) the physical you must eliminate, pretend that it does not exist.

Unfortunately, physicalism is woefully inadequate to account for the world as it really is. Here are four things that exist that cannot be reduced, eliminated, or adequately explained in a physicalist view of reality:

Consciousness. You can't get something from nothing, in this case, mind from matter, so if you start with matter and simply rearrange it according to natural law, you will end up with increasingly complex arrangements of brute matter. But consciousness will not come to be. Atheist philosopher Paul Churchland acknowledges:

The important point about the standard evolutionary story is that the human species and all of its features are the wholly physical outcome of a purely physical process.... If this is the correct account of our origins, then there seems neither need, nor room, to fit any nonphysical substances or properties into our theoretical account of ourselves. We are creatures of matter. And we should learn to live with that fact.[9]

Secondary qualities. Primary qualities—size, shape, mass, location, being in motion or at rest—are those thought to characterize matter. Secondary qualities are features like colors, smells, tastes, sounds, textures. As with consciousness, if you start with matter bereft of secondary qualities and your creation account tells a story about the rearrangement of matter into increasingly complex structures, there will be no account of the origin of secondary qualities (and, no, color is not a wavelength of light! The two may be correlated, but they are different!).

Interestingly, secondary qualities are what make the world fun and interesting—imagine a world with no smells, colors, or tastes. Christian thinkers like John Locke explained their existence theologically: It was God's good pleasure to put them into his world because they make the world beautiful and pleasant. This is, indeed, the most rational explanation for secondary qualities. Naturalists are unable to provide any explanation of irreducible secondary qualities.

Normative properties. Normative properties give their owners intrinsic value. There are three kinds of normative properties: ethical (goodness, rightness), aesthetic (beauty), and intellectual (being rational, being good evidence). Naturalism can describe only what is the case, not what ought to be the case. It can (allegedly) account only for how things are, not how they should be.

The Grand Story itself. Why is there any physical universe at all? Why did the initial conditions of the Big Bang take place? Why are the laws of nature as they are? Why are the fundamental and fine-tuned constants of nature what they are? Since the Grand Story includes a beginning to time (the Big Bang), what caused it? Don't bangs have to have bangers? These are legitimate questions, queries that can be explained if there is a God but which have no explanation within the constraints of naturalism.

People pretend that there are no serious implications for individual and social life that follow from accepting a naturalist worldview. Nothing could be further from the truth. In this case, you cannot have your cake and eat it too. Let's look at some of the important implications of taking the naturalistic turn.

CRUCIAL IMPLICATIONS
OF A NATURALIST WORLDVIEW

The worldview of naturalism presents a thin world. Accordingly, a number of troublesome results are most naturally taken to follow from it. Some naturalists pretend to accept these results and not to be bothered by them. Others say they are bothered but live as if they aren't. Still others, such as one of my atheist professors in graduate school, see the implications and commit suicide. Many can't face these implications, so they try to fiddle with naturalism so as to avoid them, but these adjustments are contrived, ad hoc, and entirely unconvincing.

As we saw in chapter 1, there can be no real drama in a thin world because such a world does not exhibit the features necessary for objective meaning to life. Indeed, secularized folk are truly at a loss when it comes to giving an intellectually satisfying and psychologically livable view of the meaning of life. A number of years ago, *The Rocky Mountain News* featured a story on the meaning of life by exhibiting several prominent answers to the question "What is the meaning of life?"[10] Here were some of the answers:

> "Life is a slow walk down a long hall that gets darker as you approach the end."
>
> "If there is meaning in life, maybe the purpose is to find it."
>
> "Well, my goodness! 'What is the meaning of life?' you ask. What is the 'meaning' in your question? And whose life? A worm's? Or yours? In any case, enjoy it."

The first response is a trivial, superficial answer to a crucial question. The second response is incoherent and circular. The third response is so general and inadequate that it could be satisfied by Adolph Hitler, as long as he enjoyed his hideous life.

At the end of the day, the naturalist answer to the question doesn't get much better than a slogan I recently saw in a Valvoline commercial: "You're born, you die; in between, you work on cars." There are six key factors that must occur if there is to be rich, objective meaning to life that can be known and realized in our lives. Naturalism fails to provide a satisfying account of these factors.

1. *Free will to ground responsibility, creativity, praise, and blame.* Most commonsense folk know that freedom is incompatible with one's "actions"

being determined by factors outside their control. If a scientist planted an electrode in your brain and could cause your body to move by hitting the right button, then if he caused your arm to move and a person's face was hit, you would not really be responsible, nor would you be the proper object of blame. Only if we are the ultimate source of our actions, only if the buck stops with us, only if we can act without those "acts" being caused by factors outside our control are our actions free and meaningful.

But as we have already seen, human actions are determined in a naturalist worldview such that there is no room for freedom. Thus, as naturalist philosopher John Searle says, "our conception of physical reality simply does not allow for radical [libertarian] freedom."[11] According to naturalist John Bishop, "the idea of a responsible agent, with the 'originative' ability to initiate events in the natural world, does not sit easily with the idea of [an agent as] a natural organism.... Our scientific understanding of human behavior seems to be in tension with a presupposition of the ethical stance we adopt toward it."[12] Finally, Cornell professor William Provine flatly asserts that "free will as traditionally conceived ... simply does not exist. There is no way the evolutionary process as currently conceived can produce a being that is truly free to make choices."[13]

Among the reasons for incarcerating people — rehabilitation, deterrence, protection of society, and punishment — only the first three make sense in a naturalist view of things. Genuine retributive justice is a thing of the past. Naturalist philosopher Daniel Dennett tries to preserve a remnant of retributive punishment on a naturalist view, but his solution may fairly be taken as a reductio ad absurdum against naturalism (if naturalism implies Dennett's absurd view, then naturalism is false).[14]

Dennett acknowledges that both alcoholics and child abusers are equally determined to act as they do by forces outside their control. If we wish, we can continue to peel back the layers of people engaged in each action and find the genetic or other determining factors producing the behavior. Still, we draw a metaphysically arbitrary line between the two, and we hold child abusers and not alcoholics responsible for their behavior, preferring to treat the latter as a disease. What justifies us in drawing the line where we do? Dennett explicitly appeals to a utilitarian justification, claiming that it maximizes the greatest amount of good for the greatest number of people (e.g., it serves to deter other acts of child abuse) if we act *as if* child abusers are responsible but the same cannot be said for alcoholics.

Utilitarian justifications of this sort are inadequate for several reasons, not least of which is that, if accepted, they justify horrendous moral evils. Thus, suppose a serial rapist is active in a major city and, as a result, many people are needlessly worried and anxious insofar as the odds of their being a victim are small. As a result of this worry, scores of women limit their activities and stay cooped up at home and, further, a small number of divorces take place because of the increased tension throughout the city. Under these conditions, it could easily maximize utility if the police catch and punish an innocent homeless man, keep what they have done as a secret, and continue to look for the real criminal.

In the meantime, such an act will deter other crimes by sending a message of police competency, it may deter the serial rapist himself, and it calms numerous people who are needlessly worrying; it will also prevent other harmful effects like broken homes. Remember, the police keep all of this a secret as they continue to look for the real rapist; if caught, they will frame him for a different crime. No one will know the difference. Punishing an innocent man could maximize the common good and, given a utilitarian view of justice, human rights, and punishment, it could easily be the right thing to do. But no matter how useful, it is wrong to punish an innocent man in this way, and utilitarianism is the worse for suggesting otherwise.

2. *Real intrinsic value that can be known and factored into our lives.* If your life is to have objective meaning, then three things must be true regarding value. First, some things have to be intrinsically good, right, reasonable, and beautiful. There have to be ends in themselves, things of worth for their own sakes. Second, human faculties have to be such that we can grasp and know what is and what is not intrinsically valuable. Part of what makes human life objectively meaningful is the knowledgeable, deliberate attempt to be about good and to defeat evil. Finally, human actions, projects, relationships, products, and humans themselves must be among the items that have intrinsic value. In grounding meaning to life, it would be of no help if there were intrinsic value in the cosmos that was utterly unrelated to human beings.

Naturalists cannot give an adequate account of these three factors. I will address the relationship between intrinsic value and human beings below, so let's set this issue aside for the moment. Regarding the existence of intrinsic value, Bertrand Russell's depiction of the universe cited in chapter 1 is the most consistent one for a naturalist to adopt. The universe and we are just here. The history of the universe is a history of mere descriptive facts that does not include the appearance of prescriptive, intrinsic value.

As J. L. Mackie, one of the leading intellectual atheists of the twentieth century, noted: "Moral properties constitute so odd a cluster of properties and relations that they are most unlikely to have arisen in the ordinary course of events without an all-powerful god to create them."[15] Mackie's naturalistic "solution" was to opt for subjectivism about values—a solution, I suppose, that the Los Angeles rioters following the Rodney King beating could have nicely appropriated had they taken the time to read Mackie.[16]

Regarding our ability to know what has intrinsic value, the various brain mechanisms relevant to human behavior in general, and rational and ethical behavior in particular, are what they are because they aided (or at least did not hinder) their possessors in adapting to recurring problems over the long course of evolutionary history in feeding, reproducing, fighting, and fleeing, which in turn, aided their possessors in the struggle for differential reproductive advantage. The blind processes of evolution selected sensory and mental faculties apt for interacting with the sense perceptible world so organisms could survive to live another day.

However, the ability to be aware of intrinsic value goes far beyond sense experience and, in any case, the accurate perception of value would be epiphenomenal in a world whose successive states are governed by the laws and states of physics. Thus, as evolutionary naturalist Michael Ruse notes,

> morality is a biological adaptation no less than are hands and feet and teeth. Considered as a rationally justifiable set of claims about an objective something, ethics is illusory. I appreciate that when somebody says "Love thy neighbor as thyself," they think they are referring above and beyond themselves. Nevertheless, such reference is truly without foundation. Morality is just an aid to survival and reproduction ... and any deeper meaning is illusory.[17]

3. *The ability to acknowledge the reality of evil, provide an explanation of its origin, and offer hope that it is ultimately redeemed and defeated.* Suffering and evil are real. A satisfying view of meaning to life must not dismiss evil as an illusion, and it must offer a rational account for hope in the midst of suffering, hope that the suffering can be of ultimate significance. But the naturalist can offer no account of how there could be such a thing as real evil, much less offer hope in the midst of it.

To see this, consider the fact that evil is when things are the way they are not supposed to be, or they aren't the way they are supposed to be. Neither a rock nor a colorblind child can see red, but only in the latter case is there an evil defect precisely because it is a situation in which things aren't the way they are supposed to be. Now we quite literally say that a carburetor on an automobile can function properly or be dysfunctional, and when we say the latter, we are saying that it isn't functioning the way it is supposed to function. And when we say that, we are stating that it isn't functioning the way it was designed to function. The most plausible account of evil requires reference to a Designer.

Naturalists cannot help themselves to this depiction of the nature of and grounds for proper functioning, the good life, and real evil. While not all naturalists agree about the nature of morality and the good life—how could they when it is hard enough to have any clear room for objective value in a naturalist view of things?—many tough-minded naturalists opt for a view of morality that Daniel Callahan calls "minimalist ethics": One may act in any way one chooses so far as one does not do harm to others.[18] Unfortunately, such an ethic draws too sharp a distinction between public and private morality, it reduces humans to isolated moral atoms who create their own moral universe, and it deprives us of meaningful and true ways to discourse about the good life of virtue in its individual and communal forms. Other naturalists follow Alasdair MacIntyre and take virtues and the good life of human excellence to be mere expressions of value relative to one's culture and tradition (presumably, not Nazi culture) or to one's private beliefs and choices (presumably, not Jeffrey Dahmer's.)[19]

As for hope in the midst of suffering, about all the naturalist can say is that stuff happens, we do the best we can to deal with it, and that's the end of the matter. Charles Darwin noted in his *Autobiography*:

> [Consider] ... the view now held by most physicists, namely that the sun with all the planets will in time grow too cold for life, unless indeed some great body dashes into the sun and thus give it fresh life.... Believing as I do that man in the distant future will be a far more perfect creature than he now is, it is an intolerable thought that he and all other sentient beings are doomed to complete annihilation after such long-continued slow progress.[20]

This is hardly a robust word in a world where people need real, sensible hope to cope with suffering. In such cases, people regularly assure themselves by saying that things happen for a reason and, thus, there must be a redemptive reason for this suffering. But such a claim is empty and delusional in the thin world of naturalism.

4. *Human beings must have equally intrinsic value simply as such.* Speciesism is, allegedly, a form of racism, which amounts to an unjustified bias toward the value of your own species. Apparently, only humans can be guilty of it. But as Helga Kuhse and Peter Singer have noted, the most plausible way to justify the claim that humans have intrinsic value as such, that they have equal value as humans, and that humans have greater value than other biological beings, is to argue that humans were created in the image of God. Given that this is false, they claim, it is racist to continue to assert these theses.[21]

Indeed, it is not clear how, on a naturalist view, humans have *any* value at all as human beings. If Darwin's point above is correct, then we current humans have less value than future humans and, in fact, may be properly treated as means to the end of evolving greater creatures. We stand in relation to future products of evolution as amoebas stand in relation to us. Indeed, scientists John Barrow and Frank Tipler draw precisely this conclusion.[22] They argue that humans are just one fleeting stage in evolutionary development that is moving toward higher and higher life forms. All intermediate stages from amoebas to humans have only instrumental value as they contribute to later stages. Earlier stages do *not* have intrinsic value. In fact, Barrow and Tipler claim that it is only the DNA program *in* humans that has intrinsic value, and we exist to perfect that program to bring about future life.

A popular naturalist move is to say that we get our value by being persons and not by being humans, and naturalists offer various criteria for personhood: self-awareness, self-control, a sense of the future, ability to make plans, ability to relate to others, and so forth. But apart from the fact that such a move merely helps itself to the existence of intrinsic value with no naturalist justification for it, it suffers from three further difficulties.

First, the selection of such criteria is itself speciesist. How curious it is that persons select criteria of personhood instead of criteria like adaptability and longevity that favor bacteria and insects. Second, vulnerable people at the edges of life, who are still bearers of the image of God, fail to have value on these criteria. Finally, the criteria are degreed properties, like the property of being cloudy—something does not merely have the property; rather, it possesses it to a greater or lesser degree. Humans do not equally possess self-awareness, the ability to formulate plans, and so forth. This would mean that we should not all have equal rights; indeed, according to these criteria, half the freshmen at Biola University would fail to qualify as persons during finals week! But any account of objective meaning to life must recognize that we humans are fundamentally relational beings and that rich relationships flower only in the soil of equal value. It is only if we can rationally believe that we are all equal in a fundamental sense that genuine, flourishing community is possible.

5. *There must be teleology (things that happen for a purpose or future goal) and purpose in the cosmos relevant to human life.* The ascendancy of naturalism in the West squeezed out the so-called teleological outlook. What Newton did to motion at the transition into the eighteenth century, Darwin did to living organisms in the nineteenth century and B. F. Skinner did to humans and their actions in the twentieth century. Let me explain.

Aristotle distinguished an efficient from a final cause. An efficient cause is that by means of which an effect is produced. When ball A moves ball B, A is the *efficient* cause of B's motion. A *final* cause is that for the sake of which an effect is produced; that is, Ball A was made to hit ball B in order to put B in the side pocket. We can cite efficient causes for what makes water boil and we can refer to final causes when we give the reason why it is boiling (e.g., to make tea). Teleology refers to something taking place for an end, a purpose, a goal, a final cause.

Aristotle claimed that objects move in order to reach their proper location. He did not mean they did this consciously; he simply thought that a principle of teleology was embedded in material objects. Newton rejected final causes for motion and explained motion by way of efficient causes in terms of the force of gravity. Darwin did the same to living organisms and their parts. Instead of explaining the eye's existence and nature as being there in order for the organism to see, Darwin told a story about the eye coming to be what it is solely in terms of efficient causes — mutation, variation, natural selection. Drawing to a climax the long war against teleology in human action started by Freud, B. F. Skinner and others of the early and mid-twentieth century claimed that no one really acts for the sake of an end. Instead, actions are efficiently caused by various motives, drives, and so forth.

Newton's perspective seems to me to be fair enough, though chemists do talk of chemical change taking place in certain ways *in order to* distribute charge most widely or to reach the most energetically feasible state. But the shift with Darwin and Skinner are hard sells, indeed. Contemporary Darwinist Richard Dawkins acknowledges that biologists must be vigilant to keep in mind that the things they study that seem to have been made for a purpose really are not. I leave to your reflection whether or not you have ever really acted for the sake of an end, but you may wish to start by asking why you are reading this book.

It is fair to say that efficient and final causality can both be true, but such a response misses the point. Final causality is not at home in a naturalist worldview. As philosophers Joshua Hoffman and Gary Rosenkrantz note, attempts to slap teleology onto a naturalist framework really amount to the abandonment of naturalism:

> Aristotle's account [of natural function and teleology] does *not* provide a naturalistic reduction of natural function in terms of efficient causation. Nor do characterizations of natural function in terms of an irreducibly emergent purposive principle, or an unanalyzable emergent property associated with the biological phenomenon of life, provide such a reduction. Theistic and vitalistic approaches that try to explicate natural function in terms of the intentions of an intelligent purposive agent or principle are also nonnaturalistic. Another form of nonnaturalism attempts to explicate natural function in terms of nonnatural evaluative attributes such as intrinsic goodness.... We do not accept the anti-reductionist and anti-naturalistic theories about natural function listed above. Without entering into a detailed critique of these ideas, one can see that they either posit immaterial entities whose existence is in doubt, or make it utterly mysterious how it can be true that a part of an organic living thing manifests a natural function.... The theoretical unity of biology would be better served if the natural functions of the parts of organic life-forms could be given a reductive account completely in terms of nonpurposive or nonfunctional naturalistic processes or conditions.[23]

In my view, this admission applies to other naturalist attempts to adjust their worldview in order to avoid untoward consequences—for example, to embrace moral realism and irreducible intrinsic value within a naturalist framework. Such attempts are ad hoc and contrived. They do not follow naturally from their worldview. And they are question-begging in light of Christianity as a powerful alternative.

If there is no purpose, no goal, no end in the cosmos, then the same must be said for human life and action. The late Harvard evolutionist Stephen Jay Gould understood this. When asked why we are here, he gave this reply:

We are here *because* one odd group of fishes had a peculiar fin anat-
omy that could transform into legs for terrestrial creatures; *because*
the earth never froze entirely during an ice age; *because* a small and
tenuous species, arising in Africa a quarter of a million years ago, has
managed, so far, to survive by hook and by crook. We may yearn for a
"higher" answer — but none exists. [italics mine][24]

I doubt that Gould really yearned for a higher answer because he goes
on to say that his views are actually liberating and exhilarating. One of my
philosophy professors at USC gave essentially Gould's take on meaning in
life, and he finished class by saying that the lack of ultimate purpose and
meaning was liberating to him because it meant that he could do anything
he wanted to without worrying about any ultimate consequences of his
actions. This attitude may not have characterized Gould, but I suspect it is
true of no small number of naturalists.

Note carefully that the question put to Gould — "Why are we
here?" — is an irreducibly teleological one. The questioner is asking, "Is
there some purpose or end for the sake of which we are here?" But Gould,
understanding clearly the implications of Darwinian naturalism, did not
answer this question. Instead, he changed the subject and told an efficient
causal story of how we got here (the italicized words in his statement all
cite efficient causes). That's the best a naturalist can do.

That said, it is ironic that when Gould's funeral was reported in the
newspaper, all his naturalistic friends employed teleology to eulogize his life:
He lived *in order to* combat ignorance, promote genuine science education,
and defeat creationism. Here is the unavoidable hunger for drama, a hunger
that can be neither explained nor satisfied in a naturalist worldview.

6. *There must be a satisfying answer to the question "Why should I be
moral?"* An adequate philosophy of life should include an answer to the question of why one should be moral. But the question "Why should I be moral?"
needs clarification. Three points should help to clarify the question.

First, one can distinguish specific moral acts (an act of kindness or of
self-sacrifice) from what philosophers call the moral point of view. The
question "Why should I be moral?" is really asking, "Why should I adopt
the moral point of view?" Thus, it is important to understand what the
moral point of view is. If you adopt the moral point of view, then you do
the following: You subscribes to normative judgments (judgments about
what is right and wrong, about what you should and should not do) about

actions, things (persons, the environment), and motives; you are willing to universalize judgments (if something is right or wrong for me, then it is right or wrong for everyone in a morally relevant situation); you seek to form moral views in a free, unbiased, enlightened way; you seek to promote the good.

In other words, if you adopt the moral point of view, you submit to and seek to promote the dictates of normative, universalizable morality in a mature, unbiased, impartial way. You embrace the dictates of morality and seek to live in light of the moral point of view. Such a viewpoint governs your life and priorities. So understood, the question "Why should I be moral?" becomes the question, "Why should I adopt the moral point of view as a guiding force over my life?"

Second, you can distinguish between motives and reasons for adopting the moral point of view. Regarding the former, the question is asking what motivates you to adopt the moral point of view. Motives do not need to be rational factors. For example, you could say that you are motivated to adopt the moral point of view because it gives you approval with your parents and with society or simply because of a certain urge or feeling to do so. Regarding reasons, the question is asking what rational justification can be given for adopting the moral point of view. The question is usually framed in terms of reasons, but both reasons and motives are relevant to a full discussion of why one adopts the moral point of view.

Third, it is not clear what kind of justification the question is seeking. What kind of "should" is involved in "Why should I be moral?" If it is a moral "should," then the question is asking for a moral justification for adopting the moral point of view. If a moral "should" is used in the question, then some philosophers think that the question involves a pointless self-contradiction. For you are then asking for a moral reason for accepting moral reasons. In other words, if you are using a moral "should" in the question, then you are already reasoning from within the moral point of view, since you are already willing to acknowledge a moral answer to a moral question. But if you have already adopted the moral point of view, then there is not much point in asking for a moral reason for doing so.

About the only answer you could give to the question posed would be that it is simply morally right to adopt the moral point of view. But if you are willing to adopt the moral point of view because such an act is morally right, then you have already adopted the moral point of view without knowing it. So the question "Why should I be moral?" is not really using a moral sense of "should," and if it is, the only answer is that such an act is just the morally right thing to do.

But there is a different notion of "should" that is better suited as a part of the question. This is a *rational* sense of "*should*." According to this sense of "should," you are not asking the question "Why should I be moral?" from within the moral point of view, but from outside the moral point of view altogether. In other words, you are asking the question: "What rational justification can be given to me as to why it would be reasonable for me to adopt the moral point of view rather than some other point of view, say, an egoistic, self-interested point of view where I govern my life for my own best interests without regard for the moral point of view at all?" As you seek to formulate a *rational life plan* for yourself, a well thought-out, reasonable approach to the way you will live your life so as to be a rational person, why should the moral point of view be a part of that rational life plan? In sum, the question "Why should I be moral?" is asking for the motives, but more importantly, the reasons why someone should adopt the moral point of view as a part of a rational plan of life.

Part of the rational assessment of an ethical theory or, more generally, an entire worldview is the evaluation of the answer that theory or worldview provides to the question "Why should I be moral?" Different answers have been given to the question, but the two most prominent have been the egoistic and theistic replies. Naturalism cannot give a satisfying answer to the question, and the most fitting naturalist response is the egoistic one. Roughly, the egoistic response says that you ought to be moral just in case it is in your best interests to do so. But this answer is inadequate because it really says that you should fake caring about morality as long as such faking pays off; otherwise, you should just set morality aside when that pays off.

In one way or another, theistic responses incorporate reference to the existence of God. For example, you ought to be moral because the moral law is true and is constituted by the nonarbitrary commands of a good, just, wise, and loving God or because the moral law is grounded in the way we were designed by such a God to function properly. For the Christian, we should be moral for the same reason that a car should be driven on the road and not on the bottom of the ocean. That is the proper, true, flourishing way we're made to function, and by so functioning we get in touch with reality and bring honor to our wonderful Creator.

NATURALISM AND OUR FIVE CRUCIAL QUESTIONS

We have seen why naturalism is a thin worldview. I want to close this chapter by putting our five crucial questions to naturalism to provide a capstone to our analysis of its inadequacies.

1. What is real?
2. What are the nature and limits of knowledge?
3. Who is well off? What is the good life?
4. Who is a really good person?
5. How does one become a really good person?

Naturalism implies that the physical world is all there is; that knowledge occurs only or most ideally within the bounds of the senses and the methods of science; that the good life is whatever you freely choose for yourself, for example, a life of social recognition and success (most likely, financial, academic, or artistic success); that a really good person is one who is true to his or her own ideals (whatever they are) and is tolerant of others; and there is virtually no advice given for how to become a good person.

In light of these five questions, naturalism is exposed as the shallow, destructive fraud that it really is. By contrast, the worldview of Jesus provides deep, satisfying, true answers to these questions. For Jesus, the basic reality is the Triune God and his wonderful Kingdom. We have knowledge of a wide variety of things, including theological and ethical knowledge. The well-off person is anyone who is alive in the Kingdom of God, irrespective of his or her life's circumstances. The good person is the one who is pervaded with agape love and who manifests the fruit of the Holy Spirit (love, joy, peace, patience, kindness, goodness, faithfulness, gentleness, and self-control, Gal. 5:22–23). The way to become a good person is to enlist as an apprentice of Jesus in Kingdom living.

By comparison with naturalism, it becomes obvious that the way of Jesus is the only game in town! Today, Jesus stands at the center of the world and its history, just as he predicted he would. Jesus simply towers over any other figure in world history. In the last fifty years, his church has experienced the greatest expansion in two thousand years, and there are no signs that this harvest is going to slow down.

While I have offered criticisms of naturalism from time to time, that has not been my main purpose. I have done that elsewhere.[25] My purpose has been to make plain the implications of the worldview that now dominates our universities, public schools, and the media. Naturalism is a razor-thin worldview, and one would think that its bleakness would cause cultural leaders to reexamine the thick worldview of Christianity. But many have refused, opting instead for a second thin worldview that, together with naturalism and Christianity, is in a three-way race for the hearts, minds, and souls of our families, friends, and social institutions. It is more slippery than naturalism, but we will try to get a hold of it in the next chapter.

Questions for Personal Reflection or Group Discussion

1. What do you understand by *naturalism*? What are its characteristics? How do media pundits and the intellectual class often exhale naturalism whenever they comment on human experience, values, the origins of the universe, pain, suffering, and justice? Bring to your group at least one example of naturalist thinking you have found in the media.

2. Naturalism's theory of knowledge (epistemology) is called *scientism*. What is scientism? What reasons and evidence could be given to support what is wrong with scientism? How and where were you exposed to naturalism and scientism? How have you inhaled its ideas?

   Why is scientism so culturally pervasive and attractive to so many people? Does this epistemology strike you as arrogant and condescending? If you were to adopt this epistemology, would it be conducive to freely and virtuously evaluate beliefs, reasons, and evidence that are either independent of, or contrary to, naturalism?

3. Naturalism's epistemology acts as certainty to its creation story, which is proffered by a naturalistic evolutionary theory (pages 44–46). Its epistemology and creation story discount or diminish the likelihood of moral and theological knowledge as an authoritative explanation for the origin of the universe. Do you find naturalism to be amiable to considering what is real? Do you think that theistic evolution (at least of the John Haught sort) does a better or worse job at being amiable to following the evidence where it leads?

   Assess your own worldview. Do you have explanations that are "bootstrapped" to a particular epistemology, such that you do not allow yourself to consider and evaluate all the relevant data or evidence concerning what, how, and why something is the case?

4. The author presents four things that exist but that cannot be reduced, eliminated, or adequately explained in a physicalist view of reality: consciousness, secondary qualities, normative properties, and the Grand Story itself (page 47). Interact with each of these. Compare and

contrast what are their similarities and differences. Can you think of other things that exist but that do not submit to physicalism's view of reality?

If physicalism is true, how can one explain what is the good, the lovely, and the beautiful? If there are things that do exist but that defy physicalism's epistemology and metaphysic to say that they exist, is it intellectually responsible to still maintain a commitment to physicalism? Why or why not?

5. Is human freedom incompatible with one's "actions" being determined by factors outside their control (see pages 49–50)? For example, what is meant by "freedom" or "free will"? Why is "determinism" contrary to making our actions meaningful? Do you think "determinism" of the scientific sort is similar to a determinism of the theological sort, the difference being that God does the determining and not some impersonal cause? Would our actions be meaningful if God determined them?

Can a naturalist honestly make a distinction between, say, alcoholics and child abusers, since according to this worldview both would be equally determined to act as they do by forces outside of their control?

6. Naturalism fails to provide a satisfying account of what is "real intrinsic value that can be known and factored into our lives" (pages 50–51). What is "real intrinsic value"? Why is this important to any life that desires to flourish? Can you think of any fictional stories, movies, or music that have tried to capture what it would be like to live a meaningless existence in a meaningless world?

7. The author says that "evil is when things are the way they are not supposed to be" (page 52). Does this statement have commonsensical appeal as you consider cases of evil historically or in our own era? Can a naturalist really provide a satisfying account of proper functioning (or the lack thereof) in the absence of an intelligent designer?

Consider and evaluate Daniel Callahan's "minimalist ethics" (page 52). Can you live your life as it was meant to be lived in light of it? Could you raise a family or lead a nation with it? Could you go to war or keep the peace? Would it give you real hope in the midst of injustice?

8. On a naturalist account, is it possible for human beings to have any intrinsic value, especially if they are seen as part of some fleeting stage in evolutionary development that is moving toward higher and higher life forms?

   a. Do you treat yourself or others as though they only have instrumental value? Have you ever been treated as a means toward an end? Have you ever been loved or accepted only because of your abilities or lack thereof? Have you in your heart or mind begun to treat other people as though they were a commodity to be exploited for your purposes?

   b. Naturalists sometimes claim that we get our value by being persons and not by being human. Usually, they then offer diverse criteria for personhood. What is fundamentally wrong with this view? What are some of its implications?

9. Naturalism fails to provide a satisfying account of the fact that "there must be teleology (things that happen for a purpose or future goal) and purpose in the cosmos relevant to human life" (pages 54–56). Aristotle distinguished an efficient cause from a final cause. How does this distinction help to clarify the fact that there must be teleology in the cosmos? Do you think it is freeing or debilitating to live your life as though there were no final causes?

10. Naturalism fails to provide a satisfying account to the question, "Why should I be moral?" (page 56–57). The author distinguishes between "motives and reasons for adopting the moral point of view" (page 57). What does this mean? Does it make sense to you?

CHAPTER 3

THE POSTMODERN STORY

I watched with sadness the movie during an eastbound flight in the summer of 2002. The plot for *Stolen Summer* features Pete, an eight-year-old Catholic boy living in suburban Chicago during the 1970s, and his attempt to convert Danny, a boy of the same age and a rabbi's son, during their summer break from school. Pete's efforts are motivated by a desire to follow the Lord and to bring salvation and a hope for heaven to Danny. Pete is an exclusivist — Jesus Christ is the only way to God. Unfortunately, Danny becomes seriously ill and passes away during the summer. As the movie closes, Pete attends Danny's funeral, meets his family and offers an apology. He now knows that it does not matter what one believes about God, that all roads lead to him, and that sincerity is really what matters. What was really stolen that summer was Pete's exclusivism. He ends up being a politically correct pluralist who has learned not to "force his views on others." Those like me who are exclusivists are demeaned, misrepresented, and depicted as arrogant, intolerant, and naively misguided. It was very, very sad.

During the fall of 2000 when the presidential race between George W. Bush and Al Gore was heating up, I witnessed three similarly saddening events on television. The first was an interview on NBC during the Republican Convention of four swing voters — citizens who had voted for Bill Clinton twice but now were voting for Bush. Each voter, interviewed separately, gave the same reason for his/her swing — Gore was boring, Bush was more likeable, came across better on television, and seemed more interesting and trustworthy. Clearly, these are inadequate reasons for voting for any candidate, much less for one to fill one of the most powerful political positions in the world. For the swing voters, the make-up man was more important than the speech writer. Feelings, image, and likeability guided their decisions more than ideas and substance.

Shortly thereafter during the Democrat's convention, the most effective campaign move was a lengthy kiss that Al Gore laid on his wife in front of the cameras. The next day I listened to a three-hour talk radio show that only accepted callers for whom the kiss had been significant. Caller after caller gushed that Gore's kiss motivated them to vote for him because it made him seem real, likeable, spontaneous, and concerned about family values.

A few weeks later after the third presidential debate, Sam Donaldson and Cokie Roberts were processing the debate when Roberts said something truly shocking. "Sam," she said, "it is too early to tell who won. We'll have to wait until David Letterman and Jay Leno have their comedic say tonight, because it is often what the comedians do with the debate that more significantly influences voters than the substance of the debate itself."

What do these three political events have in common with *Stolen Summer*? Given that knowledge is limited to empirical science, realms of public discourse outside science—especially religious, ethical, and political discourse—are not aspects of life in which truth can be known. Thus, decision-making in these areas cannot be guided by any hope of cognitive success. As a result, tolerance and pluralism must prevail and rhetoric, image, and their kin trump reason, ideas, and knowledge. The makeup man is more important than the speech writer.

The public square is, as some commentators refer to it, "naked." The public square is that arena in which people with various perspectives must come together—public schools, political structures, courtrooms. And discourse in the public square is naked—it is not informed by a robust view of human and social flourishing, character, and virtue, because such a view entails that there is knowledge about human nature, ethics, and proper/improper individual and social human functioning. The public square, along with debates about religion, ethics, and politics, turns out to be about power (the ability to enforce compliance) and not about authority (the right to be believed and followed based on possession of the relevant knowledge).

This is one reason why political correctness is about power, not truth, and this is why the media, university culture, and political interaction have become secular. Radicals and activists in the 1960s sought to change the world, but given their perhaps unwitting adoption of scientism, the only way they could accomplish their aims was through power and not through the promotion of nonempirical knowledge. Cultural power is available in university, media, and political careers, and having absorbed scientism, when the activists of the sixties stormed these social structures, the inevitable result was their secularization and the emergence of coercive, politically correct utilizations of power. In a naturalist world, the will-to-power is all there is; authority is unavailable.

This is a dangerous situation, and it is not the first time in recent memory that it has happened. In the mid-1930s, philosopher Edmund Husserl pondered the question of just how it could be that arguably the most educated society in history (Germany) could have been so easily led by powerful leaders into some of the most barbarous actions and values the world had ever seen. His work (*The Crisis of European Sciences*) was as an expression of his reflections on this and related questions.

According to Husserl, the main culprit was the emergence of a view of the nature and limits of knowledge that had come to occupy culture generally—knowledge is to be identified with mathematical physics and the hard sciences.[1] For Husserl, this meant that pressing questions of human significance—those about values, meaning in life, God, the afterlife, the proper nature of the state—were not capable of being answered in a way in which those answers would be regarded as items of objective knowledge. The effect of this was to privatize ethical and theological issues and to set up a cultural context in which people could be manipulated by powerful leaders (the makeup man became more important than the speech writer!) since there was no knowledge of moral and religious truths that could be raised against them. Little did Husserl know when he wrote this what was about to come—another war whose intellectual inspiration lay in the conceptual relativism of Nietzsche. If Germany's scientific positivism was the disease, Nietzsche was the cure that killed the patient.

How Should We Then Live?

Knowledge is an important basis for acting with authority. We allow dentists and not lawyers to fix our teeth, not because the former have a set of sincere beliefs, but because they possess the relevant knowledge. Knowledge is also a crucial component for living wisely. It is crucial, therefore, for Christians to pay close attention to views about the nature and limits of knowledge inside and outside of the Christian community.

How should we Christians respond to the widespread dominance of naturalism and its scientistic view of knowledge? I will attempt to answer this question directly in chapters 4 and 5, but in this chapter I want to warn you about the dangers of opting for postmodernism as an appropriate form of self-understanding by the Christian community. A growing number of Christian intellectuals are opting for some form of postmodernism; more importantly, one of the fastest growing segments of the Christian community—the Emerging church—appears to have hitched its wagon to postmodernism in a way that is fraught with difficulties seldom appreciated.

I do not wish to be harsh or inappropriately critical of my brothers and sisters who are part of the Emerging church. There is much good in the problems they are bringing to the surface and in some of the solutions they are offering.[2] For now, I simply register my concern about what I believe is their unnecessary association with postmodern language and thought. If you are inclined in this direction, I ask that you give me a fair chance to suggest a different way to accomplish your goals, many of which I share. To facilitate dialog, let me begin with a true story, one that I believe illustrates in microcosm what I believe has been happening before our very eyes in the broader culture.

My story is about the journey of one of the leading philosophers of the last fifty years, Harvard philosopher Hilary Putnam.[3] Around 1980, Putnam attended a dinner party at which the hostess remarked that science has taught us that the universe was an uncaring, purposeless, valueless machine.[4] The statement stuck with Putnam and, in my view, played a role in the development of his thought, which moved from strict naturalism to a form of relativistic constructivism regarding truth, reality, reference, reason, and value.[5] Apparently, Putnam could not face the meaninglessness of life in a cold, blind, material universe. Sadly, he did not reconsider theism, especially Christian theism. Instead, he moved in a postmodern direction according to which reality, value, and truth are arbitrary conventions relative to different cultures.

To be sure, postmodernism is a variegated movement with many stripes. But if we take postmodernism to include a rejection (1) of objective truth construed as a correspondence with reality, (2) of the rational objectivity of reason, and (3) of the reality of simply seeing and the human ability to be aware of and know reality directly, unmediated by "conceptual schemes," language, or their surrogates, then Putnam's move is postmodern despite its analytic philosophical trimmings.

Curiously, truth is a casualty in both scientific naturalism and postmodernism and, along with it, reason and objective rationality. The Baconian/Cartesian identification of power[6] over nature as the goal of science is still with us, and the postmodern preoccupation with the power dynamics of language is well known.

Putnam's way out — moving from the meaningless worldview of naturalism to relativism without reconsidering Christianity and the existence of God — is sad at many levels. At one level, it reminds me of the supposed virtues of Buddhist justifications for ecology heralded in the late 1960s. The claim was that Buddhism replaces the Christian chauvinism of humans vis-à-vis nature and levels the playing field. What escaped notice, however, was that the field was no longer worth playing on because nothing is of any real value if everything is relative. Similarly, it is small comfort to those suffering from real evil to be told not to worry about the meaninglessness of it all because we now know that value, every bit as much as "reality," is linguistically constructed.

But what concerns me more is that, apparently, Putnam could not see a more satisfying third option right in front of him. He should have rejected the naturalist theory of knowledge and reality, retained the human ability to gain nonempirical knowledge of immaterial reality (including theological and ethical knowledge), and pondered what sort of worldview made the most sense of this ability. I think such a move would have led him to theism. *I am concerned that the turn to postmodernism in the culture generally, and the Emerging church particularly, parallels Putnam's journey with all the attendant land mines and booby traps that undermine the possibility of a powerful, confident, knowledgeable, vibrant Christian community.*

Putnam's story helps to set the stage for my treatment of postmodernism. But one more prop needs to be added before I examine this ideological movement directly, and that is a larger story than Putnam's.

The Decline of the American Uni-versity

In a recent column, civil libertarian Nat Hentoff noted that while our universities may exhibit increasing racial diversity, there is one sort of diversity that they leave out — a diversity of ideas.[7] Hentoff reports that both the Chronicle of Higher Education and the American Council on Education acknowledge that American universities are so dominated with a liberal, secular presence and ideology that secular group-think and monolithic indoctrination are widespread. In classroom after classroom, politically and religiously conservative students are "intimidated into silence, ignored or occasionally ridiculed."

How did we get into this situation, and what bearing does it have on our culture's view of the reality of moral and religious knowledge? Hentoff does not raise these issues, but those of us in love with Jesus must raise and seek to answer them, and that's what I will attempt to do in this section.

In her authoritative work *The Making of the Modern University*, Harvard professor Julie Reuben describes in painstaking—and for Christians, painful—detail the transition from the American liberal arts college to the modern research university from 1880 to 1930.[8] Reuben's work is a must-read for Christians interested in how our culture got in its current mess, and I urge my brothers and sisters with postmodern leanings to consider Reuben's insights carefully.

Reuben divides this time of upheaval into three overlapping periods: the Religious Stage (1880–1910), the Scientific Stage (1900–1920), and the Humanities and Extracurricular Stage (1915–1930). During the first period, colleges took themselves to have two mandates: the impartation of wisdom and knowledge and the tools needed to discover them, and the development of spiritually, morally, and politically virtuous graduates who could serve God, the state, and the church well.

Note carefully that the college's purpose was filled with material content and was normative: *People should be taught how to live well, and knowledge was available to give content to what this should look like.* Because the Christian God was a single, unified mind and the source of all truths, the curriculum was unified in that every discipline was expected to shed light on and harmonize with every other discipline. College faculty and administrators were confident that knowledge existed in all the fields of study. In particular, spiritual, ethical, aesthetic, and political truth and knowledge were real and on a par with truth and knowledge in other disciplines, including science. Front and center was the importance of teaching, of gaining a breadth of knowledge, and of fostering spiritual and moral virtue.

This perspective changed, however, as a result of several factors, especially the need to develop technology for industry and defense and the increased specialization occurring in the sciences. As time went on, a fact/value distinction arose according to which truth and facts, along with the knowledge thereof, was the sole domain of empirical science. Religion and ethical claims were reduced to private feelings, individual attitudes, and personal perspectives. The realm of religion and values became noncognitive (knowledge is not possible in these domains) and nonfactual (their claims are neither true nor false); the function of religion and ethics is to help people live better lives (whatever that means). The idea that there exists a stable body of knowable truths gave way to the notion that truth changes constantly, that progress, not wisdom, is what matters, and that university education should focus on method and "learning how to think," rather than trying to impart knowledge and wisdom to students, especially outside the empirical sciences. Academic freedom, "open" inquiry, a spirit of skepticism, and specialized research became the central values of American universities.

The abandonment of Christian monotheism from the cognitive domain meant that there was no longer a basis for a unified curriculum. Without a single, rational God, why think that there is a unity to truth, that one discipline should have anything at all to do with another discipline? Thus, uni-versities gave way to plural-versities, and we have lived with fragmentation in our schools ever since the 1930s. No longer did possession of a body of knowledge distinguish college graduates from those without such an education. Instead, the main gift of a college education, besides helping one get a job, was the impartation of a vague "scientific attitude," of the mental discipline to "think for oneself," of a spirit of open inquiry, and of an attitude of tolerance for various viewpoints.

Great hostility arose to natural and revealed theology and their claim to provide knowledge of God and related matters; instead, religion was tolerated as long as it did not claim to be cognitive or factual. As the fact/value distinction prevailed, scientism won the day, and along with it, the widespread view that there is no such thing as nonempirical knowledge. Because it is difficult to sustain the notion that in a domain of life, such as the religious and ethical domains, there are truths but no one can know what they are, the denial of nonempirical knowledge resulted in the denial of truth outside the empirical sciences. At the same time, in many religious studies departments, courses centered not on the study of theology as such but on the history of religions, where empirical knowledge was available.

So far we have noted two important, related shifts: (1) from a unified curriculum, grounded in a monotheistic God, in which knowledge and truth was present in all areas of study, to plural-versities with a fragmented curriculum in which electives and specialization proliferated and in which knowledge was limited to the empirical sciences; (2) from a cognitivist view of theological and ethical claims according to which these claims are often both true and items of knowledge, to a fact/value distinction according to which empirical science is the sole domain of facts and knowledge, and nonempirical fields (especially religion and ethics) study the realm of "values," that is, nonfactual, private feelings, attitudes, and behaviors, which are not topics for which knowledge is available.

These shifts left university presidents and administrators in a pickle, and the sad manner in which they tried to address the problem should be a lesson to all who would seek to remove theology and ethics from the domain of objective knowledge. Remember the two purposes of college/university education? The first one (about acquiring knowledge and the tools necessary to obtain it) was retained, though in a modified form. The new goal was not the discovery of truth, but the facilitating of research that could provide useful information against a background of changing truth. This was easy to accomplish in the sciences and, as a result, the better scientific scholars were increasingly rewarded with not having to teach. The humanities were left with shuffling paradigms and teaching students new and different language games. If science is the sole domain that studies reality, then the humanities are the domain that studies how we talk about reality and other things.

The second purpose was simply impossible to achieve — the development of spiritually, morally, and politically virtuous graduates who could serve God, the state, and the church well. For a moment, forget about spirituality, God, and the church. The development of morally and politically virtuous graduates who could serve their culture requires an assumption — the existence of a body of moral knowledge — that is inconsistent with the modern university, which eschews any sort of dogmatism and values diversity, tolerance, and academic freedom.

Given the fact/value distinction and the noncognitivist attitude towards religion and morality, the universities did the best they could, I suppose, but the history of their attempt to satisfy this second goal is pathetic. At the beginning of the period, all fields of study were understood to be relevant to religious and moral knowledge and training, so this second mandate was integrated throughout the curriculum. This is as it should be if the domains are cognitive ones. But along the way, the scientists wanted to get rid of religious and ethical ideas in their fields and, along with them, the need to teach students how to live. So the responsibility for moral and religious development fell to the humanities. Administrators looked to professors in literature, art, history, language, and philosophy to unify the lives of students and teach values for university life in general, and the curriculum in particular.

There was just one problem. Professors in the humanities had accepted the noncognitivist view of these domains and, thus, they could not find any basis for agreement about whose values, whose justice, whose religion should be taught. The attempt to teach character was inconsistent with the other values of the university, namely, tolerance, academic freedom, and a spirit of nondogmatic and free inquiry. So professors in the humanities couldn't mount a robust, common vision of moral and religious truth and knowledge apt for fulfilling this mandate. As a result, ethical and religious training was punted to extracurricular activities.

Universities sought to provide a unifying, distinct university experience that would convey a sense of community and spiritual/moral values by developing these extracurricular structures:

1. faculty advising that was to go beyond academic aid and include personal mentoring
2. the expansion of dorms and an emphasis on living in dorms as vehicles for creating a sense of community in which students from various fields could enrich each other and learn spiritual and moral lessons in a community atmosphere
3. the office of Dean of Students, which arose at Yale in 1919, whose job was to facilitate spiritual and ethical community among students
4. freshman orientation, instituted as a means of socializing new students into the university community and orienting them to important spiritual and moral values

Once again, these efforts failed because no one could agree on exactly what spiritual and moral values these programs should aim to foster. More importantly, by shifting moral and spiritual training from classroom to extracurricular venues, the noncognitivist, nonfactual, purely private nature of religion and ethics was underscored.

All of this signifies the development away from the conviction that there is truth and knowledge in religion and ethics to the view that spiritual and moral guidance is so subjective that it is best left for extracurricular specialists like the Dean of Students. The university's second mandate to impart moral and spiritual knowledge to its students devolved into the vague aim of developing a rich student life as part of the college experience. Given the scientism that filled the atmosphere, morality soon became morale or school spirit, and the goal of making a college education a distinct experience turned out to revolve around athletic teams and the school spirit associated with supporting them. As scientism permeated American universities, the second mandate went out with a whimper. The moral and spiritual wisdom of Plato, Aristotle, Moses, Solomon, and Jesus was replaced with football and the school spirit.

A few years ago and perhaps in a fit of frustration, the president of a major Eastern university bemoaned the fact that because the universities had abandoned a Judeo-Christian worldview, they were now turning out highly skilled barbarians—graduates technically trained but with no chests (centers of moral and spiritual awareness), as C. S. Lewis put it. I would add that if the students aren't barbarians when they enter the university, there are many forces on campus that will do everything they can to be sure they are barbarians when they graduate. This was one theme of a recent work by Ben Shapiro on the widespread celebration of and addiction to sexual perversion and pornography in Western culture.[9] Nowhere, says Shapiro, is such debauchery celebrated more than on our college campuses where random sexual encounters are both frequent and regularly endorsed by university professors in a zoo-like atmosphere sustained by resentment of all things traditional.

To his credit, Shapiro locates a major source of campus debauchery in the loss of belief in objective truth in our universities, along with the promotion of a politically correct form of tolerance that inevitably degenerates into nihilistic, narcissistic, and hedonistic forms of chaotic subjectivism. He also tethers this shift to the fact that "traditional authority figures— parents, community leaders, even God—have been discarded."[10] What Shapiro fails to see, however, is that the ultimate locus of responsibility for the ethics of sexual perversion characteristic of our universities is the shift in understanding regarding ethical and, ultimately, theological knowledge in those institutions.

A similar blindness afflicts David Horowitz's otherwise courageous and accurate description of the grotesquely secularized, leftist liberalism that dominates the American university in *The Professors: The 101 Most Dangerous Academics in America*.[11] I am a fan of Horowitz and have enjoyed his book immensely. I also appreciate his spirited defense of this book during multiple appearances on Fox News program *Hannity and Colmes*. Horowitz correctly points out that the universities are now the powerbase for the secular left, and the American university has become an indoctrination center for political correctness and its loathing for traditional values, the Judeo-Christian religion, and conservative ethical, religious, and political thought.

He also offers a useful sociological analysis of why this has happened—for example, that the radicals of the 1960s infiltrated the professoriate and have continued to hire leftist look-alikes up to the present.

But such sociological analyses do not go far enough, and Horowitz does not mention the shift in epistemology (the emergence of scientism that eliminates ethical, religious, and political knowledge) that greased the skids for the radicals in the first place. Indeed, he seems guilty of accepting this shift himself. Thus, he says that professors "have professional obligations as teachers, whose purpose is the instruction and education of students, not to impose their biases on students as though they were scientific facts." In other words, ethical, religious, or political perspectives do not rise to the level of scientific certainty and, thus, should not be "imposed" on students.[12] Again, he opines that "there are no 'correct' answers to controversial issues, which is why they are controversial: scholars cannot agree. Answers to such questions are inherently subjective and opinion-based."[13]

Apart from the self-refuting nature of this claim (if there are no correct answers on controversial issues, then his own statement, indeed, his entire book, cannot be offered as correct because it is surely controversial as much as the professors he correctly targets), it seems to presuppose that if scholars cannot achieve consensus on a topic, then there is either no correct answer or no one can know what the correct answer is. But this criterion—that consensus among experts is a necessary condition for either truth or knowledge—is a fairly recent one in the history of thought, and it is far from obvious. After all, there could be a nonrational reason for why consensus has not been achieved regarding some topic besides the fact that no one viewpoint is true or capable of being known.

Indeed, Horowitz's own book is an exceptional example of precisely this: locating the subjectivist, biased, agenda-driven group-think that dictates what is the "correct" viewpoint to hold in proper academic company and what makes rational appraisal of alternatives all but impossible. Besides, this criterion (that experts must reach consensus before truth or knowledge can be achieved) is also self-refuting (experts do not agree about the criterion itself and, thus, by its own standard of acceptability, it cannot be true or known to be true).

But I must stop shadow-boxing with Horowitz. The important point for our purposes is that his own theory of knowledge undermines the very thing that is needed to restore the plural-versities of our time to uni-versities in which civil argumentation, not indoctrination, can flourish. Such a theory of knowledge underwrites the reality of nonempirical knowledge, which, together with producing spiritually, morally, and politically flourishing graduates, can provide the only appropriate purpose for a university education. And if a Christian worldview is the best way to make sense of how such knowledge and truth could exist and how there could actually be meaning to life, including meaning to social institutions (the university included), then so be it.

Even though Horowitz fails to see the basic issue, his book is an encouraging step forward in exposing the bankruptcy of the contemporary secular university. Even more encouraging is C. John Sommerville's latest book, *The Decline of the Secular University*.[14] Sommerville is professor emeritus of history at the University of Florida, and his book is a scathing critique of the secularization of western universities. The publisher has provided a summary of this book with these words:

> The American university has embraced a thorough secularism that makes it increasingly marginal in a society that is characterized by high levels of religious belief. The very secularization that was supposed to be a liberating influence has resulted in the university's failure to provide leadership in political, cultural, social, and even scientific arenas.
>
> In *The Decline of the Secular University*, C. John Sommerville explores several different ways in which the secular university fails in its mission through its trivialization of religion. He notes how little attention is being given to defining the human, so crucial in all aspects of professional education. He alerts us to problems associated with the prevailing secular distinction between "facts" and "values." He reviews how the elimination of religion hampers the university from understanding our post-Cold War world. Sommerville then shows how a greater awareness of the intellectual resources of religion might stimulate more forthright attention to important matters like our loss of a sense of history, how to problematize secularism, the issue of judging religions, the oddity of academic moralizing, and the strangeness of science at the frontiers.
>
> Finally, he invites the reader to imagine a university where religion is not ruled out but rather welcomed as a legitimate voice among others. Sommerville's bracing and provocative arguments are sure to provoke controversy and stimulate discussion both inside and outside the academy.[15]

Yeah, verily, and amen! My only word of caution is to be sure we argue for the importance of a Christian worldview for the university's mission on the grounds that it is rational, defensible, and arguably true, and not simply because of the good results that follow when religion gets a place at the table. We Christians must defend the objectivity of ethical and theological knowledge no matter what the cost or how embarrassing it is for some Christian intellectuals who have already given up this ground. Luther once said that if we defend Christ at all points besides those at which he is currently being attacked, we have not really defended Christ. Luther may have overstated the issue, but there is an important insight here: In presenting our lives and defending our ideas to the culture, we must direct most of our efforts toward the central tension points blocking our efforts. As go the universities, so goes the culture, and the Christian must keep in mind the tensions between Christian claims and competing worldviews currently dominating the culture, especially views of knowledge and reality that constitute the universities.

As we have just seen, there is an important cultural fact that Christians must face, especially in light of Luther's dictum: *There simply is no established, widely recognized body of ethical or religious knowledge now operative in the institutions of knowledge in our culture, for example, the universities.* Ethical and religious claims are placed into what Francis Schaeffer used to call the upper story, and they are judged to have little or no epistemic authority, especially compared to the authority given to science to define the limits of knowledge and reality in those same institutions. This raises pressing questions: *Is Christianity a knowledge tradition or merely a faith tradition, a perspective that, while true, cannot be known to be true and must be embraced on the basis of some epistemic state weaker than knowledge? Is there nonempirical knowledge, including knowledge of value and nonphysical, immaterial matters?*

There are at least two reasons why these may well be *the* crucial questions for Christians to keep in mind as they sift through the ideas extant in our culture. First, Christianity claims to be a knowledge tradition and places knowledge at the center of proclamation and discipleship. The Old and New Testaments, including the teachings of Jesus, claim not merely that Christianity is true, but that a variety of its moral and religious assertions can be known to be true.

Second, knowledge is the basis of responsible action in society (recall the example above about dentists and lawyers). If, then, Christians do little to deflect the view that theological and ethical assertions are merely parts of a tradition, ways of seeing the world from a Christian "perspective" that fall short of conveying knowledge, they inadvertently contribute to the marginalization of Christianity precisely because they fail to rebut the contemporary tendency to rob it of the very thing that gives it the authority necessary to prevent that marginalization (i.e., its legitimate claim to give us moral and religious knowledge).

Both in and out of the church, Jesus has been lost as an intellectual authority, and the Christian should weigh ideas in light of this fact. *It is because of this broad context regarding the nature and limits of knowledge that Christian acceptance of and association with postmodernism in both its strong and weaker incarnations is irresponsible and results in the church becoming its own grave-digger.*

THE POSTMODERN TURN

Postmodernism is a loose coalition of diverse thinkers from several different academic disciplines, so it is difficult to characterize postmodernism in a way that would be fair to this diversity. Still, it is possible to provide a fairly accurate characterization of postmodernism in general, since its friends and foes understand it well enough to debate its strengths and weaknesses.[16]

Postmodernism is both a historical, chronological notion and a philosophical ideology. Understood historically, postmodernism refers to a period of thought that follows, and is a reaction to, the period called *modernity*. Modernity is the period of European thought that developed out of the Renaissance (fourteenth to seventeenth centuries) and flourished in the Enlightenment (seventeenth to nineteenth centuries) in the ideas of people like Descartes, Locke, Berkeley, Hume, Reid, Leibniz, and Kant. In the chronological sense, postmodernism is an era that began after and, in some sense, replaces modernity.

As a philosophical ideology, postmodernism is primarily a reinterpretation of what knowledge is and what counts as knowledge, though postmodernists don't like to talk in this way. More broadly, it represents a form of cultural relativism about such things as reality, truth, reason, value, linguistic meaning, the self, and other notions. On a postmodern view, there is no such thing as objective reality, truth, value, reason, and so forth. All these are social constructions, creations of linguistic practices, and as such are relative not to individuals, but to social groups that share a narrative. Roughly, a narrative is a perspective such as Marxism, atheism, or Christianity that is embedded in the group's social and linguistic practices. A narrative is the community's story by which it expresses its shared concerns. Important postmodern thinkers are Friedrich Nietzsche, Ludwig Wittgenstein, Jacques Derrida, Thomas Kuhn, Michel Foucault, Martin Heidegger, and Jean-Francois Lyotard. Two aspects of postmodern thought are worthy of special attention.

1. *Postmodernism and the denial of objective knowledge and reason.* Many, if not most, postmodernists deny that people can function objectively when it comes to rationality and knowledge. According to Emergent church leader Brian McLaren, making absolute truth claims becomes problematic in the postmodern context.

> I think that most Christians grossly misunderstand the philosophical baggage associated with terms like *absolute* or *objective* (linked to foundationalism and the myth of neutrality).... Similarly, arguments that pit absolutism versus relativism, and objectivism versus subjectivism, prove meaningless or absurd to postmodern people.[17]

Postmodernists often reject the notion that rationality is objective on the grounds that no one approaches life in a totally objective way without bias. Thus, objectivity is impossible, and observations, beliefs, and entire narratives are theory-laden. There is no neutral standpoint from which to approach the world. Therefore, observations, beliefs, and the like are perspectival constructions that reflect the viewpoint implicit in one's own web of beliefs. For example, the late Stanley Grenz claimed that postmodernism rejects the alleged modernist view of reason which "entails a claim to dispassionate knowledge, a person's ability to view reality not as a conditioned participant but as an unconditioned observer—to peer at the world from a vantage point outside the flux of history."[18]

Regarding knowledge, postmodernists believe that there is no point of view from which one can define knowledge itself or what counts as knowledge without begging the question in favor of one's own view. "Knowledge" is a construction of one's social, linguistic structures, not a justified, truthful representation of reality by one's mental states. For example, knowledge amounts to what is deemed to be appropriate according to the professional certification practices of various professional associations. As such, knowledge is a construction that expresses the social, linguistic structures of those associations, nothing more, nothing less.

Let's focus on the question of objectivity. (I will address the nature of knowledge in chapter 5.) People can fail to be objective in one of three senses. One can lack psychological objectivity, rational objectivity, or in some way be cut off from direct access to a language- or mind-independent real world — a world that exists and is what it is, quite independently of our talking and thinking about it. Let's focus on the first two senses — psychological and rational objectivity — and leave access to the external world to chapter 5.

Postmodern claims about objectivity often exhibit deep confusion. As a first step toward clearing away this confusion, we need to clarify the distinction between psychological and rational objectivity, a distinction that postmodernists often miss.

Psychological objectivity is detachment, the absence of bias, a lack of commitment either way on a topic. Do people ever have psychological objectivity? Yes, they do, typically in areas in which they have no interest or about which they know little or nothing. Note carefully two things about psychological objectivity. For one thing, it is not necessarily a virtue. It is there if one has not thought deeply about an issue and has no convictions regarding it. But as one develops thoughtful, intelligent convictions about a topic, it is wrong to remain "unbiased," that is, uncommitted regarding it. Otherwise, what role would study and evidence play in the development of one's approach to life? Should one remain "unbiased" that cancer is a disease, that rape is wrong, that the New Testament was written in the first century, that there is design in the universe, if one has discovered good reasons for each belief? No, one should not.

For another thing, while it is possible to be psychologically objective in some cases, most people are not psychologically objective regarding the vast majority of the things they believe. In these cases, it is crucial to observe that a lack of psychological objectivity does not matter, nor does it cut one off from knowing or seeing the world directly the way it is, or from presenting and arguing for one's convictions. Why? *Because a lack of psychological objectivity does not imply a lack of rational objectivity, and it is the latter that matters most, not the former.* We have all had experiences where we were committed to a viewpoint and, thus, were not 50/50 about it, and later we came to hear good arguments for and against that viewpoint (as well as bad arguments for and against it!). The lack of psychological objectivity did not keep our rational faculties from working.

To understand this, we need to get clear on the notion of *rational objectivity*. Rational objectivity is the state of having accurate experiential or cognitive access to the thing itself. This entails that if one has rational objectivity regarding some topic, then one can discern the difference between genuinely good and bad reasons/evidence for a belief about that topic and one can hold the belief for genuinely good reasons/evidence. The important thing here is that bias does not stand between a knowing subject and an intentional object, nor does it eliminate a person's ability to assess the reasons for something. Bias may make it more difficult, but not impossible. If bias made rational objectivity impossible, then no teacher — including the postmodernist herself — could responsibly teach any view the teacher believed on any subject! Nor could the teacher teach opposing viewpoints, because she would be biased against them!

2. *Postmodernism and the denial of objective, absolute truth.* The second troublesome feature of much postmodern involvement is the denial of the notion of objective truth, especially the correspondence theory of truth. Accordingly, our descriptions of the world are neither true nor approximately true. Moreover, we are trapped behind our language (theories, conceptual schemes, narratives) and cannot get to the thing-in-itself, so for all purposes, questions about the existence and nature of the "real world" are moot.

A bit more needs to be said about the correspondence theory of truth. In its simplest form, the correspondence theory says that a proposition is true to the extent that it corresponds to reality, when what it asserts to be the case is indeed the case. More generally, truth occurs when a truth-bearer stands in an appropriate correspondence relation to a truth-maker:

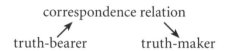

correspondence relation

truth-bearer   truth-maker

What is the truth-bearer? It is the thing that is true or false. Moreover, the thing that is either true or false is not a sentence but a proposition. A proposition is the content of a sentence. For example, "It is raining" and "Es regnet" are two different sentences that express the same proposition. A sentence is a linguistic object consisting of a sense perceptible string of markings formed according to a culturally arbitrary set of syntactical rules, a grammatically well-formed string of spoken or written scratchings/sounds. Sentences are true to the extent that they express a true proposition or content.

What about truth-makers? What is it that makes a proposition true? The best answer is facts. A fact is some real state of affairs in the world — for example, grass's being green, an electron's having negative charge, God's being all-loving. Consider the proposition *that grass is green.* This proposition is true just in case a specific fact, namely, grass's being green, actually occurs in the real world. If Sally has the thought *that grass is green*, the specific state of affairs, (grass actually being green) "makes" the propositional content of her thought true just in case the state of affairs actually is the way the proposition represents it to be. Grass's being green makes Sally's thought true even if Sally is blind and cannot tell whether or not it is true, and even if Sally does not believe the thought. Reality makes thoughts true or false. A thought is not made true by someone believing it or by someone being able to determine whether or not it is true. Put differently, evidence allows one to tell whether or not a thought is true, but the relevant fact is what makes it true.

Our study of truth-bearers has already taken us into the topic of the correspondence relation. Correspondence is a two-placed relation between a proposition and a relevant fact. A two-placed relation, such as "larger than," is one that requires two things (say, a desk and a book) before it holds. Similarly, the truth relation of correspondence holds between two things—a relevant fact and a proposition—just in case the fact matches, conforms to, corresponds with the proposition.

What reasons can be given for accepting the correspondence theory of truth? Two main arguments have been advanced for the correspondence theory, one descriptive and one dialectical. The descriptive argument focuses on a careful description and presentation of specific cases to see what can be learned from them about truth. As an example, consider the case of Joe and Frank. While in his office, Joe receives a call from the university bookstore that a specific book he had ordered—Richard Swinburne's *The Evolution of the Soul*—has arrived and is waiting for him. At this point, a new mental state occurs in Joe's mind—the thought that Swinburne's *The Evolution of the Soul* is in the bookstore.

Now Joe, being aware of the content of the thought, becomes aware of two things closely related to it: the nature of the thought's intentional object (Swinburne's book being in the bookstore) and certain verification steps that would help him to determine the truth of the thought. For example, he knows that it would be irrelevant for verifying the thought to go swimming in the Pacific Ocean. Rather, he knows that he must take a series of steps that will bring him to a specific building and look in a certain place for Swinburne's book in the university bookstore.

So Joe starts out for the bookstore, all the while being guided by the proposition *that Swinburne's* The Evolution of the Soul *is in the bookstore*.

Along the way, his friend Frank joins him, though Joe does not tell Frank where he is going or why. They arrive at the store and both see Swinburne's book there. At that moment, Joe and Frank simultaneously have a certain sensory experience of seeing Swinburne's book, *The Evolution of the Soul*. But Joe has a second experience not possessed by Frank. Joe experiences that his thought matches, or corresponds with, an actual state of affairs. He is able to compare his thought with its intentional object and "see," or be directly aware, that the thought is true. In this case, Joe actually experiences the correspondence relation itself and truth itself becomes an object of his awareness.

The dialectical argument asserts that those who advance alternative theories of truth or who simply reject the correspondence theory actually presuppose it in their own assertions, especially when they present arguments for their views or defend them against defeaters. Sometimes this argument is stated in the form of a dilemma: Those who reject the correspondence theory either take their own utterances to be true in the correspondence sense or they do not. If the former, then those utterances are self-defeating. If the latter, there is no reason to accept them, because one cannot take their utterances to be true.

Many postmodernists deny the existence of objective truth, construed along the lines of the correspondence theory, which they often equate with absolute truth. For example, Christian postmodernist Philip Kenneson flatly states:

> Let me assure you that I am not a relativist. But the reason I am not a relativist may not bring you much comfort; it is because I *don't believe* in objective truth, a concept that is the flip side of relativism and that is necessary for the charge of relativism to be coherent. In other words, one can defend objective truth or relativism only by assuming that it is possible for human beings to take up a "view from nowhere"; since I don't believe in "views from nowhere," I don't believe in objective truth or relativism. Moreover, I don't want *you* to believe in objective truth or relativism either, because the first concept is corrupting the church and its witness to the world, while tilting at the second is wasting the precious time and energy of a lot of Christians.[19]

As we saw above, Brian McLaren opines that making absolute truth claims is problematic in the postmodern context. To be sure, McLaren is not a philosopher, but I believe that his statements represent crucial data that should be taken into account by any Christian—scholar or otherwise—before they climb into bed with postmodern thought. Why? Christians are concerned about the impact their views have on the broader culture, and it is clear that postmodern ideas have influenced McLaren's understanding of truth. McLaren is an influential pastor in the Christian community, and his views of these matters are representative of many who have opted for the emerging church and its philosophy of ministry.

Unfortunately, this postmodern rejection of objective or absolute truth rests on at least two confusions. The first postmodern confusion involves metaphysical versus epistemic notions of absolute truth. In the metaphysical and correct sense, absolute truth is the same thing as objective truth. On this view, people discover truth, they do not create it, and a claim is made true or false in some way or another by reality itself, totally independently of whether the claim is accepted by anyone. Moreover, an absolute truth conforms to the three fundamental laws of logic (an assertion is identical to itself and is different from other assertions, an assertion cannot be true and false at the same time in the same sense, and an assertion has to be either true or false), which are absolute truths themselves. According to objectivism, a commitment to the absolute truth of some proposition P entails no thesis about a knowing subject's rational situation regarding P.

By contrast with the metaphysical notion, postmodernists claim that a commitment to absolute truth is rooted in Cartesian anxiety (an anxious need to be absolutely certain about something) and its need for absolute certainty; accordingly, they claim that acceptance of the absolute truth of P entails acceptance of the conjunction of P's truth in the objective sense and the possibility of a (finite) knowing subject having complete certainty with respect to P. Thus, one postmodernist recently stated that commitment to objective truth and the correspondence theory is merely "an epistemic project [that] is funded by 'Cartesian anxiety,' a product of methodological doubt."[20]

As I have already pointed out, this claim is entirely false philosophically. Advocates of a correspondence theory of objective truth take the view to be a realist metaphysical thesis and they steadfastly reject all attempts to epistemologize the view. The claim that some proposition P is an objective or absolute truth is simply the claim that P corresponds to reality. Such a claim says absolutely nothing about the speaker's degree of certainty with respect to P.

The second confusion is one about the identity of the truth-bearer. As we have already seen, the informed correspondence theorist will say that propositions are truth-bearers. What is a proposition? Minimally, it is the content of declarative sentences/statements and thoughts/beliefs that is true or false. Beyond that philosophers are in disagreement, but most would agree that a proposition (1) is not located in space or time; (2) is not identical to the linguistic entities that may be used to express it; (3) is not sense perceptible; (4) is such that the same proposition may be in more than one mind at once; (5) need not be grasped by any (at least finite) person to exist and be what it is; (6) may itself be an object of thought when, for example, one is thinking about the content of one's own thought processes; and (7) is in no sense a physical entity.

By contrast, a sentence is a linguistic type or token consisting in a sense perceptible string of markings formed according to a culturally arbitrary set of syntactical rules. A statement is a sequence of sounds or body movements employed by a speaker to assert a sentence on a specific occasion. So understood, neither sentences nor statements are good candidates for the basic truth-bearer.

It is pretty easy to show that having or using a sentence (or any other piece of language) is neither necessary nor sufficient for thinking or having propositional content. First, it's not necessary. Children think prior to their acquisition of language—how else could they thoughtfully learn language—and, indeed, we all think without language regularly. Moreover, the same propositional content may be expressed by a potentially infinite number of pieces of language and, thus, that content is not identical to any linguistic entity. This alone is not enough to prove that propositional content can exist without language. But when one attends to the content that is being held constant as arbitrary linguistic expressions are selected to express it, that content may easily be seen to satisfy the nonlinguistic traits of a proposition listed above. For example, if I have in my mind the content that snow is white, I can vary the sentence I use to express that content from "snow is white" to "Schnee ist weiss." The linguistic expressions can vary and, indeed, are arbitrary while the content of the sentences remains the same in my mind.

Second, it's not sufficient. If erosion carved an authorless linguistic scribble in a hillside, for example, "I'm eroding," then strictly speaking it would have no meaning or content, though it would be empirically equivalent to another token of this type that would express a proposition were it the result of authorial intention.

Postmodernists attack a straw man when they focus on the alleged inadequacies of linguistic objects to do the work required of them in a correspondence theory of truth. Speaking for himself and other postmodernists, Joseph Natoli claims that "no one representation, or narrative, can reliably represent the world because language/pictures/sounds (signifiers) are not permanent labels attached to the things of the world nor do the things of the world dwell inside such signifiers."[21]

Unfortunately, even granting the fact that language (and certain sensations) is problematic if taken to represent things in the world (e.g., granting that the language/world hookup is arbitrary), it follows that human subjects fail to be able to accurately represent the world only if we grant the further erroneous claim that representational entities are limited to language (and certain sensations). But this is precisely what the sophisticated correspondence theorist denies.

Again, according to Richard Rorty, "to say that truth is not out there is simply to say that where there are no sentences there is not truth, that sentences are elements of human language, and that human languages are human creations. Truth cannot be out there—cannot exist independently of the human mind—because sentences cannot so exist, or be out there.... Only descriptions ... can be true and false."[22] It should be obvious that Rorty attacks a straw man and that his argument goes through only if we grant that sentences are the fundamental truth-bearers.

POSTMODERNISM AND OUR FIVE CRUCIAL QUESTIONS

At the end of chapter 1, we cited five crucial questions that should be put to any worldview. In answering these questions now, reality for postmodernism either does not exist or we have no direct access to it. Claims to have knowledge are power moves designed to dominate those judged not to have it. More modestly, knowledge is what your community's experts will let you get away with saying without having to defend yourself further. The good life and the nature of a good person are whatever your community arbitrarily takes them to be. Moreover, there is no clear advice given as to how to become a good person. Instead, we get mantras about being tolerant and doing whatever you want as long as you harm no one else. It's all pretty thin stuff.

It is open to a postmodernist to complain that my treatment of postmodernism only addresses extreme versions of the ideology and fails to take into account weaker forms that are consistent with Christianity. This response is beside the point. For one thing, my description of postmodernism is an accurate account that fairly captures an understanding of postmodernism widely employed throughout the literature. So even if there are more conservative forms of postmodernism, I can hardly be accused of offering a caricature of the movement.

Second, there are ideas central to postmodernism, such as a lack of direct access to a language-independent world, that make it difficult, if not impossible, to prevent a more conservative postmodern perspective from sliding into a stronger relativist form. For example, if all perception and knowledge take place from within a culture, a standpoint, or a tradition, if all perception and knowledge are interpretive and laced with presuppositions, if all observations are "theory laden," then it is hard to see how people can ever compare their concepts or theories with the world as it is in itself. And if we cannot know the world as it is in itself, unmediated by language and its surrogates, then debates about whether there is a real external world are like a bunch of stray cats fighting over an old, rotting mouse carcass.

Third, given the loss of moral and spiritual knowledge that I have been at pains to describe and explain, it is irresponsible and naïve to adopt a postmodern perspective and try to harmonize it with Christianity.

Should Christians utilize postmodernist insights from time to time as they find helpful? I don't believe they should, and to see why, consider Nazi ideology. Surely, some aspects of Nazi thought — for example, a commitment to a strong national defense and to solid education for youth — are correct and appropriate. But for two reasons, it would be wrong to say that one was neutral or even favorable toward Nazi thought, rejecting its problems and embracing its advantages. First, Nazi thought is so horrible and its overall impact so harmful that its bad features far outweigh whatever relatively trivial advantages it offers. Thus, such an attitude is inappropriate toward Nazi thought. Second, neither of the advantages just cited (strong national defense and solid education) requires Nazi ideology for its justification.

The same points apply to postmodernism. Its harm to the cause of Christ and human flourishing far outweigh any advantages that may accrue to it, and whatever those advantages are, they do not require postmodernism for their justification. After all, the importance of narrative and story, and the need to be aware of the inappropriate use of power have been understood long before postmodernism came on the scene. Moreover, the way to avoid scientism and reductionism is to use the very things postmodernists deny to argue against them. The only alternative to argument is the use of mere rhetoric or sheer politically correct public power to marginalize scientism and reductionism, and this use of power is the very thing postmodernists rightly abhor.

In her provocative book entitled *Longing to Know*, Esther Meek asserts that humans as knowers exercise a profound responsibility to submit to the authoritative dictates of reality.[23] Thus, "it is not responsible to deny objective truth and reality in knowing; it is irresponsible. It is not responsible to make the human knower or community of knowers the arbiters of a private truth and reality; it is irresponsible."[24] Again, Meek claims that "good, responsible knowing brings blessing, shalom; irresponsible knowing brings curse."[25] Elsewhere Meek warns that

> the kind of freedom implied by the thought that we humans completely determine our reality leaves us with a gnawing sense of the relative insignificance of our choices. I think it leads not to total responsibility but to careless irresponsibility, both with regard to ourselves and with regard to other humans, not to mention to the world. And, paradoxically, it leads not to a deeper sense of [communal or individual] identity and dignity but to a disheartening lack of it.[26]

We need to pay careful attention to Meek's claims. As humans, we live and ought to live our lives not merely by truth but by knowledge of truth. Knowledge of truth gives us confident trust and access to reality. Moreover, those of us called to be teachers and scholars for the church and, indeed, for the unbelieving world are enjoined not only to impart and defend truth, but to impart and defend knowledge of truth, and, even more, to impart and defend knowledge of truth *as* knowledge of truth. This entails we must impart and defend the notion that we do, in fact, have knowledge of important spiritual and ethical truths. Among other things, this gives confidence in truth and knowledge to those we serve. Thus, we are irresponsible not simply if we fail to achieve knowledge of reality; we are doubly irresponsible if we fail to impart to others knowledge *as knowledge*. The corrosive affects of postmodernism eat away at the fulfillment of these duties and responsibilities that constitute our calling from Almighty God.

Meek goes on to point out that the achieving of knowledge and the teaching of it as knowledge "calls for courageous resolve. And this courageous resolve, when proven true, merits the deep admiration of others."[27] The need for such courage is especially grave today as we labor in an intellectual milieu in which the worldviews of naturalism and postmodernism both entail that there is no nonempirical knowledge, especially no religious or ethical knowledge.

Faced with such opposition and the pressure it brings, postmodernism is a form of intellectual pacifism that, at the end of the day, recommends backgammon while the barbarians are at the gate. It is the easy way out that removes the pressure to engage alternative conceptual schemes, to be different, to risk ridicule, to take a stand outside the gate. But it is precisely as disciples of Christ—even more, as officers in his army—that the pacifist way out is simply not an option. However comforting it may be, postmodernism is the cure that kills the patient, the military strategy that concedes defeat before the first shot is fired, the ideology that undermines its own claims to allegiance. As followers of the Lord Jesus, the postmodern option is a concession to our culture that goes too far, however well-intentioned it is. We can and must do better than this if we are to be up to the task of responding to the crisis of our age.

QUESTIONS FOR PERSONAL REFLECTION OR GROUP DISCUSSION

1. Postmodernism is another dominant worldview in Western culture today. It has contributed to making discourse in the public square "naked." What does that mean (pages 65–66)? How have the debates about religion, ethics, and politics turned out to be about power (the ability to enforce compliance) rather than about authority (the right to be believed and followed based on possession of the relevant knowledge)?

   Our so-called "information age" has democratized information production, dissemination, and access. Do you think this has contributed to human beings as being more wise and virtuous? If not, why not?

2. Two important shifts that have occurred in Western culture at large and in *academia* in the last one hundred years have been discussed. What are they, how did they come about, and what has been their implication (pages 69–70).

   Critique the fact/value distinction—i.e., the claim that science presents facts and theology or ethics present values (which are to be held privately because they should not have authority in the public square). Is this a false dichotomy? If so, why? How has it contributed to the view that Christianity is a faith tradition and not a knowledge tradition? Do you live your life publicly as though the fact/value distinction is true?

3. Postmodernism includes a denial of objective knowledge and reason (pages 78–80). What does it mean to reject the notion that rationality is objective? Is there any point of view from which one can define knowledge itself or what counts as knowledge without begging the question in favor of one's view?

   Interact with the author and his citations of postmodernists (page 79). How does the distinction between "psychological" and "rational" objectivity help clear away some of the entrenched historical and cultural confusion about what is meant by objective knowledge?

4. Postmodernism also advocates denying objective, absolute truth. This denial of truth involves what philosophers have called the

"correspondence theory of truth" (pages 80–82). What is meant by this theory? How does it appeal to ordinary, commonsensical experience? What is the essential relationship between a "truth-bearer," a "correspondence relation," and a "truth-maker"?

5. In light of the key terms associated with the correspondence theory of truth, the author considers two main arguments advanced for the theory: a descriptive and a dialectical argument (pages 81–82). How are these arguments different in terms of their main claim, their supportive reasons, and their approach? Which is the stronger argument? Why?

6. The author claims that the "postmodern rejection of objective or absolute truth rests on at least two confusions" (p. 83). What are they? Is absolute truth the same thing as objective truth? Do you have to be absolutely certain about something in order to accept absolute truth? Why is the epistemic notion of objectivity false philosophically?

   The second confusion is that statements are truth bearers and not propositions. Why is this false philosophically?

7. Postmodernists often confusingly assert that having or using a sentence (or any other piece of language) is a necessary and sufficient condition for thinking or having propositional content (pages 84–85). Assess the reasons the author gives to show that one can think prior to acquiring language. Have you ever encountered this postmodern confusion?

8. Review this section that gives the postmodernist's answers to the five questions (pp. 85–86): What is real? What is the nature and limits of knowledge? Who is well-off and what is the good life? Who is a really good person? How does one become a really good person?

   Given what postmodernists believe, do you think it is intellectually prudent to draw from postmodern insight and apply it to Christianity? Can one be a better apprentice of Jesus by being a postmodernist? Does postmodernism engender a greater or lesser responsibility on knowers to submit to the authoritative dictates of reality?

9. Consider the distinction between learning to live our life by truth versus learning to live our life by knowledge of the truth (page 87). Why are both necessary?

CHAPTER 4

FROM DRAMA TO DEADNESS IN FIVE STEPS

On Sunday morning May 9, 2004, I was in the Seattle airport waiting to board my flight home. Having finished a weekend of speaking, I wanted to relax, so I picked up a copy of *The Seattle Times* and made a beeline for the sports page. Before I got there, the lead editorial in the opinion section caught my eye. It was entitled "A Nation Divided," and in it Joel Kitkin argued that America is more divided today than at any time since the Civil War.[1] America is two nations, he claimed, and the fundamental dividing line is not political, economic, or racial. Rather, it is "a struggle between contrasting and utterly incompatible worldviews"—a secular perspective championed by the universities, Hollywood, and the major media, and ethical monotheism whose center of gravity—are you ready for this?—is Evangelical churches.

In my view, Kitkin was painting with too broad a brush and did so to make his point. But his fundamental idea seems to me correct. The secularized perspective is constituted by two worldviews—naturalism and postmodernism—which agree with each other over against ethical monotheism (of which Christianity is the main version) about one important point: There is no nonempirical knowledge and no objective immaterial world. This is the continental divide at the root of current public debate and discourse, and I want to expand on this center of divide by noting five crucial paradigm shifts that greased the skids from a thick world to a thin one. To some extent, these shifts have deadened all of our souls, and it is part of the drama of life in the Kingdom of God to understand and provide alternatives to these shifts.

SHIFT 1: FROM KNOWLEDGE TO FAITH

Shortly after the terrorist attack on September 11, 2001, Oprah Winfrey focused an episode of her program on the turn to God since the attack, a turn she wished to foster. For those already deadened to cultural shifts, the program was fairly uneventful, but for those with eyes to see, it was breathtaking.

To explain, let me note first what she did not do. She did not get on the air, warn that we were under threat of a terrorist smallpox attack, and urge people to seek protection from smallpox whatever that protection meant to each individual. If your truth implies that smallpox, prevention comes by eating cereal and not eggs for breakfast, then go for it. If it implies that you should attend more movies to relax your immune system, then live out your truth in this way. We shouldn't get hung up in the word we use for "smallpox prevention"—cereal, movie attendance or whatever; the important thing is to seek prevention whatever that means to you. Indeed, Oprah did not even presume to speak about smallpox prevention since she is not an expert. In fact, she brought a doctor on the show to address the issues. This is because we assume that the issue of smallpox prevention is one of objective fact, that there is a body of knowledge relevant to the issue and that some folks—experts—have the knowledge needed to address the problem.

Instead, here is what she did. She urged people to seek God, "whatever he, she, it, or they mean to you." We should not get hung up in the word we use for him, her, it, or they, she cautioned. The important thing is that we all seek our own truth with renewed vigor. Now what assumption— most likely subconscious—must Oprah Winfrey and her editorial crew be making about religion and the audience's understanding of it? Just this: Religious claims are neither factual in nature nor subject to rational evaluation. Religion is not a domain of fact and knowledge, so there are no experts. Thus, a talk show host's feelings about her own truth regarding religious matters is just as "valid" as anyone else's.

In such a context we now live and move and have our being, and this context undermines the religion of Jesus and his Kingdom gospel. Thus, it is more than ironic to see the Evangelical community widely adopt a perspective perilously close to Oprah's. While most Evangelicals reject pluralism and do, in fact, take Christianity to be true, without knowing it, they accept the claim that religion is a matter of faith and not knowledge. In chapter 5, I will clarify the nature of faith and its relationship to knowledge, and I will describe ways to develop faith. But for now, I note that the current definition of faith sees it as a brute decision of the will to believe something without that choice being informed by knowledge or reason.

To illustrate the widespread acceptance of a noncognitive view of faith among us, consider a trip I took several years ago. I went to Schenectady, New York, to conduct a series of evangelistic messages for a church. The series was in a high school gym, and several believers and unbelievers came each night. The first evening I gave arguments for the existence of God from science and philosophy. Before closing in prayer, I entertained several questions from the audience. One woman (who was a Christian) complained about my talk, charging that if I "proved" the existence of God, I would leave no room for faith. I responded by saying that if she were right, then we should pray that currently available evidence for God would evaporate and be refuted so there would be even more room for faith! Obviously, her view of faith utterly detached it from reason and knowledge and, as Archie Bunker put it, faith is believing something because it's in the Bible that nobody would believe otherwise!

Here's another consideration. Evangelical institutions of learning from elementary school to Christian colleges and universities are rightly concerned with integrating Scripture and Christian theology with other fields of study to help students form a Christian worldview. So far, so good. But note the ubiquitous language used to describe the integrative endeavor: *the integration of faith and learning*. What does this communicate? It implies that insights gained from various disciplines from chemistry to literature deserve the cognitive label "learning," while biblical assertions are named "faith." When push comes to shove and there are tensions between "faith" and "learning," guess who wins? The academic discipline in question will carry greater cognitive authority than biblical teaching, which, conveniently, will be placed in some complementary upper story of meaning and value, while the factual, intellectual labor will come from the academic discipline. Theistic evolution is the classic expression of this intellectual pacifism that results from depicting integration as a task of relating "faith" and "learning."

The sad result of this understanding of faith is the loss of an Evangelical mind. As Mark Noll bemoaned,

> the scandal of the evangelical mind is that there is not much of an evangelical mind.... Despite dynamic success at a popular level, modern American evangelicals have failed notably in sustaining serious intellectual life. They have nourished millions of believers in the simple verities of the gospel but have largely abandoned the universities,

the arts, and other realms of "high" culture.... The historical situation is ... curious. Modern evangelicals are the spiritual descendants of leaders and movements distinguished by probing, creative, fruitful attention to the mind.[2]

This, in turn, creates a plausibility structure in culture in which actions such as Oprah Winfrey's pass without notice, a structure in which Christian ideas are no longer taken as factual or items of knowledge. For example, as philosopher John Hick pointed out regarding the afterlife, the "considerable decline within society as a whole, accompanied by a lesser decline within the churches, of the belief in personal immortality clearly reflects the assumption within our culture that we should only believe in what we experience, plus what the accredited sciences certify to us."[3] In such a context, Christians must stop talking about "belief" in life after death, heaven and hell, and must reexpress their views on these and related matters as expressions of knowledge of reality. In chapter 5, I will provide some aid in this task.

SHIFT 2: FROM HUMAN FLOURISHING TO SATISFACTION OF DESIRE

Another modern trend is a change in what people mean by "the good life." From Old Testament times and ancient Greece until this century, the good life was widely understood to mean a life of human flourishing constituted by intellectual and moral virtue. The good life is the life of ideal human functioning according to the nature that God himself gave to us.

On this view, prior to creation God had in mind an ideal blueprint of human nature that he used to create each and every human being. Happiness was understood as a life of virtue, and the successful person was the person who knew how to live life well according to what we are by nature because of the creative design of God. When the Declaration of Independence says that we are endowed by our Creator with certain inalienable rights, among them the right to pursue happiness, it is referring to virtue and character. So understood, happiness involves suffering, endurance, and patience because these are important means to becoming a good person who lives the good life.

But as we saw in chapter 1, this notion of happiness as human flourishing has been replaced with a new understanding. The old definition presupposes the availability of the moral and spiritual knowledge needed to grasp the nature of human flourishing and the journey required to achieve it. However, under the pressure of naturalism and postmodernism and their denial of nonempirical knowledge, in the last hundred years or so, happiness has come to mean something quite different, and the shift in meaning is destroying people's lives.

A recent dictionary definition of happiness is "a sense of pleasurable satisfaction."[4] This definition is far from arbitrary. It captures accurately our day-to-day usage of "happiness" as seen in statements like these:

> I just got my semester grades and I am so happy!
>
> My team won the Superbowl and I am so stoked, so happy!
>
> I can't wait to go on vacation. Just the thought of it makes me so happy!

Note carefully that happiness is identified with a feeling, and more specifically, a feeling close to pleasure. So understood, the essence of happiness becomes the unbridled satisfaction of desire. Pleasurable satisfaction makes a poor lifetime goal; it is, however, a wonderful byproduct of striving after happiness in the classical sense. Think about it. If happiness is having an internal feeling of fun or pleasurable satisfaction and if it is our main goal, where will people place their focus each day? It will be on them, and the result will be a culture of self-absorbed narcissists who cannot live for something bigger than they are.

To see this, consider the current preoccupation with physical appearance and exercise. Far too often today, the exercise craze is an expression of empty selves trying to be happy by indulging a narcissistic, self-absorbed emphasis on body image and sexual attraction as the holy grail of life's most important quest—the satisfaction of immediate bodily desire. It is no accident that the emergence of the empty self and the inordinate preoccupation with exercise and jogging coincide. This, I take it, is the bad news about the current exercise craze.

Does it follow that there is no good news? Certainly not. In its proper place in a life well lived, exercise can be of immense benefit to one's health and overall flourishing. I also believe that exercise can be a strategic part of an overall employment of spiritual disciplines that, taken together, can help to produce virtuous, flourishing people of wisdom and character. But the current overemphasis on exercise is the result of a preoccupation with body image and sex as means to desire satisfaction, social power—in short, happiness. This, in turn, is a result of the loss of moral and spiritual knowledge. In chapter 6, we will investigate the role of spiritual disciplines as a way of resisting current preoccupation with "happiness" and the slide toward Gomorrah it signifies.

SHIFT 3: FROM DUTY AND VIRTUE TO MINIMALIST ETHICS

The loss of moral knowledge has meant a shift from a view of the moral life in which duty and virtue are central to a minimalist ethical perspective to be described shortly. If duty and virtue are of central concern to the moral life, then there must be moral knowledge available to know what duties and virtues are correct and how one can become a righteous, virtuous person. Remember, moral rules without knowledge degenerate into customs such as "don't eat your peas with a knife," and customs are too trivial to marshal the courage and effort needed to live by and internalize them.

Knowledge of duty and virtue is no longer seen as a possibility, and the impact of the shift to minimalist ethics is disastrous. I will illustrate this disaster by showing how it informs the pro-life cause. A salient feature of the success of any social, religious, or moral movement is the degree to which its advocates understand, shape, and employ the flow of ideas that forms the intellectual backdrop against which those advocates carry out their work. Setting aside Marxist and other self-refuting materialist forms of social determinism, it seems clear that ideas are among the primary things that impede or facilitate revolutionary movements.

Nowhere is this more evident than the pro-life cause. But just exactly what ideas constitute the core components of the milieu in which pro-life advocates live and move and have their being? In 1981, Daniel Callahan, who at that time served as director of The Hastings Center, published an important article entitled "Minimalist Ethics."[5] Callahan's central thesis was that contemporary American culture had come to stress the transcendence of the individual over the community, the importance of tolerating all moral viewpoints, the autonomy of the individual as the highest human good, and the voluntary, informed consent contract as the model of human relationships. These diverse moral positions, argued Callahan, are not part of a list of isolated ideas; rather, they constitute different aspects of a widely accepted moral axiom — minimalist ethics — that can be expressed in a single proposition: *One may morally act in any way one chooses so long as one does not do harm to others.*

Sadly, Callahan provided no analysis of the connection between this axiom and other ideas extant in the culture at that time. Indeed, this lack of analysis blunted the force of his own solution to the problem, which essentially amounted to the claim that we need to set aside the assumption of minimalist ethics in favor of richer moral convictions because a minimalist ethic will not sustain us over the long haul.

What are those ideas that Callahan failed to weave into his analysis? Among a small handful of worthy candidates, I want to focus on one that I take to be the primary hindrance to persuading people to adopt a richer ethical stance than minimalist ethics and, a fortiori, to adopting a pro-life perspective. One might think that it is the loss of belief in moral truth to which I refer. This is, indeed, a serious problem and worthy of analysis, but it is not, in my view, the foundational culprit. After all, if pressed, most moral philosophers and theologians would eschew ethical relativism in its various forms for reasons discussed below.

Rather, at the risk of undue repetition, I repeat a major theme of the first three chapters: The main intellectual factor left out of Callahan's analysis and one that hinders the pro-life movement is *a loss of belief among cultural elites in particular, and the broader public in general, in the existence of nonempirical, nonscientific* **knowledge**, *especially of moral and religious* **knowledge**. Since we know that water is H_2O, no one thinks you are legislating chemistry by insisting on this truth. But if you insist on abortion being immoral, you are accused of legislating morality precisely because (allegedly) no one can know whether or not this is true.

Interestingly, Callahan himself seemed to accept the absence of moral knowledge in his article. He makes reference to the fact that when John Stuart Mill first advanced his harm principle in 1859, he could "assume a relatively stable body of moral conviction below the surface."[6] Later, he advises that we bring "all the public and private opinion we can" against a minimalist ethic.[7] Note carefully Callahan's selection of terms: moral *conviction* and public/private *opinion*. These are hardly robust cognitive labels.

There are several examples in the literature of this ubiquitous denial of ethical knowledge that provides the context in which minimalist ethics can flourish. For example, in a widely used text in ethics, utilitarian Tom L. Beauchamp considers and rejects an objective theory of value because, among other things, he thinks it is futile and presumptuous to attempt to develop such a general theory.[8] As a replacement, Beauchamp proffers subjective preference utilitarianism, according to which the value of an act lies in its maximization of the satisfaction of desires and wants that express individual preferences.

Beauchamp recognizes that, so defined, this theory suffers from some fairly obvious counterexamples; for example, in a possible world where most prefer child molestation, it would justify such an act under certain conditions. So Beauchamp supplements the principle of subject preference such that the justification of an act is spelled out in terms of the maximization of those subjective preferences that it is rational to have.

Now just exactly how is "rationality" functioning here? To answer this, let us distinguish prescriptive and descriptive rationality. Prescriptive rationality is the ability to have insights into or form justified beliefs with respect to what is intrinsically valuable. This cannot be what Beauchamp means since, if it were, his theory would be circular. Clearly, he means descriptive rationality: the ability to select efficient means to accomplish arbitrarily preferred ends and the formation of only those desires that normal people desire, which, in turn, would be cashed out statistically or in terms of evolutionary advantage, or in some similar sort of way.

My purpose here is not to evaluate Beauchamp's subjective preference theory as a theory of value, though it is clearly deficient on this score. Among other things, if the processes of evolution or the statistically regular means of socialization produced Nazis or child molesters, then Beauchamp's theory of value would entail the moral correctness of such acts. Rather, I want to call attention to the impact on the availability of moral knowledge that Beauchamp's analysis has. By defining rationality in the descriptive and instrumental way he does, he severs the connection between rationality and moral truth and, thus, implicitly denies the possibility of moral knowledge. In such a context, those like the pro-life movement, who take a stand that assumes the existence of moral truth and knowledge, will be marginalized and disregarded. Thus, part of the pro-life effort must include the reinstatement of moral knowledge.

SHIFT 4: FROM CLASSIC FREEDOM TO CONTEMPORARY FREEDOM

Classically, freedom meant the power to do what one ought to do. Thus, one is free to play the piano if one has the skills, training, and knowledge necessary to play it. Similarly, one is free in life if one has the power to live *the way one ought to live*. Sexual freedom in this context means the power to live a chaste, holy life and to engage skillfully in sexual activity in the way in which we were designed by God—in heterosexual marital union. Classic freedom is liberating, indeed, but a necessary condition of such freedom is the availability of the relevant sort of knowledge. Absent such knowledge, freedom has come to be understood as the right to do *what one wants to do*. Sexual freedom in this context means the right to satisfy one's desires in any way one wishes, with the possible exception of not harming others.

In my view, the contemporary view of freedom makes it difficult to justify resistance to a wide range of immoral practices, including, for example, the practice of adults having sex with minors, including children. If this is what adults want to do to satisfy their desires, who are we to judge? Now someone could respond that on the contemporary view of freedom sexual activity should be limited to contact among consenting adults and that children are not mature enough to give informed consent. Thus, the contemporary view of freedom, along with the concept of informed consent, does have the resources needed to justify resistance to sex with children.

But such a response is inadequate. We do not require informed consent from children when it comes to giving them vaccinations or requiring them to attend school. Consent is a factor only if we have already judged that the activity in question is harmful or wrong in some way. But absent the existence of moral absolutes and the knowledge thereof, it is hard to see how such a judgment can be made. What if one were to argue that sex with children actually helps them overcome oppressive fundamentalist hang-ups with enjoying their bodies and, like vaccinations, it is actually good for children?

Lest you think that this line of argumentation is far-fetched, understand that some today are making precisely this argument. A Christian worldview has the intellectual resources needed to refute such attitudes, but it is far from clear that our current milieu and its view of freedom have such resources. I don't want to press the point further, but Christians should understand that in the thin atmosphere of contemporary secularism, if freedom means the right to do whatever I want, any attempt to limit freedom, especially if such a limitation is grounded in a substantive moral claim, will be greeted with a burden of proof that is hard to meet in a thin world.

Shift 5: From Classic Tolerance to Contemporary Tolerance

Finally, there is widespread confusion today about the nature and value of tolerance, a confusion that results from conflating the classic and contemporary understandings of this term. By failing to keep them distinct,

Christians quite understandably experience the injunction to be tolerant with a certain degree of ambiguity. On the one hand, we intuitively sense that tolerance is a good thing. On the other hand, there's something fishy with the way it is used today. The way out of this confusion is to distinguish two forms of tolerance, reject the contemporary sense, and retain the classic version. Before I distinguish the two, it will be helpful to offer a characterization and critique of moral relativism because one version of tolerance is consistent with objective moral values while the other version expresses and fosters moral relativism.

Moral relativism is widely espoused today. This thesis holds that everyone ought to act in accordance with the agent's own society's code (or, perhaps, with the agent's own personal code). What is right for one society is not necessarily right for another society. For example, society A may have in its code that "adultery is morally permissible," and society B may have that "adultery is morally forbidden." In this case, adultery is permissible for members of A and forbidden for those in B.

Put differently, moral relativism implies that moral propositions are not simply true or false. Rather, the truth values (true or false) of moral principles themselves are relative to the beliefs of a given culture/individual. For example, "murder is wrong" is not true plain and simple; it is "true for culture A" but, perhaps, "false for culture B." The point here is not just that there is a certain relativity in the *application* of moral principles. For example, two cultures could both hold that "one should maintain sexual fidelity in marriage," but apply this differently because of factual differences about what counts as a marriage (e.g., one wife or several wives). Factual diversity can lead to differences in the way a moral rule is applied.

Moral relativism goes beyond this type of diversity and asserts that the truth values of moral principles themselves are relative to a given culture. For example, whether one ought to maintain sexual fidelity itself could be true relative to one culture and false relative to another culture. There is a difference between individual moral relativism (also called *subjectivism*) and cultural moral relativism (also called *conventionalism*). The former says that the truth of moral rules is relative to the beliefs of each individual; the latter makes moral truth relative to entire cultures or societies.

For at least four reasons, moral relativism is irrational and false. First, it is difficult to define what a society is or to specify in a given case which society is the relevant one. Consider societies A and B above. If a man from A has extramarital sex with a woman from B in a hotel in a third society C with a different view from either A or B, which is the relevant society for determining whether the act was right or wrong? Moreover, we are often simultaneously a member of several different societies, which may hold different moral values: our nuclear family, our extended family, our neighborhood, school, church, or social clubs, our place of employment, our town, state, country, and the international community. Which society is the relevant one? What if I am simultaneously a member of two societies and one allows but the other forbids a certain moral action? What am I to do in this case?

Second, moral relativism suffers from a problem known as the Reformer's Dilemma. If relativism is true, then it is logically impossible for a society to have a virtuous, moral reformer like Jesus Christ, Gandhi, or Martin Luther King. Why? Moral reformers are members of a society who stand outside that society's code and pronounce a need for reform and change in that code. However, if an act is right if and only if it is in keeping with a given society's code, then the moral reformer is by definition an immoral person, for his views are at odds with those of his society. Moral reformers must always be wrong because they go against the code of their society. But any view implying that moral reformers are impossible is defective.

Put differently, moral relativism implies that neither cultures (if conventionalism is in view) nor individuals (if subjectivism is in view) can improve their moral code. The only thing they can do is change it. Why? Consider any change in a code from believing, say, racism is right to racism is wrong. How should we evaluate this change? All the moral relativist can say is that, from the perspective of the earlier code, the new principle is wrong and from the perspective of the new code, the old principle is wrong. In short, there has merely been a change in perspective. No sense can be given to the idea that a new code reflects an improvement on an old code because this idea requires a vantage point outside of and above the society's (or individual's) code from which to make that judgment. And it is precisely such a vantage point that moral relativism disallows.

Some relativists respond to this by claiming that moral reformers are allowed in their view because all moral reformers do is to make explicit what was already implicit but overlooked in the society's code. Thus, if a society already has a principle that persons ought to be treated equally, then this implicitly contains a prohibition against racism even though it may not be explicitly recognized by society. The moral reformer merely makes this explicit by calling people to think more carefully about their own code. Unfortunately, this claim is false. Many moral reformers do, in fact, call people to alter their codes. They do not merely make clear what was already contained in preexisting codes.

Other relativists claim that they can allow for the existence of moral reformers by recognizing that societies may contain, implicitly or explicitly, a principle in their code that says "follow the advice of moral reformers." But, again, this response does not work. For one thing, what does it mean to call these reformers "moral" if they do not keep the rest of their society's code, which, by definition, they do not keep? If, however, the reformer does keep and believe in the rest of his or her society's code, how could a change in that code count as a moral improvement? A reformer could have the *power* to bring change, but how could he or she have the moral *authority* to do so? And why call the change a moral improvement?

Moreover, moral reformers can exist without any such principle being in a society's code, so the presence or absence of such a principle is irrelevant. And what if there are two or more moral reformers operating at the same time? Which one do we follow? Finally, the presence of such a principle in a society's code places all the other moral principles in jeopardy, for they would be temporary principles subject to the whims of the next moral reformer. In fact, before someone could honestly follow a principle in one's society's code, one would have to make a good faith effort to make sure a moral reformer had not changed that part of the code that day.

Third, some acts are wrong regardless of social conventions. The simple fact is that all people can know that some things are wrong, such as torturing babies for fun, stealing as such, greed as such, and so forth without first having to have criteria for knowing how it is that they do, in fact, know such things. Thus, an act (e.g., torturing babies for fun) can be wrong and known to be wrong even if society says it is right, and an act can be right and known as such even if society says it is wrong. In fact, an act can be right or wrong even if society says nothing whatever about that act.

Fourth, if moral relativism is true, it is difficult to see how one society could be justified in morally blaming another society in certain cases. According to moral relativism, I should act in keeping with my society's code and others should act in keeping with their society's codes. If Smith does an act that is right in his code but wrong in mine, how can I criticize his act as wrong?

One could respond to this objection by pointing out that society A may have in its code the principle that one should criticize acts of, say, murder regardless of where they occur. Thus, members of A could criticize such acts in other societies. But such a rule further reveals the inconsistency in normative relativism. If normative relativism is true and is embraced by members of A, those in A seem to be in the position of holding that members of society B ought to murder (since B's code says it is right), and I ought to criticize members of B because my code says I should. Thus, I criticize members of B as immoral and at the same time hold that their acts should have been done. Further, why should members of B care about what members of A think? After all, if relativism is true, there is nothing intrinsically right about the moral views of society A. For these and other reasons, moral relativism must be rejected.

We are now in a place where we can fruitfully discuss tolerance. The principle of tolerance is often associated with the debate about relativism. It is often thought that this principle is implied by relativism but is at odds with some form of absolutism because the latter is dogmatic and judgmental while the former is more tolerant in orientation. In order to evaluate this claim, we need to get clear on what the principle of tolerance is.

As already noted, two senses can be distinguished. According to the classical sense of the principle of tolerance, a person holds that his own moral views are true and those of his opponent are false. But he still respects his opponent as a person and his right to make a case for his views. Thus, someone has a duty to tolerate a different moral view, not in the sense of thinking it is morally correct but quite the opposite, in the sense that a person will continue to value and respect one's opponent, to treat him with dignity, to recognize his right to argue for and propagate his ideas, and so forth. Strictly speaking, on the classic view, one tolerates persons, not ideas.

In this sense, even though someone disapproves of another's moral beliefs and practices, he or she will not inappropriately interfere with them. However, it is consistent with this view that a person judges his opponent's views to be wrong and dedicates himself to doing everything morally appropriate to counteract those views, such as using argument and persuasion. It should be clear that the classic sense of tolerance is really an absolutist position and is inconsistent with relativism. If a person does not hold another position to be morally false, what is there to tolerate? Surely, it is not just the fact that one doesn't like the view in question, but that he judges it mistaken.

The contemporary version of tolerance, popular in the general culture, goes beyond the classical version in claiming that one should not even judge that other people's *viewpoints* are wrong. How does this view square with relativism? It is not at all clear. For one thing, this principle of tolerance does not follow from the simple fact that cultures sometimes differ regarding the moral rules they accept. From the fact that cultures differ in basic ethical judgments, no moral duties whatever follow. Second, moral relativism implies that one ought to be tolerant if the principle of tolerance is in that person's social code and one ought to be intolerant if the principle of intolerance is in that person's social code. Moral relativism does allow for the principle of tolerance, but it also allows for the principle of intolerance in the same way.

Combinatorial relativism means and so implies that we ought not to pass judgment on the freely chosen understanding of the good life of others. Finally, the moral duty to be tolerant does not follow from naturalist or postmodern skepticism regarding moral knowledge because no moral duties follow from such skepticism. It seems, then, that the contemporary notion of tolerance is not an easy fit with different versions of relativism, in spite of what many think.

"WE GOTTA GET OUTTA THIS PLACE IF IT'S THE LAST THING WE EVER DO"

As I have already noted, Professor Martin Seligman is a leading expert on happiness.[9] For at least thirty years, he has been warning us that the various shifts in our culture since the 1960s, including some I have mentioned in this chapter, have led to a growing sense of depression, despair, and meaninglessness in our culture. For Seligman, these shifts have brought about a replacement of a sense of objective meaning and purpose to life in serving God, one's country, and one's family with the narcissistic preoccupation with one's own private success and pleasure.

In 2001, Hollywood publicist Michael Levine wrote a cover article in *Psychology Today* in which he argued that constant exposure to beautiful women has made single men less interested in dating and married men less interested in their wives.[10] According to Levine, since about 1950, the average male has been exposed to hundreds upon hundreds of beautiful women as a result of airplane and automobile travel as well as television and movies. Levine refers to research involving men who were exposed to (nonpornographic) pictures of beautiful actresses. After the exposure, single and married men were asked to rate the desirability of a typical woman in their social environment or of their wives, respectively. In both cases they were much less interested in the women available to them.

Levine observes that prior to the automobile and television, men were exposed to few people in general and extremely beautiful women in particular. Limited in travel and with no television, most men learned to relate to women on a basis other than beauty. But today, most men observe numerous beautiful women each night on television. As a result, they begin to lose interest in the more "ordinary" women around them.

None of this will strike you as particularly surprising. What is surprising, however, is his explanation for this loss of interest: Television exposure did not cause more "ordinary" women to appear less attractive to the men studied. Rather, men began to think: "My partner is fine, but why settle for fine when there are so many beautiful women out there! I can do a lot better than this!"

Levine's analysis stops here, but the insights provided in this chapter offer a more penetrating analysis than Levine's. Why is it that men think this way? Answer: The shift in worldview from a Judeo-Christian thick world to a naturalist or postmodern thin world has brought about the five shifts noted above and with them, a cultural milieu that lacks the resources needed to resist the drift towards the proliferation of empty selves. In this context, men are empty selves gorged on and dulled by seeking happiness and, as a result, are individualistic, narcissistic, infantile people who approach others as objects that exist merely to make them happy. Slowly but surely, the contemporary Zeitgeist is killing our lives, our religious fervor, and our relationships. As the song put it, "we gotta get outta this place, if it's the last thing we ever do." The second half of the book provides direction for doing just that.

Questions for Personal Reflection or Group Discussion

1. Because of naturalism and postmodernism, Western culture has undergone five important shifts. The first is from knowledge to faith (pages 91–94). How does the ubiquitous language of "integration of faith and learning" exemplify this shift? How has this shift contributed to what historian Mark Noll has called "the scandal of the evangelical mind"?

   Do you conceive of Christianity as a faith or a knowledge tradition? Assess why. If the former, what motivates this position for you?

2. Another important shift is from an emphasis on human flourishing as happiness to happiness as the satisfaction of desire (page 94–96). How does this shift relate to the first shift? If the resources of Christianity produces mere privatized faith, does this encourage an emphasis on flourishing in virtue and character formed by wisdom, or does it encourage simply the satisfaction of felt needs or desires? What are some contemporary popular cultural habits and experiences that model the shift to happiness as pleasurable satisfaction?

3. The third shift is from duty and virtue to a "minimalist ethics" (page 96–98). How has a loss of belief in the existence of nonempirical, nonscientific knowledge contributed to the hindrance of a richer ethical viewpoint? Is a "minimalist ethic" an unlivable position to maintain individually or in a society? Is so, explain how and why.

4. A fourth shift is from classical freedom to a contemporary sense of freedom. What is the essence of this shift (pages 98–99)? How have the previous shifts given birth the contemporary sense of "freedom"? Do you think the contemporary notion is more plausible if a "thin" or a "thick" world exists?

   If "whatever you want to do" is a necessary condition for freedom, what role is there for virtue or doing the right thing? Should a democratic society promote a freedom that is formed in virtue?

5. The final shift is from an emphasis on classical tolerance to an affirmation of contemporary tolerance. This shift has led to a widespread moral relativism (page 100–104). What is moral relativism? How is it related to a notion of freedom gone amuck or freedom unconstrained by virtue? What is the difference between subjectivism and conventionalism?

6. The author offers four reasons why moral relativism is irrational and false. The first reason is that "it is difficult to define what a society is or to specify in a given case which society is the relevant one" to morally choose (page 100). How does this reason lead to moral confusion and chaos? Is there a way to maintain moral relativism but successfully avoid this objection? What kind of view of human relationships and community must a moral relativist maintain in order to avoid this objection?

7. A second reason why moral relativism is false is that it suffers from a problem known as the "Reformer's Dilemma." What is that, and how and why does moral relativism suffer from it (pages 101–102)? How can a moral relativist accurately state that heroes or moral exemplars are important to follow? How does a moral relativist seek to solve the Reformer's Dilemma, and why does the author consider these examples unsuccessful (pages 101–103)?

8. A third reason for why moral relativism is false is that "some acts are wrong regardless of social conventions" (page 102). Does moral relativism do a good job of preserving or contradicting our deeply held moral intuitions about what is right and wrong (e.g., torturing babies for fun)? If it contradicts these intuitions, what does this tell us about the explanatory adequacy and liveability of moral relativism as an ethical theory?

9. A final reason for why moral relativism is false is that if it were true, "it is difficult to see how one society should be justified in morally blaming another society" (page 102). Why isn't moral relativism a good candidate for helping to spread democratic governance amidst terrorist or politically oppressive regimes? How might this fourth reason address the political and moral problems of multiculturalism as an ideology that attempts to address cultural pluralism without urging that one culture is "better" than another?

PART 2

CHARTING A WAY OUT: THE
KINGDOM TRIANGLE

CHAPTER 5

THE RECOVERY OF KNOWLEDGE

We all sense the craziness of our culture. I certainly do, and my heart is saddened by the fractured lives and decadent social structures that proliferate around us. Sometimes the forces aligned against the Kingdom look overwhelming, and it is tempting to see the church's role as a rescue mission for a straggler here and there as we wait for the world to end. However understandable such sentiments are, they are premature, misguided, and unworthy of the Lord Jesus and his Kingdom. If the statistics are even approximately accurate, there are a lot of us who have enlisted as Jesus' apprentices.

In chapter 7, you will be truly startled when I show you that the best-kept secret of the last fifty years is the incredible explosion of believing Christianity all over the world. Make no mistake about it: Aslan is afoot with unmistakable power—everywhere, that is, except in Western culture. Still, there are many of us Westerners who have not bowed the knee to Baal, and if we redouble our efforts to find ways to band together, the Western church has a significant amount of mileage in it yet for the Kingdom.

So what do we do? I think we need to return to the first four centuries of Christianity and take some lessons from the early church. During that time, our brothers and sisters faced odds of success more incredible than ours, and yet they were so victorious that today we name our children Peter and Paul and our dogs Caesar and Nero!

In a 2003 revised edition of his magisterial work *Evangelism in the Early Church*, a book that must be regarded as the single most authoritative treatment of the spread of the gospel in the first four centuries, Michael Green highlights three factors central to the church's explosive success in her first four centuries: (1) the church's ability to engage in persuasive apologetics and outthink her critics; (2) the transformed character and biblical compassion of believers; and (3) the manifest power of the Kingdom of God by the Spirit through healings, demonic deliverance, and prophetic ability clearly from another realm.

Regarding persuasive apologetics and the church's ability to outthink her critics, consider the following statement from Justin Martyr in A.D. 155. In it he appeals to the Roman emperor Hadrian to give Christianity a fair hearing:

> Reason requires that those who are truly pious and philosophers should honor and cherish the truth alone, scorning merely to follow the opinions of the ancients, if they are worthless.... In these pages we do not come before you with flattery, or as if making a speech to win your favor, but asking you to give judgment according to strict and exact inquiry—not moved by prejudice or respect for superstitious men, or by irrational impulse.[1]

How refreshing! A knowledgeable Christian leader appealing not to faith but to reason! It is incredible to me that when Catholics or Jews present their community's views before the nation, their spokespersons are university professors, trained ethicists, and highly qualified intellectual advocates for their viewpoints. But when Larry King or MSNBC seeks Evangelical perspectives on today's issues, our community puts forth megachurch pastors. These men are to be honored and thanked for the great job they are doing in pasturing their flocks. But frankly, they simply are not qualified to speak about abortion, homosexuality, church/state issues, or a host of other topics that must be carefully nuanced and articulated if a solid Christian perspective is to be presented.

That the media selects communicators and not scholars and that the communicators either do not think to defer to Evangelical scholars or do not have a way to do so tell us something about how different we are from Justin Martyr and those made out of the same cloth as him. The makeup man is more important than the speech writer (or something like that). Since knowledge and faith are the central topic of this chapter, I will return to these matters shortly.

Regarding character and biblical compassion, I cite one example of the moral impact of the early Christian community. Decades ago Herbert Henson observed that paganism during this period was distinguished by callousness and cruelty toward children, especially baby girls. Infanticide and the exposure of infants were widely accepted.

Many of the exposed children were trained for purposes of prostitution, and many perished, immersing those who exposed them in the guilt of homicide. The compassion of Christians went forth to these abandoned little ones, doomed by their parents to vice and death. The widows and virgins of the Church included among their regular works of piety the care of these outcast babes. Among the first recorded charitable institutions we find mention of children's homes or orphanages.[2]

Henson goes on to argue that the minute and scrupulous care of human life by the early church, especially in its most vulnerable forms — slaves, gladiators, infants, various outcasts — was both foreign to paganism and part of what made vibrant Christianity triumphant over its enemies. I will address the formation of character in chapter 6.

Regarding the manifestation of Kingdom power, consider the statement by Quadrantus in the early second century. He emphasizes that some whom Jesus had healed were still around, and their presence strengthened the faith of the church: "But the works of our Savior were always present, for they were true, those who were cured, those who rose from the dead, who not merely appeared as cured and risen, but were constantly present, not only while the Savior was living, but even for some time after he had gone, so that some of them survived even to our own time."[3]

In his attempt to defend Christians against Roman persecution, Tertullian (155–230) points out the foolishness of such persecutions:

> But who would rescue you [if Christians were to withdraw] from those secret enemies that everywhere lay waste your minds and your bodily health? I mean, from the assaults of demons, whom we drive out of you, without reward, without pay. Why, this alone would have sufficed to avenge us — to leave you open and exposed to unclean spirits with immediate possession.[4]

In a similar vein, in his letter to the Roman official Scapula, Tertullian refers to the healings of well-placed Roman citizens:

> For, the secretary of a certain gentleman, when he was suffering from falling sickness caused by a demon, was freed from it; so also were the relatives of some of the others and a certain little boy. And heaven knows how many distinguished men, to say nothing of common people, have been cured either of devils or of their sickness.[5]

I will take up the topic of Kingdom power in chapter 7.

THE RECOVERY OF KNOWLEDGE BY THE CHRISTIAN COMMUNITY

Overview of Knowledge

Given the crisis of knowledge in our time, it is crucial that the church recover her confidence that she is in possession of *spiritual and ethical knowledge* in Holy Scripture primarily, but also in the history of her thought about God, moral issues, the spiritual life, and other important topics. For example, the Bible's teaching about the nature and proper functioning of the self, the family, and the life of virtue and spiritual formation, along with crucial information about developing an interactive relationship with God and his Kingdom, is not merely a set of ideas from the "Christian tradition." *Just as the history of chemistry provides us with knowledge of reality, so the history of Christian thought on these topics, rooted in the inerrant Word, provides knowledge of God and these related matters.*

To facilitate this recovery, the place to start is by gaining clarity about the nature of knowledge itself, so people will know what it means to have it. In essence, *knowledge is the ability to represent things as they are on an appropriate basis of thought and experience.* The possession of knowledge is crucial for life. Knowledge provides truth about reality along with the skillful ability to interact with reality. It is so important that Hosea 4:6 categorically asserts:

> My people are destroyed for lack of knowledge.
> Because you have rejected knowledge,
> I will also reject you from being My priest.
> Since you have forgotten the law of your God,
> I also will forget your children.

Note carefully that Hosea does not say the people have rejected faith. It is far worse than that. They have rejected the only appropriate ground for faith — knowledge. It comes as a surprise to people that Scripture has as much or more to say about knowledge than faith. Consider the following passages:[6]

> "I *know* you are a beautiful woman" (Gen. 12:11).

> [Abram] said, "O LORD God, how may I *know* that I shall possess it?" So he said to him ... (Gen. 15:8–9).

> "Now I *know* that the LORD is greater than all other gods; indeed, it was proven when they dealt proudly against the people" (Ex. 18:11).

Moses said to the LORD, "See, You say to me, 'Bring up this people!' But You Yourself have not let me *know* whom You will send with me" (Ex. 33:12).

Moses said, "By this you shall *know* that the LORD has sent me to do all these deeds; for this is not my doing. If these men die the death of all men or if they suffer the fate of all men, then the LORD has not sent me. But if the LORD brings about an entirely new thing and the ground opens its mouth and swallows them up with all that is theirs, and they descend alive into Sheol, then you will *understand* that these men have spurned the LORD"(Num. 16:28–30).

Know therefore today, and take it to heart, that the LORD, He is God in heaven above and on the earth below; there is no other (Deut. 4:39).

He said to sons of Israel, "When your children ask their fathers in time to come, saying, 'What are these stones?' then *you shall inform* your children [lit., let them know], saying, 'Israel crossed this Jordan on dry ground'" (Josh. 4:21–22).

"... *know with certainty* that the LORD your God will not continue to drive these nations out from before you" (Josh. 23:13).

Yet David vowed again, saying, "Your father *knows well* [lit., certainly knows] that I have found favor in your sight" (1 Sam. 20:3).

"But my lord is wise, like the wisdom of the angel of God, to *know* all that is in the earth" (2 Sam. 14:20—even if the claim is hyperbolic flattery).

"For your servant *knows* that I have sinned; therefore behold, I have come today, the first of all the house of Joseph to go down to meet my lord the king" (2 Sam. 19:20).

"For it will happen on the day you go out and cross over the brook Kidron, you will *know for certain* that you shall surely die; your blood shall be on your own head" (1 Kings 2:37).

"Now let him come to me, and he *shall know* that there is a prophet in Israel" (2 Kings 5:8).

"Do you not *know* that the LORD God of Israel gave the rule over Israel forever to David and his sons by a covenant of salt?" (2 Chron. 13:5).

But *know* that the LORD has set apart the godly man for Himself; the LORD hears when I call to Him (Ps. 4:3).

The lips of the righteous *bring forth* [lit., know] what is acceptable (Prov. 10:32).

"And all flesh *will know* that I, the LORD, am your Savior, and your Redeemer, the Mighty One of Jacob" (Isa. 49:26).

"Only *know for certain* that if you put me to death, you will bring innocent blood on yourselves, and on this city, and on its inhabitants; for truly the LORD has sent me to you to speak all these words in your hearing" (Jer. 26:15).

"I will satisfy My wrath on them, and I will be appeased; then they *will know* that I, the LORD, have spoken in My zeal" (Ezek. 5:13).

"Then they will comfort you when you see their conduct and actions, for you *will know* that I have not done in vain whatever I did to it," declares the LORD God (Ezek. 14:23).

"All the choice men in all his troops will fall by the sword, and the survivors will be scattered to every wind; and you *will know* that I, the LORD, have spoken" (Ezek. 17:21).

"... the great God *has made known* to the king what will take place in the future; so the dream is *true*, and its interpretation is *trustworthy*" (Dan. 2:45).

"Then I desired to *know* the exact meaning of the fourth beast" (Dan. 7:19).

"So you are to *know* and *discern* that ..." (Dan. 9:25).

"Then I will dwell in your midst, and you *will know* that the LORD of hosts has sent Me to you" (Zech. 2:11; cf. 4:9).

"To you it has been granted to *know* the mysteries of the kingdom of heaven, but to them it has not been granted" (Matt. 13:11).

"Teacher, we *know* that You are truthful and teach the way of God in truth" (Matt. 22:16—even though the context shows that Jesus' enemies were lying through their teeth when they said this, the context also presupposes they should have been sincerely confessing this!).

"You are mistaken, not *understanding* the Scriptures nor the power of God" (Matt. 22:29—a fine combination of propositional and experiential knowledge).

"But *be sure* [lit., know] of this, that if the head of the house *had known* at what time of the night the thief was coming, he would have been on the alert" (Matt. 24:43).

It seemed fitting for me as well ... to write it out for you in consecutive order, most excellent Theophilus; so that you may *know* the exact truth about the things you have been taught (Luke 1:3–4).

Zechariah said to the angel, "How *will I know* this for certain?" (Luke 1:18).

"Rabbi, we *know* that You have come from God as a teacher; for no one can do these signs that You do unless God is with him" (John 3:2).

The woman said to Him, "I *know* that Messiah is coming (He who is called Christ); when that One comes, He will declare all things to us" (John 4:25).

"If anyone is willing to do His will, he *will know* of the teaching, whether it is of God or whether I speak from Myself" (John 7:17).

"However, we *know* where this man is from; but whenever the Christ may come, no one *knows* where He is from" (John 7:27—another instance of a false claim that nevertheless discloses the nature of the presupposed epistemology).

"When you lift up the Son of Man, then you *will know* that I am He, and I do nothing on My own initiative, but I speak these things as the Father taught Me" (John 8:28).

"We *know* that this is our son, and that he was born blind; but how he now sees, we *do not know*; or who opened his eyes, we *do not know*" (John 9:20–21).

"We *know* that God has spoken to Moses, but as for this man, we *do not know* where He is from" (John 9:29).

"... that you may *know* and understand that the Father is in Me, and I in the Father" (John 10:38).

This is the disciple who is testifying to these things and wrote these things, and we *know* that his testimony is true (John 21:24).

"Men of Israel, listen to these words: Jesus the Nazarene, a man attested to you by God with miracles and wonders and signs which God performed through Him in your midst, just as you yourselves *know* ..." (Acts 2:22).

"Brethren, you *know* that in the early days God made a choice among you, that by my mouth the Gentiles would hear the word of the gospel and believe" (Acts 15:7).

"May we *know* what this new teaching is which you are proclaiming? For you are bringing some strange things to our ears; so we *want to know* what these things mean" (Acts 17:19–20).

"You yourselves *know,* from the first day that I set foot in Asia, how I was with you the whole time" (Acts 20:18).

But on the next day, wishing to *know for certain* why he had been accused by the Jews, he released him (Acts 22:30).

"But we desire to hear from you what your views are; for concerning this sect, *it is known to us* that it is spoken against everywhere" (Acts 28:22).

Now we *know* that whatever the Law says, it speaks to those who are under the Law, so that every mouth may be closed and all the world may become accountable to God (Rom. 3:19).

For we *know* that the Law is spiritual (Rom. 7:14).

For we *know* that the whole creation groans and suffers the pains of childbirth together until now (Rom. 8:22).

And we *know* that God causes all things to work together for good to those who love God, to those who are called according to His purpose (Rom. 8:28).

We *know* that we all *have knowledge* (1 Cor. 8:1).

If anyone supposes that he *knows* anything, he has *not yet known* as he ought *to know* (1 Cor. 8:2—which simultaneously pricks the pretensions of those who are proud in their little knowledge and rebukes them for not knowing more).

We *know* that there is no such thing as an idol in the world, and that there is no God but one (1 Cor. 8:4).

But I want you to *understand* [lit., know] that ... (1 Cor. 11:3).

For we *know in part* and we prophesy in part (1 Cor. 13:9).

Therefore, my beloved brethren, be steadfast, immovable, always abounding in the work of the Lord, *knowing* that your toil is not in vain in the Lord (1 Cor. 15:58).

For we *know* that if the earthly tent which is our house is torn down, we have a building from God, a house not made with hands, eternal in the heavens (2 Cor. 5:1).

Therefore, *be sure* [lit., know] that it is those who are of faith who are sons of Abraham (Gal. 3:7).

For this you *know* with certainty, that no immoral or impure person or covetous man, who is an idolater, has an inheritance in the kingdom of Christ and God (Eph. 5:5).

Convinced of this, I *know* that I will remain and continue with you all for your progress and joy in the faith (Phil. 1:25).

For our gospel did not come to you in word only, but also in power and in the Holy Spirit and with *full conviction* (1 Thess. 1:5 — here "conviction" means not "conviction of sins," but "being convinced").

We had already suffered and been mistreated in Philippi, as you *know* (1 Thess. 2:2).

We *know* that the Law is good, if one uses it lawfully (1 Tim. 1:8).

… [people] who forbid marriage and advocate abstaining from foods, which God has created to be gratefully shared in by those who believe and *know* the truth (1 Tim. 4:3).

But *realize* [lit., know] this, that in the last days difficult times will come (2 Tim. 3:1).

For you *know* that even afterwards, when he desired to inherit the blessing, he was rejected (Heb. 12:17).

… *let him know* that he who turns a sinner from the error of his way will save his soul from death and cover over a multitude of sins (James 5:20).

… *knowing* that you were not redeemed with perishable things like silver or gold from your futile way of life inherited from your forefathers, but with precious blood, as of a lamb unblemished and spotless, the blood of Christ (1 Peter 1:18–19).

By this we *know* that we have come to *know* Him, if we keep His commandments (1 John 2:3 — a matchless example of propositional knowledge, personal knowledge, and moral ground).

… even now many antichrists have appeared; from this we *know* it is the last hour (1 John 2:18).

We *know* that when He appears, we will be like him (1 John 3:2).

By this we *know* that we love the children of God, when we love God and observe His commandments (1 John 5:2).

These things I have written to you who believe in the name of the Son of God so that you may *know* that you have eternal life (1 John 5:13).

And if we *know* that he hears us in whatever we ask, we *know* that we have the requests which we have asked from Him (1 John 5:15).

But these men revile the things which they *do not understand* [lit., know]; and the things which they *know* by instinct, like unreasoning animals, by these they are destroyed (Jude 10).

"And I will kill her children with pestilence, and all the churches will *know* that I am He who searches the minds and hearts; and I will give to each one of you according to your deeds" (Rev. 2:23).

Given the magnitude of the role that knowledge plays in life and discipleship, it is important to get clear on what knowledge is and is not. Much confusion abounds today about the nature of knowledge, a confusion that hurts people and prevents them from growing in Christ with the sort of confidence that is their birthright in the way of Jesus.

There are three kinds of knowledge. The first is *knowledge by acquaintance*. This happens when we are directly aware of something; for example, when I see an apple directly before me or pay attention to my inner feelings, I know these things by acquaintance. One does not need a concept of an apple or knowledge of how to use the word "apple" in English to have knowledge by acquaintance with an apple. A baby can see an apple without having the relevant concept or linguistic skills. *Knowledge by acquaintance is sometimes called "simple seeing," being directly aware of something.*

The second is *propositional knowledge*. This is knowledge that an entire proposition is true. For example, knowledge that "the object there is an apple" requires having a concept of an apple and knowing that the object under consideration satisfies the concept. *Propositional knowledge is justified true belief; it is believing something that is true on the basis of adequate grounds.*

The third type is *know-how*. This is the ability to do certain things, such as using apples for certain purposes. We may distinguish mere know-how from genuine know-how or skill. The latter is know-how based on knowledge and insight and is characteristic of skilled practitioners in some field.

Mere know-how is the ability to engage in the correct behavioral movements, such as following the steps in a manual, with little or no knowledge of why one is performing these movements. Before I elaborate on these three sorts of knowledge, I want to get three general features of knowledge before your mind.

Certainty, Confidence, and Simply Knowing

First, *knowledge does not require certainty*. Something is certain if it is utterly impossible that one be mistaken about it. In this sense, few things can be known with certainty. Among them are that I exist, that basic principles of math are true (2 + 2 = 4), and that the fundamental laws of logic are correct (something cannot be true and false at the same time in the same sense). That's about it. But knowledge does not require certainty, as Paul's remark in Ephesians 5:5 suggests: "For this you know *with certainty*, that no immoral or impure person or covetous man, who is an idolater, has an inheritance in the kingdom of Christ and God." If knowledge is simply a sort of certainty, then to assert "you know with certainty" would be redundant.

This is no small point. Among other things, it means that one's degree of knowledge can grow or diminish over time. It also means that one can know something and, at the same time, acknowledge that one might be wrong about it. Indeed, the presence of doubt, the awareness of disagreements among experts, or the acknowledgment of arguments and evidence contrary to one's view on something does not necessarily mean that one does not have knowledge of the thing in question.

When we seek knowledge of God, specific biblical texts, morality, and a host of other things, we should not assume that our search requires reaching a state with no doubt, no plausible counterarguments, no possibility of being mistaken. When people believe that knowledge *requires* certainty, they will fail to take themselves to have knowledge if they lack certainty. In turn, this will lead to a lack of confidence and courage regarding one's ability to count on the things one knows. I am not suggesting that certainty is a bad thing—not for a second. I'm merely noting that it is not required.

Second, *you can know something without knowing **that** you know it*. Consider Joe, who is about to take his history final. He has true beliefs about the answers to the test on the basis of solid, adequate justification. In short, he has done his homework and knows the answers. However, because of a poor self-image, when a friend asks Joe if he knows the answers, he may say that he does not. In this case, Joe knows the answers but does not know that he knows them.

To see the incredible importance of this simple point, consider these three tasks of teaching. First, there is the impartation of truth, which consists in conveying what one should believe. Second, there is the impartation of knowledge of truth, which consists in conveying why one should believe various truths. Third, there is the impartation of confidence that one knows the truth, which consists in conveying that one can know that one knows the truth. In my view, most people know many things relevant to a Christian worldview, such as that there is a God, life after death, absolute morality, and so forth. But few people know that they know these things. They would never admit to knowing them because our naturalist and postmodern cultural elites have indoctrinated many into believing that these just aren't the sorts of things people can know.

Confidence comes not merely from possessing knowledge, but in knowing that one has knowledge. One role that Christian intellectuals and scholars play in the church is to assure believers that they do, indeed, have knowledge—that is, to give average Christians the confidence that comes from knowing that we Christians actually know the things we claim to know.

Finally, *you can know something without knowing **how** you know it*. We have all met skeptics who in one way or another have raised doubts about what we can know or reasonably believe. When you assert something, the skeptic responds with "Says who?" or "How do you know?" There are many different forms of skepticism, and I cannot describe and critique all of them here. For our purposes, let us define the skeptic as someone who does not believe that people have knowledge or rationally justified beliefs. Some skeptics are global skeptics; they hold their skepticism about all beliefs whatever, from religion to science. Other skeptics are local in orientation; they may allow for knowledge in certain areas, say in science or mathematics, while confining their skepticism to such areas as ethical or religious claims.

It is important to begin our critique of skepticism by clarifying what is called "the problem of the criterion." We can distinguish two different questions relevant to the human quest for knowledge. First, we can ask, "What is it that we know?" This is a question about the specific items of knowledge we possess and about the *extent* or *limits* of our knowledge.

Second, we can ask, "How do we decide in any given case whether or not we have knowledge in that case? What are the criteria for knowledge?" This is a question about our *criteria* for knowledge.

Now suppose that we wish to sort all of our beliefs into two groups — the true or justified ones and the false or unjustified ones — in order to retain the former and dispose of the latter in our entire set of beliefs. Such a sorting would allow us to improve our rational situation and grow in knowledge and justified belief.

But a problem arises regarding proceeding in this sorting activity. It would seem that we need an answer to at least one of our two questions above in order to proceed. But before we can have an answer to our first question about the extent of our knowledge, we would seem to need an answer to our second question about our criteria for knowledge. Yet before we can have an answer to the second question, we seem to require an answer to our first question. This is the problem of the criterion.[7] If we don't know how we know things, how can we know anything at all or draw limits to human knowledge? But if we don't know some things before we ask ourselves how we can have knowledge in the first place, on what basis will we answer that question?

There are three main solutions to the problem. First, there is *skepticism*. The skeptic claims, among other things, that no good solution to the problem exists and, thus, there is no knowledge.

The other two solutions are advocated by those who claim we do have knowledge. The second solution is *methodism* (not the denomination), and it has been advocated by philosophers such as John Locke and René Descartes. According to methodism, one starts the enterprise of knowing with a criterion for what does and does not count as knowledge; that is, we start with an answer to question two and not question one. Methodists claim that before I can know some specific proposition P (e.g., there is a tree in the yard), I must first know some general criterion Q and, further, I must know that P is a good example of or measures up to Q. For example, Q might be, "If you can test some item of belief with the five senses, then it can be an item of knowledge," or perhaps, "If something appears to your senses in a certain way, then in the absence of reasons for distrusting the lighting or your senses, you know that the thing is as it appears to you."

Unfortunately, methodism is not a good strategy because it leads to a vicious infinite regress. To see this, note that in general, methodism implies that before I can know anything (P), I must know two other things: Q (my criterion for knowledge) and R (the fact that P satisfies Q). But now the skeptic can ask how it is that we know Q and R, and the methodist will have to offer a new criterion, Q', which specifies how he knows Q and R', that tells how he knows that Q satisfies Q'. Obviously, the same problem will arise for Q' and R' and a vicious regress is set up.

Another way to see this is to note that there have been major debates about what are and are not good criteria for knowledge. Locke offered something akin to the notion that an item of knowledge about the external world must pass the criterion of deriving that item of knowledge from simple sensory ideas or impressions (roughly, testing it with the senses). By contrast, Descartes offered a radically different criterion: The item of knowledge must be clear and distinct when brought before the mind. If we are methodists, how are we to settle disputes about criteria for knowledge? The answer will be that we will have to offer criteria for our criteria, and so on. It seems, then, that methodism is in trouble.

The third solution to the problem is known as *particularism*, advocated by philosophers such as Thomas Reid, Roderick Chisholm, and G. E. Moore. According to particularists, we start by knowing specific, clear items of knowledge: that I had eggs for breakfast this morning, that there is a tree before me, that $7 + 5 = 12$, that mercy is a virtue, and so on. I can know some things directly and simply without having to have criteria for how I know them and without having to know how or even that I know them. We know many things without being able to prove that we do or without fully understanding the things we know. We simply identify clear instances of knowing without having to possess or apply any criteria for knowledge. We may reflect on these instances and go on to develop criteria for knowledge consistent with them and use these criteria to make judgments in borderline cases of knowledge, but the criteria are justified by their congruence with specific instances of knowledge, not the other way around.

For example, I may start with moral knowledge (murder is wrong) and legal knowledge (taxes are to be paid by April 15) and go on to formulate criteria for when something is moral or legal. I could then use these criteria for judging borderline cases (intentionally driving on the wrong side of the street). In general, we start with clear instances of knowledge, formulate criteria based on those clear instances, and extend our knowledge by using those criteria in borderline, unclear cases.

The skeptic can raise two basic objections against the particularist. First, the particularist allegedly begs the question (assumes the very thing that needs to be proved, namely, that we do, in fact, have knowledge) against the skeptic by simply assuming his answer to the point at issue — whether we have knowledge. How does the particularist know that we have this? Isn't it possible in the cases cited above that the particularist is wrong and he only thinks he has knowledge here?

Particularists respond to this objection as follows. First, regarding begging the question, if the skeptic doesn't offer a reason for his skepticism (and just keeps asking "How do you know?" each time the particularist makes a knowledge claim), his skepticism can be ignored because it is not a substantive position or argument. If, however, his skepticism is the result of an argument, then this argument must be reasonable before it can be held as a serious objection against knowledge. However, if we did not know some things, we could not *reasonably* doubt anything (e.g., the reason for doubting my senses now is my justified belief that they have, or at least may have, misled me in the past). Unbridled skepticism is not a rationally defensible position, and it cannot be rationally asserted and defended without presupposing knowledge.

Second, the skeptic tries to force the particularist to be a methodist by asking the "how-do-you-know?" question, since the skeptic is implying that before you can know, you must have criteria for knowledge. The skeptic knows he can refute the methodist. But the particularist will resist the slide into methodism by reaffirming that he can know some specific item without having to say how he knows it. For example, the particularist will say, "I know that mercy is a virtue and not a vice even if I don't know how it is that I know this. But, Mr. Skeptic, why do you think that I have to know how I know this *before* I can know it?"

Furthermore, the particularist argues that just because it is merely possible that he is mistaken in a specific case of knowledge, that does not mean he is mistaken or that he has any good reason to think he is wrong. And until the skeptic can give him good reason for thinking his instances of knowledge fail, the mere possibility that he is wrong will not suffice.

Suppose I claim to know when I first went to Disneyland several years ago and the skeptic tries to show I don't really know this by raising the possibility that I might have been born five seconds ago with a memory and that my memory is deceiving me. The particularist will respond this way: Just because the statement "J. P. Moreland was born five seconds ago with a memory" is not a logical contradiction (like "J. P. Moreland is and is not a human being") and *could* be true as a bare, logical possibility, that does not mean we have good reasons for actually believing the statement is correct. The particularist will insist that unless there are good reasons for believing the skeptic's claim (and the skeptic doesn't give such reasons), the bare possibility that it might be true is not sufficient to call into question what I actually know about my Disneyland visit.

The particularist and skeptic have very different approaches to knowledge. For the skeptic, the burden of proof is on the one who claims to know something. If it is logically possible that one might be mistaken, then knowledge is not present because to the skeptic knowledge requires complete, 100 percent certainty. Of the two main tasks in the quest for knowledge (obtaining true or justified beliefs and avoiding false or unjustified beliefs), the skeptic elevates the latter and requires that his position be refuted before knowledge can be justified. To refute something is to show that it is wrong. The skeptic thinks avoiding error is better than gaining truth and thinks he must be shown wrong before anyone can claim to know anything.

The particularist elevates the value of gaining as many truths as are available in the world and tries to rebut the skeptic. To rebut something is not to show it is wrong, but simply to show that it has not done an adequate job of showing that it is true. After all, the particularist recognizes that we all know many things before we ever talk to skeptics. He places the burden of proof on the skeptic and requires the skeptic to show that his skepticism is true and should be taken seriously before he allows the skeptic to bother him about knowledge. The particularist does not need to refute the skeptic (show skepticism is false); he merely needs to rebut the skeptic (show that the skeptic has not adequately made his case for skepticism). Given that the skeptic cannot consistently *argue for* his skepticism, there is no reason to deny what is obvious to all of us: that we do know many things even if we don't know how we know them. This is one reason why particularism is widely favored as the proper solution to the problem of the criterion.

The Three Kinds of Knowledge

Now that we have probed the three general features of knowledge, we can return to elaborate on the three sorts of knowledge: knowledge by acquaintance, propositional knowledge, and know-how. *Knowledge by acquaintance* is knowledge by simple seeing—when one is directly aware of or directly experiences something. One can think of a tree, God, or whether one is angry, but these are all different from directly being aware of the tree, God, or one's inner state of anger. Knowledge by acquaintance is an important foundation for all knowledge, and in an important sense, experience or direct awareness of reality is the basis for everything we know.

However, one should not limit what one can see or directly be aware of to the five senses. One can also be directly aware of one's own soul and inner states of thoughts, feelings, desires, beliefs, and so forth by intro-spective awareness of one's inner life. One can be directly aware of God, of his speaking to one in guidance, of the Spirit's testimony to various things, and so forth. From Plato to the present, many philosophers have believed—correctly in my view—in what is called *rational awareness*, that is, the soul's ability to directly be aware of aesthetic and moral val-ues, numbers and the laws of mathematics, the laws of logic, and various abstract objects such as humanness, wisdom, and so forth. *The important thing to note is that we humans have the power to "see," to be directly aware of, to directly experience a wide range of things, many of which are not subject to sensory awareness with the five senses.*

Given the reality and nature of knowledge by acquaintance, it follows that knowledge does not begin with presuppositions, language, concepts, one's cultural standpoint, or anything else. It starts with awareness of real-ity. Indeed, it is because there is such a thing as knowledge by acquaintance that we regularly experience times in which we can compare our con-cepts or thoughts about something with the thing itself as it is in reality, and thereby correct or confirm our thoughts by comparing them with the things themselves. Knowledge by acquaintance gives us direct access to reality as it is in itself, and we know this to be the case in our daily lives.

To see this, consider the following examples offered by philosopher Scott Smith, which, because of their richness and practical importance, I quote in full:[8]

> 1. *How a toddler learns to identify an apple.* I have enjoyed watching my two-year-old daughter develop her understanding of what apples are. When she was quite young, my wife and I would show her a book that helped her learn what different fruits look like. There are about twenty-four pictures of Red Delicious apples, oranges, grapes, and bananas on two adjacent pages. We would start by pointing to a pic-ture of an apple on the left page, and we would then say "apple." Then we would point to another apple picture and say "apple" again. We would repeat this through all the apple pictures, as well as the oranges and so on. Later, we would return to this book and ask her, "Where

are the apples?" She would point to one, and we would affirm her by saying "Good!" Then I might ask, "Where is another apple?" As she has grown older, she has developed the ability to identify all the other apples pictured there. She also would get to see different apples we would eat at home, not all of which were Red Delicious.

What was going on? She had to see each apple picture for *what it is*, hear the word "apple" uttered for *what it is*, learn to associate the apple's picture with the word "apple," and then develop a concept of what an apple is from many observations. She then could go into the grocery store's produce section and be able to pick out as apples not just Red Delicious ones, but also Gala, Golden Delicious, Fuji, and more.

2. *The prescription refill example.* I use my telephone to call in refills for prescriptions. I bring the vial with me to the phone while I call, and I am prompted by the system to enter certain information, starting with my phone number. I have to look at the phone's keypad, notice which keys are for which numbers, and then press the correct numbers in sequence. How do I (or anyone else) do that? I am thinking of a number, then I see which key is for that number, and then I direct my finger to that key and press it. After doing that for all the digits, I hear the number replayed back to me, and again I have to verify that I entered the number correctly. How do I do that? I listen to the digits, and then I compare the numbers spoken back to me in a sequence with those of my phone number. I have to be able to hear the numbers for what they are, compare them with what I know to be my number, and see that they match up.

The same follows when I enter the prescription number, which in turn is repeated back to me. Again, I have to be able to see the number, this time on the vial, as it really is, then see which keys are for which numbers, and then direct my finger to press the right keys. If I make a mistake, I can know that because I see that I pressed the wrong one. I must be able to see the numbers for what they are on the vial, do the same with the keypad, and then match up the audio feedback with the number as I read it on the vial. In all cases, I have to be able to see the numbers for what they are, in order to match them up.

3. *The example of reading a text aloud.* Suppose you are reading a passage of Scripture aloud in your church's worship service, and your passage is Romans 1:16–17 (NASB): "For I am not ashamed of the gospel, for it is the power of God for salvation to everyone who believes, to the Jew first and also to the Greek. For in it the love of God is revealed

from faith to faith; as it is written, 'But the righteous man shall live by faith.' " Suppose you read the passage just like that. Now, you may notice that some people look up at you with a puzzled look on their faces. You might start to wonder why. Then, maybe someone pulls you aside and, to your surprise, tells you that you read it wrong, that you substituted "love" for "righteousness" in the last verse.

How would people present know whether what you read was right or not? Somehow they have to hear the sounds you uttered for what they are, see what the word in the passage actually is, compare the two, and then express their thoughts properly in language (e.g. "you misspoke," not "great job!"). I did this intentionally in a philosophy class one day, to see how attentively my students were following my reading, and to force them to pay attention to their awarenesses — what they heard, what they read, their comparison of the two, and their judgment. How could we ever correct anyone if we do not have access to these things as they really are, and that we can each see what is indeed the case?

What should we make of these case studies? In each case, we have to be able to see a thing for what it is. From many noticings, we develop a concept of what that thing is. We also must see that a particular object of our awareness is another instance of that kind of thing (perhaps a Golden Delicious apple). We learn to associate a term with our awareness of the object by hearing the term for what it is, seeing the object for what it is, and then comparing them and seeing that, yes, this object is indeed that kind of thing. That is, we can see that an object of our awareness fulfills the concept, and then we can see that the thing in question is indeed such-and-such.

I have belabored the reality of knowledge by acquaintance because it is so widely dismissed today. Yet it is of such crucial importance for the Christian life. Among other things, such knowledge places us in direct contact with God, physical and spiritual reality, our own souls, and a host of other things. Knowledge by acquaintance is not infallible — it can be distorted, blurred, and so on, because of our finiteness and fallenness — but it is available. By way of application, it would be a useful exercise to think through how knowledge by acquaintance is essential to learning to hear God's voice on a daily basis within the boundaries set by Holy Scripture.[9]

The other two forms of knowledge require only a brief comment. *Propositional knowledge* consists in a true belief based on adequate justification or grounds. If I know that it is raining outside, I must believe it is raining, that belief must be true, and I must have adequate grounds for the belief. Remember, propositional knowledge does not require certainty, so that one's grounds for a belief that, say, it is raining or that God is leading me to do such and such, or that abortion is wrong do not need to make the belief absolutely certain. Moreover, what counts as adequate grounds will vary from circumstance to circumstance, depending on whether the context is art and beauty, chemistry, the reality of whether an event happened in history, knowledge that God is real, and so forth.

Skill is know-how based on knowledge. In fact, wisdom may fairly be defined as skill regarding how to live life well. So understood, it follows that one can have knowledge without wisdom but not vice versa. This is important, because so many today wrongly divorce wisdom from knowledge.

I have been at pains to clarify exactly what knowledge is and is not, as well as what is and is not required to have it. If we are going to grow in our spiritual and moral knowledge and confidence that we actually have it, it is important to have some idea of what knowledge itself is.

I suspect that this section has been tough sledding for some of you, and if so, I want to challenge you with one thing. As you know, the nature and limits of knowledge are at the core of spiritual warfare in our culture, and the local church can no longer afford to conduct its business in disregard of this conflict. Therefore, *it is crucial that we call the Christian community back to its place in the world as a group that, on the basis of revelation in creation, religious experience, and, most importantly, the inerrant Word of God, presents religious, ethical, and other forms of knowledge to the world. Our religion is a religion of knowledge, not private faith, and we must teach people the ins and outs of knowledge as part of the recovery of our heritage as the sons and daughters of God.*

Because knowledge is the basis of faith, I will provide suggestions for strengthening faith and growing in the knowledge of God and his truth after we have had a chance to look briefly at the nature of faith.

How to Strengthen Your Faith
The Nature of Faith

The essence of faith—biblical or otherwise—is confidence or trust, and one can have faith in a thing (such as a chair) or a person (such as a parent, the president, or God), and one can have faith in the truth of a proposition, such as confidence that the following are true: "Statins help lower cholesterol," "Mutual Fund X is a good investment," or "God was in Christ reconciling the world unto himself." When trust is directed toward a person/thing, it is called "faith in"; when it is directed toward the truth of a proposition, it is called "faith that."

In Scripture and ordinary life, appropriate faith is grounded in knowledge and it is as good as its object. It is on the basis of knowledge about a chair, statins, or God that one is able to exhibit confidence in the respective object or possess a readiness to act as if the relevant proposition is true. I am not suggesting that a person who exercises faith always or even usually understands everything about what is going on at that moment or in the future. Abraham placed faith in God though there was much he did not understand. But Abraham's faith was still grounded on things he knew about God. It is a great misunderstanding of faith to oppose it to reason and knowledge. Nothing could be further from the truth. In actual fact, faith — confidence, trust — is rooted in knowledge. Even in cases of misplaced faith, people usually root that faith in what they *take themselves to know*, perhaps mistakenly.

Confidence is inextricably wrapped up with beliefs — a person will have confidence in the truths he or she believes and the objects of those truths. Beliefs are the rails on which our lives run. We almost always act according to what we really believe. It doesn't matter much what we say we believe or what we want others to think we believe. When the rubber meets the road, we act out our actual beliefs most of the time. That is why behavior is such a good indicator of a person's beliefs. It is also why, if you want to really come to the point where your confidence in God and Christian truths is strong, you must learn to distinguish what you believe from what you say you believe. To grasp faith in order to cultivate its growth in one's soul, it is important to ponder three aspects of belief.[10]

1. *The content of a belief.* The *content* of a belief helps determine how important the belief is for our character and behavior. *What* we believe matters — the actual content of what we believe about God, morality, politics, life after death, and so on will shape the contours of our life and actions. In fact, the contents of our beliefs are so important that according to Scripture, our eternal destiny is determined by what we believe about Jesus Christ.

Today, people are inclined to think that the sincerity and fervency of one's beliefs are more important than the content of the beliefs themselves. As long as we believe something honestly and strongly, we are told, that is all that matters. Nothing is further from the truth. Reality is basically indifferent to how sincerely we believe something. I can believe with all my might that my car will fly me to Hawaii or that homosexuality is caused solely by the brain, but that fervency doesn't change a thing. As far as reality is concerned, what matters is not whether I like a belief or how sincere I am in believing it, but whether or not the belief is true. I am responsible for what I believe and, I might add, for what I refuse to believe because the content of what I do or do not believe makes a tremendous difference to what I become and how I act.

There is a powerful implication of this for your life and for the life of your church in the Kingdom of God: It is important that you grow in the clarity and depth of understanding of the specific things you believe about God and related matters. You really cannot believe something that is vague. For example, to the degree that there is fog in what actually comes before your mind when you remind yourself that prayer works or that God is sovereign, to that degree these items will have little affect on how you really live and think about life. Discipleship unto the Lord Jesus is a thoughtful life. The simple truth is that those who are not thoughtful about the real content of what they actually believe about God will not actually believe very much.

2. *The strength of a belief.* In addition to content, a belief also exhibits some degree or other of *strength.* To see what I mean here, consider the fact that we all believe things without being absolutely certain that they are true. If you believe something, then you are at least more than 50 percent convinced the belief is true. If it were 50–50 for you, you wouldn't really hold the belief in question. You would still be evaluating the claim to see whether or not you should believe it. A belief's strength is the degree to which you are convinced it is true. As you gain evidence and support for a belief, its strength grows for you. That belief may start off as plausible and later become fairly likely, quite likely, beyond reasonable doubt, or completely certain. The more certain you are of a belief, the more it becomes a part of your very soul, and the more you rely on it as a basis for action.

3. *The centrality of a belief.* Finally, there is the belief's *centrality.* The centrality of a belief is a measure of how crucial the belief is for supporting your other beliefs. The more central a belief is, the greater will be its impact on your worldview if the belief were given up. My belief that tulips are better than roses is a fairly strong one for me but it is not central. I could give it up and I would not have to abandon or adjust many other beliefs I hold.

But my beliefs in the existence of God and Jesus Christ is very central for me, more central now, in fact, than just after my conversion in 1968. If I were to lose these beliefs, my entire set of beliefs would undergo a radical reshuffling, more so now than, say, in 1969. As I grow, these beliefs come to play a more central role in the entire way I see life.

Three Ways to Grow in Knowledgeable Confidence in God and His Truth

It is possible to develop a solid knowledge of God and his ways and the strength of confidence in him and his truth needed to sustain a vibrant life that is worthy of the Lord, a life that embodies the nature and power of the Kingdom of God. Here are three ways to grow in your knowledge of and confidence in God and his truth.

1. *Be ruthless in assessing the precise nature and strength of what you actually believe and develop a specific plan of attack for improvement.* You need to get away for a period of personal reflection and ask yourself some hard questions. Often, our congregations are not safe places for such self-examination, but if you have friends who can help you here, by all means, invite them into the process.

Your goal is to diagnose your current condition on two fronts. First, select a set of target beliefs and try to be precise and clear about what you actually think of when these target topics come before your mind: What is God really like? Is the Bible really a reliable guide to life? What, precisely, do you mean when you say that God is sovereign and in control? Does God answer prayer, and in what precise sense do you think he does? Come up with your own list in light of what your specific journey and stage of life require. The goal here is not to surface what you are supposed to believe about these subjects. Rather, it's to find out what you really do think about them. Remember, you can't believe something that is vague, so the more clarity you gain about what really comes to mind regarding your targeted beliefs, the more you can improve them.

Here are two questions to ask yourself about a specific topic you are diagnosing. When you think about the topic, is it more of a slogan to you, or is it perhaps a vague, unclear string of words you utter in mantra-like fashion as a substitute for clear thinking about it? Or do you have a clear idea in your mind about the topic? Can you write on paper exactly what the topic means to you and what you think about it (e.g., What does prayer accomplish? Does it change God's mind? Does it change what happens in the world? Is it merely trying to align oneself with what God's will already is?)? Next, what friends do I have with whom I can gather for an afternoon with paper and pen in hand and probe each other about a particular topic to surface what we actually think about it?

Second, try to assess how strongly you believe them, recalling that faith can grow in strength. Are you 51 percent confident that God answers prayers, 75 percent confident, or what? Don't lie to yourself. In assessing the precise content and strength of your beliefs, you must distinguish what you say you believe from what you actually believe, what you want to believe from what you actually believe, how much you believe something from what you want others to think about the strength of your faith. Be authentic and brutally honest with yourself, and don't be discouraged if things aren't what you have been telling yourself. This exercise is the beginning of a way forward; it is not an occasion to wallow in self-pity.

Once this is done, develop a strategy for clarifying and strengthening specific beliefs important to your discipleship unto the Lord Jesus. For years, I kept a list of questions, doubts, confusions, and so forth, and I took it with me everywhere in my Bible. I was constantly on the lookout for things to read, people to query, insights to be gained about my list.

Why don't you do the same thing? Seek out people and books with answers and insights, and don't stop until you have answers that satisfy you. Doubt your doubts, as C. S. Lewis advised. That is, list on paper why you doubt that God is real, or whether he really forgives you, and so on, and list reasons why this doubt is, itself, a foolish thing to believe. Don't let this rest. I assure you that progress can be made and, in fact, has been made by many of your brothers and sisters who have been serious about growing in their faith. Read, think, ask questions, and keep checking things off your list. Don't settle for Christian slogans. Get real answers to your questions. Be a learner and see all this as an invitation to a journey of growth in confidence and knowledge.

2. *Take appropriate yearly risks that stretch your faith.* John Wimber used to say that faith is spelled "R-I-S-K," and there is an important insight to this saying. Faith grows as we step out, put ourselves in situations in which God must show up, wait to see what happens, and learn from our experience. There is a balance between being too kind to yourself and being too demanding and harsh. That's why I recommend that you start by setting yearly "risk" goals that are slightly beyond your comfort level but not so far that you brutalize yourself. Each year, I set forth certain

goals — professional, financial, familial, and so forth — in which I plan to attempt things by way of action or concentrated prayer. If these things happen, I will know God was involved, and if they don't happen, I will be able to learn from my mistakes.

Each year, I ask myself this question: How much of my life and ministry last year required the existence of the Christian God to explain it? How much would have happened if God did not exist? Here's the point: Life in the Kingdom — corporately in our churches and individually — is a supernatural colaboring with God in which we both matter. I matter because God wants to use *me* — not just Billy Graham or some other well-known Christian leader. So I get to count.

But I should also expect and look for where the Kingdom is breaking out around and in my life, and I should expect that the effects produced by my life and efforts should not be explainable solely by my talent. So each year, you too should gently and wisely place yourself in risk situations. If God does not show up as you had trusted, don't give up. Instead, try to learn as best you can why things failed to happen as you had risked. This is a learning process, but I assure you that if done with wisdom and balance, it will greatly strengthen your faith. By the way, I urge you to keep a prayer journal even if you only write in it from time to time. You want a record of your own book of Acts in which you record answers to prayer and various miracles in your life, so your yearly "risks" can be recorded in such a way that you remember the acts of God's Spirit in your life.

3. *Read books about and share stories of God's miraculous actions in other people's lives as an encouragement to your own faith.* We wrongly get the idea that God is relatively inactive in the world today, but this false impression is a result of our lack of awareness of the incredible things God is doing in and through his children's lives all around us on a daily basis. In chapter 7, I will suggest some books to read that give reliable testimony to the miracles of healing, deliverance, and answers to prayer that are happening all over the world today. For now, let me illustrate the point with a personal story.

I was speaking to a church staff about developing trust in God in their congregation for the coming year, and I included the importance of providing means by which people could share on a regular basis the answers to prayer and other encouraging things God had been or was doing for them. At the break, one staff member approached me with his own story. A few years earlier, a machine had fallen on him and fractured his chest and hands. He was rushed to the doctor, x-rayed, and scheduled for surgery the next day. That evening, a group of believers came to his home and prayed for his healing. At once the pain left and he felt healed. The next day, the surgeons took new x-rays before the surgery, and the fractures were completely healed. Like an idiot I asked him how he knew this. He answered that the doctors compared the new x-rays with the ones taken the day before, and it was obvious that he had been miraculously healed! The fracture-lines were gone!

Here's the punch line: He had never shared this with anyone in the church! He didn't want to talk about himself. How are we going to encourage each other that the Christian life is a supernatural journey if we don't share these sorts of things with each other? We need to provide opportunities for credible testimonials to be given to each other on a regular basis, because they strengthen people's confidence in God and his Word.

Here's another event that happened to me at the beginning of my ministry. In 1971 as a young Christian on staff with Campus Crusade for Christ, I was assigned to work at the Colorado School of Mines in Golden, Colorado, just outside of Denver. I began to pray specifically that God would provide me and my roommate with a white house with a white picket fence in the front yard about two to three miles from campus, costing no more than $115/month (this was 1971!). I told no one that I was praying about this.

When I arrived in Golden in late August, I looked for three days for a place to live. I must have seen fifteen different places. I found nothing at all in Golden, but there was a two-bedroom apartment ten miles away in Denver for $130/month. Frustrated, I told the manager I would take it. She informed me that the apartment was the only one left but that a couple had seen it that morning and had that day to decide to move in. If they did not take it, it was mine. She called me around five o'clock in the afternoon, informing me that the couple had moved in. I was back to square one.

That evening, I received a phone call from a fellow Crusade staff member, Kaylon Carr. Keep in mind that no one, not even my roommate, knew anything at all about my prayer request. Kaylon asked if I still needed a place to live and proceeded to tell me that that very day, she had gone to Denver Seminary, looked on their bulletin board, and spotted a pastor who wanted to rent a house in Golden to Christians. Needless to say, I called the pastor, got directions, and planned to meet him at the house the next morning at nine o'clock. I drove up to a white house with a white picket fence that was two miles from campus and rented it for $110/month! Ray Womack and I lived there for the year and had a home to which we could invite students for ministry. By meditating on this and other answers to prayer, I have often recalled that God is, indeed, a supernatural Father, and my faith has been strengthened. Such sharing is a powerful way to strengthen our faith.

I have tried to explain the nature of knowledge and faith and provide help in growing in them. People perish for lack of the knowledge of God. The devil is waging war against the possibility of knowledge of God. This is no time for the church to adopt an anti-intellectual approach to knowledge and faith. I trust that you see this, and I invite you to be part of the recovery movement.

Questions for Personal Reflection or Group Discussion

1. According to Michael Green, three factors were central to the early church's explosive success: persuasive apologetics, transformed character and biblical compassion, and the manifest power of the kingdom of God by the Spirit of God (pages 111–112). How are these factors interrelated? Are these factors reproducible in our own context? In which of these three do you sense the need for greater attention and growth today?

2. What is the author's definition of knowledge (page 114)? Does this definition help to clarify why Christianity is fundamentally a knowledge tradition and not simply a faith tradition? Reread the biblical passages that focus on knowledge and choose five that particularly stand out to you. How is the author's definition of knowledge represented in those examples?

3. The author presents three general features of knowledge: Knowledge does not require certainty; you can know something without knowing *that* you know it; and you can know something without knowing *how* you know it (pages 121–122). Consider several things you know but do not know them with certainty or even know how you know them. Organize these things according to degrees of knowledge and observe how your knowledge has grown or diminished over time.

   How does knowledgable confidence inform and form the tasks of teaching (page 122)? Consider how it impacts the role of parenting and belief formation.

4. What is "the problem of the criterion"? Describe briefly the three main solutions to this problem: skepticism, methodism, particularism (pages 122–124). What are the fundamental problems with these solutions? Why do they deter us from actually obtaining knowledge?

   Have you ever functioned as a skeptic or an epistemological methodist? What was your reason or motivation for thinking that you could not know something without first knowing how you knew it? Were you motivated out of a desire for certainty or eagerness to control?

5. Particularism is the best strategy for solving "the problem of the criterion." What are the author's reasons for claiming this? What examples does he offer?

   What objections does the skeptic raise against particularism (pages 124–126)? How does the author respond to these objections? Consider, interact with, and evaluate those responses.

6. The author explains three kinds of knowledge: knowledge by acquaintance, propositional knowledge, and know-how (pages 126–130). What is knowledge by acquaintance? Why is it the basis for all other kinds of knowledge? How does it differ from "propositional knowledge" and "know-how"? If "simple seeing" is true, what are its implications for the postmodernist claim that presuppositions, language, concepts, and one's cultural standpoint stand between you and external reality? Interact with the author's plentiful examples from philosopher Scott Smith on this issue (pages 127–129).

7. What's the difference between when trust is directed toward a person or a thing and when it is directed toward the truth of a proposition? How is faith related to knowledge? In what way is confidence inextricably important to beliefs? How are the content, the strength, and the centrality of a belief interrelated, and what do you think is the importance of this interrelationship for spiritual formation (pages 130–133)?

8. One way to grow in knowledgeable confidence in God and his truth is to be ruthless in assessing the precise nature and strength of what you actually believe and to develop a plan for improvement (pages 133–134). Experiment with the author's suggestion to experience some personal reflection and to ask yourself some hard questions about what you actually believe. On any topic that you believe, is it more of a slogan to you, a vague, unclear string of words you utter in mantra-like fashion as a substitute for clear thinking about it, or do you have a clear idea in your mind about what you believe and why?

   Gather with some friends and probe each other about a particular topic. Try to assess how strongly you believe what you believe, recalling that faith can grow in strength. Also, develop a strategy for clarifying and strengthening specific beliefs important to your Christian discipleship.

9. A second way to grow in knowledgeable confidence in God and his truth is to take appropriate yearly risks ("R-I-S-K") that stretch your faith (pages 134–135). Faith grows as we step out, put ourselves in situations in which God must show up, wait to see what happens, and learn from our experience. Set for yourself yearly "risk" goals that are slightly beyond your comfort level. Keep a prayer journal, even if you only write in it from time to time, so that you can record the acts of God's Spirit in your life.

10. A third way to grow in knowledgeable confidence in God and his truth is to read books about God's transforming work in other people's lives (pages 135–136). Document how you see the reality of God's Kingdom breaking out around you in the lives of friends, relatives, coworkers, churches, etc. Encourage your church to set aside time on Sunday or during the week to ask, "In what way is the Lord working in our midst?" May this be a consistent lead question in your fellowship with other people.

CHAPTER 6

RENOVATION OF THE SOUL

The empty self is now an epidemic in America (and much of Western culture), and we have all been affected to some degree by this plague. Because it is so clear, I repeat a statement by Philip Cushman to which I referred earlier:

> The empty self is filled up with consumer goods, calories, experiences, politicians, romantic partners, and empathetic therapists.... [The empty self] experiences a significant absence of community, tradition, and shared meaning ... a lack of personal conviction and worth, and it embodies the absences as a chronic, undifferentiated emotional hunger.[1]

It should be obvious that the empty self undermines growth as a disciple.

The empty self is actually a ubiquitous incarnation of what is more broadly called the false self. Roughly, the false self is the self we present to others, perhaps unconsciously, in order to make the world safe for us, to allow us to be in control of things, to gain attention or be ignored depending on our strategy, and to hide from others and ourselves what we are really like. The false self is a tangled web of internal tapes created by childhood struggles, pain, embarrassment, anxiety, and fear. The true self is the person we really are, and if a person has not heard from himself for some time, it is entirely possible for someone not to have a clue about one's true self.

Since the empty self is a major form of the false self, all of us who hunger for increasing spiritual authenticity and real intimacy with God and others need to be on the lookout for ways we have become empty selves. Our practice of discipleship and spiritual formation must be done with a clear view of the empty self and its negative impact on our individual lives and church structures. Here are four traits of the empty self that undermine authentic spiritual formation.[2]

The empty self is inordinately individualistic. Years ago my wife and I attended a D.A.R.E. graduation (a public school program designed to help children say no to drugs) for my daughter's sixth grade class. According to the program, some students were going to share with the audience their reasons for rejecting drugs. With a twinkle in my eye, I turned to the couple sitting next to me and boldly announced a prediction: Each student would reject drugs for what would ultimately be the same reason — self-interest.

Sure enough, student after student said that he or she would refuse drugs because of a desire to stay healthy, become a doctor or athlete, or do well in school. Not one student made as much as a small reference to virtue or duty to community. Not one student rejected drugs simply because it is wrong to take them! Not one student rejected drugs because of the shame it would bring to family, community, or God. Individualistic reasons were the only ones given. A healthy form of individualism is a good thing. But the empty self ubiquitous today is a self-contained individual who defines one's own life goals, values, and interests as though one were a human atom, isolated from others, with little need or responsibility to live for the concerns of the broader community.

The empty self is infantile. Today, people carry adolescent personality features well into their thirties. The infantile person is controlled by infantile cravings and constantly seeks to be filled up with and made whole by food, entertainment, and consumer goods. The infantile self needs to be soothed and must have its desires instantly satisfied. Such a person is preoccupied with sex, physical appearance, and body image and the need to feel good all the time. For the infantile personality type, pain, endurance, hard work, and delayed gratification are simply out of the question. Pleasure is all that matters, and it had better be immediate. Boredom is the greatest evil, amusement the greatest good.

The empty self is narcissistic. Narcissism is an inappropriate sense of self-infatuation in which the individual is driven by and only by his or her own self-interest and personal fulfillment.[3] The narcissist manipulates relationships with others (including God) to validate his or her own need for power and for admiration from others. The narcissist is superficial and regards others as mere objects, mere means to his or her own selfish ends. Self-denial is out of the question. Spiritually, the narcissist dethrones God and his purposes in history from the center of the religious life and places his or her own personal fulfillment in the middle. God exists to meet the narcissist's needs, and woe to the Creator if he doesn't live up to those expectations!

The empty self is passive. Finally, the empty self is passive in the sense that he or she would rather do nothing and let life pass them by than to get involved. From watching television to listening to sermons, the empty self's primary agenda is to be amused and entertained with a minimum of energy expended. The passive individual is a self in search of pleasure provided by others. Such an individual increasingly becomes a shriveled self with less and less ability to be proactive and take control of life.

Given the impact of the empty self on all of us, we can no longer afford to do church the way we have frequently done it. We can no longer afford to build churches largely around powerful communicators who do our studying and thinking for us, and we can no longer build our services around providing bits of entertainment for an hour or so once a week. Already addicted to passivity and entertainment, these are precisely what empty selves are looking for.

There is nothing wrong with having an excellent communicator or an entertaining service each week. All things being equal, I would rather have an interesting teacher on Sunday than someone to whom it is hard to listen, and the same goes for the rest of the service. But the Sunday morning service was never intended to be the staple for growing world-changing communities or for producing radically different people under the shelter of God's wings. Those dramatic goals require a decentralized philosophy of ministry, which takes as its aim the equipping of the body for the work of ministry and the fostering of authentic Christian spiritual formation. As we continue to see our need for the renovation of our souls, I believe there are three aspects that we need to bring to the center of our efforts if we are to have a chance of becoming dramatic people fit for the Master's use.

Growing in the Art of Christian Self-Denial

I have long considered Jesus the smartest man who ever lived. Of course, I believe he was also God incarnate. But even if a skeptic takes his teachings as expressions of mere human wisdom, I believe that those teachings can be seen as superior in insight, depth, and value to those of Freud, Marx, Plato, or anyone else. Nowhere is this more evident than when Jesus is expressing his views about the way we were made to function properly and to flourish. Jesus had a grasp of human nature that has never and will never be surpassed. And it has never been more critical to weigh his words about "happiness" and one's basic approach to life than today as we live in a culture united in support of a perspective diametrically opposed to his. Consider seriously these words:

Then Jesus said to His disciples, "If anyone wishes to come after Me, he must deny himself, and take up his cross and follow Me. For whoever wishes to save his life will lose it; but whoever loses his life for My sake will find it. For what will it profit a man if he gains the whole world and forfeits his soul? Or what will a man give in exchange for his soul?" (Matthew 16:24–26)

Please ponder carefully the heart of Jesus' claims. His invitation to "follow him" is actually an invitation to enter a different kind of life and to learn from Jesus himself how to live well. Acceptance of this invitation provides the believer with the power and resources to learn how to live a radically new kind of life from above and in approximation to the sort of life Jesus himself lived. Jesus invites us to new life in the Kingdom, lived from the power of the indwelling Spirit and the resurrected power of Jesus himself. Understood in a different way, it is an invitation to a life of happiness understood in its classic sense. An important question is now forced upon us: How does the classic understanding of happiness relate to the current one?[4]

When Jesus invited people to deny themselves and follow him, he believed and taught that this was the only way they could find themselves, and in so doing, find "happiness." In his words we encounter the classic concept of happiness, one embraced by Moses, Solomon, Aristotle, Plato, the church fathers, medieval theologians, and many more. This classic concept has now given way to "pleasurable satisfaction."

According to the classic sense, happiness is a life well lived, a life of virtue and character, a life that manifests wisdom, kindness, and goodness. The life of classic happiness, the life about which to dream and for which to long, for which to hunger and seek, and which should be imitated and practiced is a life of virtue and character. The New Testament enriches this classic sense by calling it "eternal life," understood as a certain quality of life and fleshed out as a life that approximates Jesus' life and character. To be sure, such a life includes a deep sense of well-being, but this pregnant sense of well-being is not the same thing as pleasurable satisfaction.

Pleasurable satisfaction depends on external circumstances going well—for example, physical appearance, success at work, and popularity. Because of this, pleasurable satisfaction is unstable and varies with life's circumstances. Classic virtue flows from inside a person as he or she matures and develops a character formed by discipleship unto Jesus. As one progresses in the way of Jesus, classic happiness becomes less and less dependent on external circumstances.

You may recall that in C. S. Lewis's novel *The Lion, the Witch and the Wardrobe*, Turkish delight was an addictive source of immediate gratification that became less and less effective as time wore on. In the same way, "pleasurable satisfaction" becomes increasingly addictive and enslaving (and unsatisfying!) if it becomes the dominant aim of one's life. The never-ending quest for the holy grail of pleasure and good feelings creates a person who cannot live without "happiness," who is addicted to adrenaline, whose empty self must constantly be filled with calories, romance, consumer goods, and church services. In this way, "happiness" becomes addictive and enslaving.[5] Satisfaction of desire and the right to do what one wants become the goal of life.

By contrast, classical happiness brings freedom and power to live as one ought, as one increasingly becomes a unified person who lives for a cause bigger than one's self. Such a person is not preoccupied with the right to do what one wants.

One can obtain pleasurable satisfaction through some particular activity or area of success, but the gratification gained is usually limited to the area in question and does not color the rest of one's life. If your team wins or you get good grades, the excitement that ensues does not necessarily color your affective presence when you are called upon to sacrifice for and to serve others. But a life of wisdom and virtue is like background music at a restaurant; it sets the mood and texture for everything within its scope, and as you find real happiness, all aspects of your life are seasoned by it.

For Jesus, to find one's self is to find out what life is supposed to look like and to learn to live that way. It is to become like Jesus himself and have a character that manifests the radical nature of the Kingdom of God and the fruit of the Spirit; it is to find out God's purposes for one's life and to fulfill those purposes in a Christ-honoring way. This is a life of human flourishing, a life lived the way we were made to function.

This is what people hunger for whether they know it or not. We were created for drama, we were meant to live dramatic lives in the thickest world one can imagine — the world made by the Christian God and the historic struggle between God's kingdom and all who opposes it. People spend too much time and energy on things that do not matter. Naturalists and postmodernists have no other alternative because theirs is a thin world with no meaning or value. He who dies with the most toys or votes or power or ... wins. But followers of Jesus understand that they have a dramatic calling that makes the presence or absence of a fleeting amount of pleasurable satisfaction irrelevant compared to the thick happiness offered by their precious Lord.

We are to be dramatic even in the "little" things that grace the daily routines of our "ordinary" lives. As part of a pursuit of classical happiness, "little" things and "ordinary" activities quickly become big and extraordinary! No wonder people who are preoccupied with pleasurable happiness become empty selves! Their vision is too small, too confining, too mundane to justify their three score and ten years, too little to demand their best efforts over the long haul! No wonder people would rather spend themselves for an important cause—specifically, the cause of Christ and leading a life well lived—than enjoy a pampered idleness. No wonder the primary problem of contemporary culture is boredom! *A central part of the church's educational program, including its pulpit ministry, is to constantly present a vision of life in the Kingdom of God that is so rich and real that people want to give themselves away for it and in light of which the empty self is seen and felt to be the trivial fraud that it really is.*

Self-denial in Matthew 16:24–27 does not mean living without the things that bring pleasurable satisfaction. Self-denial certainly does not mean adopting the attitude of putting one's self down, nor does it mean to get rid of any personal desires. This mistaken notion is Buddhist, not Christian. Certain forms of Buddhism teach that one should get rid of all desire as a means for realizing that one does not really have a self. This greases the skids for a "deeper" realization that one does not exist and, thus, may merge with nothingness. No, the Christian disciple is to be teaming with passions and desires of all kinds in a manner fit for someone fully alive in the Kingdom. If these are what Jesus did not mean, then exactly what *did* he mean?

Note that Jesus clarifies self-denial with the phrase "taking up one's cross." Jesus did not literally mean this because Luke adds the word "daily" (Luke 9:23) to the assertion, and this is obviously impossible in a literal sense. "Taking up one's cross daily" means to form through repeated practice the daily habit of living each day with a specific attitude and outlook. More specifically, one is to form a passion for the daily practice of giving up on the failed project of making one's self the center of focus and, alternatively, to live hour by hour for God's Kingdom. It is to be preoccupied with learning skillfully to find one's place in his unfolding plan and play one's role well, to give one's life away to others for Christ's sake. A life of self-denial for Jesus' sake takes the stress away from life derived from the pressure to be "happy" all the time. It also removes the terrible burden of having to be defensive, to be constantly monitoring one's emotions, and to stay in control of every situation. In all honesty, who needs such pressure?

Pursuit of the demands of the empty self and the cultivation of a life of self-denial under Jesus' lordship constitute two very different approaches to life that produce radically different sorts of people. It is here that the two different understandings grab us by the throat, shake us to the core, and demand we make a choice of lifestyle strategies. This choice is as important as any one you will ever make, and that is not religious hype; it is the sober truth.

If pleasurable satisfaction is your goal, then from morning to night your habituated focus will be on three things—"me, myself, and I." You will constantly be monitoring your own happiness temperature, and your activities (job, recreation, church involvement) and other people (friends, spouse, children, and even God himself) will be mere things, objects that simply exist as means to your own happiness.

You will have great difficulty forming meaningful attachments to other people. If you are shy, you will withdraw from people—not to find solitude to reenter relationships with solid boundaries and emotional/ spiritual refreshment, but to attack them and find safety that keeps you from having to change. You will hide from others and fail to give them what they need from you to grow in spiritual formation and friendship. If you are outgoing, you will repress your fears and shame by becoming socially aggressive. You will talk all the time in social situations and not develop skills as a good listener, or if you do know how to listen to others, it will be a front to earn the right to turn the conversation back to you at the earliest opportunity.

After several years of this sort of life, you will become a self-absorbed, empty narcissist. A culture of people who live this way will be a culture that elevates celebrities. A celebrity is someone given attention because of his or her image or ability to get others to live their own lives vicariously through the celebrity's life, such as it is. This is an ugly form of codependence between trapped empty celebrities and passive empty fans! Empty selves exchange a life of drama for Turkish Delight.

This is an appropriate point to consider a claim I often hear people make, that "it is hard to be a dedicated disciple because it requires sacrifice and commitment and it goes against the grain of society; but it's worth the difficulty." This claim is both true and false in different senses, and we are now in a position to see why. Following the path of self-denial for Christ's sake is hard in the specific sense that learning to get good at anything is difficult in the early stages of development. If you are a novice in learning French, tennis, typing, or self-denial, you are in the difficult position of learning to form new habits to replace your old ones that already have natural inertia.

But in a different sense, the life of self-denial is, indeed, the "easy yoke." In contrast to the path of self-absorption, the path of self-denial for Jesus corresponds to the way we were made to function and to reality itself as God created it. The really hard life is the one lived in opposition to Jesus' path. All you need to do is to look at how hard life is for folks who cannot forgive others, who desperately need to be the focus of attention, who have to be in control of everything, who are driven to succeed to prove they are significant. This is the hard life, not the life of self-denial. As one gets good at self-denial for the Kingdom, life gets progressively easier.

If authentic spiritual formation, character, and deep well-being are your goal, then you will learn to see yourself in light of a larger cause, the outworking of God's plan in history. You will be absorbed by wanting to make Jesus famous and respected by everyone. You will be preoccupied with finding your role in the body of Christ and with developing the gifts and talents required to fulfill that role with excellence. Your passion will be to see all of life's activities as occasions to draw near to and become like the triune God. You will hunger to make those around you better at life because they know you and observe your wisdom and skill at living! Your long-term focus (and the simple fact that you have a long-term focus will set you apart from most people!) will be on giving yourself away to others for Christ's sake.

It is enormously important to recognize that Jesus' assertion that we lose our lives when we try to gain them, and we gain our lives when we lose them for his sake, is not a command. A command is something that one *should* obey but, at the same time, is *optional*. You can disobey it. No, this principle is not a command; it is a description of reality, an accurate characterization of the way we are made and how we do and do not flourish as image-bearers of God. It is like someone saying, "If you want to learn arithmetic, then you must do fractions and practice the multiplication table." This is not an option, something such that you can learn arithmetic whether or not you learn fractions. It is an accurate description of the very nature of arithmetic. Being rooted in reality, it describes to us the path one must take to flourish at arithmetic.

In the same way, if one wants to become a flourishing person of character with a deep sense of well-being, then one must learn to give one's life away for Jesus' sake. This is not true simply for believers; it's true for anyone whether they believe it or not. As secular scholar John Gardner acknowledged, "Existence is a strange bargain. Life owes us little; we owe it everything. The only true happiness comes from squandering ourselves for a purpose."[6] If you want to flourish as a friend and have lots of friends, you need to learn to be a friend. You will simply fail if you spend all your time trying to convince others that you are really cool, really worthy of their focused attention. Similarly, if you want to flourish as a person, you must give yourself away for Christ's sake. That brings true happiness.

Too often we shape our lives and ministries to cater to the empty self within all of us. What we must do as a central part of our mission is to teach people to grow in the skill of daily, habitual, healthy self-denial for Jesus' sake. Just as one can learn to get good at math or tennis through practice and focus, one can get good at the art of self-denial, an art that is a means to the goal of a flourishing life in the Kingdom.

Here's one simple suggestion for progress in this area. When you get up in the morning, start off with praise and thanksgiving to God for the things you honestly appreciate about him and his dealings with you. Then lift all your burdens to him until you have a sense of rest before the Lord. Then tell him that between now and, say, lunch, with his help you are going to orient your morning towards focusing on others and giving yourself away for their good.

This may mean focusing on being a servant as a mechanic, insurance salesperson, or whatever your morning station in life brings. At noon, you again lift your burdens to Jesus and focus on your own needs, fears, and problems. Once you have done that, reorient yourself to giving yourself away to others for Jesus' sake until mid-afternoon. Repeat the cycle three to five times each day, and eventually, a habit will form such that your orientation in daily life will be on extending goodness, truth, and beauty to others in the name of Jesus. There's still plenty of room for appropriate self-interest in such a life, but growth in the art of healthy self-denial provides a sure path away from being dominated by your own issues. Spiritual disciplines are intimately related to self-denial and, in fact, are effective tools for achieving facility in healthy, biblically informed self-denial.

Fostering Spiritual Disciplines in Ourselves

Think carefully about these words and see what you make of them: "Therefore I urge you, brethren, by the mercies of God, to present your *bodies* a living and holy sacrifice, acceptable to God, which is your spiritual service of worship" (Rom. 12:1, italics added). This verse is unpacked earlier in Paul's letter:

> Even so consider yourselves to be dead to sin, but alive to God in Christ Jesus. Therefore do not let sin reign in your mortal body that you obey its lusts, and do not go on presenting *the members of your body* to sin as instruments of unrighteousness, but present yourselves to God as those alive from the dead, and *your members* as instruments of righteousness to God....
>
> I am speaking in human terms because of *the weakness of your flesh*. For just as you *presented your members* as slaves to impurity and to lawlessness, resulting in further lawlessness, so now *present your members* as slaves to righteousness, resulting in sanctification. (Rom. 6:11–13, 19, italics added)

Colossians 3:5 and 1 Timothy 4:7–8 provide similar directives. For years I simply glossed over these texts with little understanding of how profound and penetrating they really are. I believe that if you follow the line of thought in the next few pages, you will be amazed at what these verses assert. The initial step in developing that line of thought requires us to unpack four concepts: *habit, character, flesh,* and *body.*

A *habit* is an ingrained tendency to act, think, or feel a certain way without needing to choose to do so. The way a person drives a car, exhibits penmanship, or typically feels upon first awakening in the morning are not things people need to think about and deliberately will to take place. For example, the way you drive a car is a habit and you are free while driving to think about other things.

Character is the sum total of one's habits, good and bad. Penmanship character is the sum total of one's good and bad writing habits; it is one's handwriting style. Note that I am using "character" to stand for all of one's habits—both good and bad—not merely for one's good habits.

Anthropological terms in the Bible such as "mind" (*nous*), "heart" (*kardia*), "flesh" (*sarx*), or "body" (*soma*) express many different meanings, and great care must be given to the context to understand the particular meaning of such terms in specific passages. For example, *flesh* and *body* may on occasion be used as synonyms, but in the passages above, each term expresses a specific meaning. *Body* is pretty obvious. In contrast to the soul, it refers to one's living, animated physical aspect. The body can be seen and touched, and it is composed of tissue, skin, bone, and various organs (e.g., the heart) and systems (e.g., the nervous system). By contrast, *flesh* means "the sinful tendencies or habits that reside in the body and whose nature is opposite that of the Kingdom of God." To see the importance of these notions, especially this usage of *flesh*, let's set aside spiritual disciplines for a moment and bring up a fairly painful topic for many: learning to play a sport, such as tennis.

In a literal sense, the beginner brings to the game a specific *tennis character*, consisting in the sum total of good and bad habits relevant for serving, using your backhand, and playing tennis in general. One's *tennis flesh* is in particular the sum of one's bad tennis habits — tendencies to hit the ball into the net or to serve outside the appropriate lines. Clearly, the goal of the novice is to develop tennis character, and this will require that person to get rid of his or her tennis flesh.

Now, exactly how does one do this? As a first step, one must answer another question: Where do these bad habits reside? Answer: They reside in specific body parts/members as ingrained tendencies. Again, there is nothing figurative about any of this. In fact, if you do not take what is being said literally, you simply will not get good at tennis (develop an excellent tennis character). Your success at tennis may be seriously compromised by bad habits in the wrists, the hips, the legs, and so on. You may have good habits in your wrists but bad habits (tennis flesh) residing in your shoulders or ankles. Tennis flesh resides in the specific members of your body, namely, those areas of the body in which bad tennis habits reside.

We are now in a position to vouchsafe a crucial insight: How does one develop a good tennis character; that is, how does one become good at tennis? Clearly it is not enough to engage in daily tennis readings, watching Wimbledon each year, and seeking constant exposure to motivational tennis music (whether it be traditional tennis hymns or contemporary tennis praise music!). No, one must present one's members to a tennis instructor at a tennis court as instruments of tennis "righteousness" instead of following one's tennis flesh as an instrument of tennis "unrighteousness" (I'm not talking John McEnroe here but being lousy at tennis!). These are not figures of speech. They are literal indeed. By so presenting one's members, one gradually gets rid of bad tennis habits and replaces them with good ones. If this is done repeatedly, tennis transformation ensues.

Now, exactly how does one present one's members to a tennis instructor? The answer consists in two crucial factors. First, a person must be committed to the pursuit of tennis righteousness (to getting good at tennis) and choose to submit as an apprentice to a master tennis instructor. Such a commitment may involve a one-time decision. But as important as such a decision is, it is not enough. Follow-through must ensue.

Thus, in addition, one must "present one's body" to a tennis instructor repeatedly by engaging specific body parts in regular activities done over and over again through repeated practice and body movement, under the watchful eye of the teacher. For example, one may present a particular body part, say the wrists, to the tennis instructor by practicing over and over again a specific wrist movement with racket in hand. The result of such habitual bodily movement will be the replacement of bad habits that dwell in the wrist with good habits. The tennis flesh that resides in the wrists will be replaced gradually by tennis righteousness in those members. Later, the instructor may require the habitual presentation of other members, say the hips or ankles, to replace bad habits that reside there.

The particular practice one must repeat will vary from time to time; that is why one needs the constant direction of a master teacher to grow in tennis character over the long haul. In general, a sport's discipline is a repeated exercise relevant to that sport—a bodily movement involving specific body parts, repeated over and over again, that is done in order to get rid of the specific sport's flesh and replace it with new habits so that sport righteousness may reside in specific body parts. A tennis discipline is done repeatedly not to get good at the discipline, but to get good at the game of tennis. Sometimes one's progress in the game of tennis is measured by the fact that a particular practice exercise is less urgent than it once was and may fruitfully be dropped for a season to concentrate on another repeated bodily movement.

It should now be clear as to how insightful the passages under consideration really are for getting good at life. When you present your body to God as a living sacrifice (Rom. 12:1), it involves not only a one-time act of dedication, but a habitual, repeated bodily exercise (1 Cor. 9:24–27; 1 Tim. 4:7–8) involving specific body parts (Rom. 6:11–13, 19) and resulting in putting to death one's bad habits (Col. 3:5)—that is, removing the flesh that resides in those body parts and replacing them with righteousness that comes to reside in the members of one's body. *A Christian spiritual discipline is a repeated bodily practice, done over and over again, in dependence on the Holy Spirit and under the direction of Jesus and other wise teachers in his way, to enable one to get good at certain things in life that one cannot learn by direct effort.*

Just as "tennis flesh" resides in specific body parts, so sinful habits often reside in specific body parts — anger in the stomach area, anxiety in the chest or shoulders, gossip in the tongue and mouth region, and lust in the eyes and other areas. A spiritual discipline is a repetitive practice that targets one of these areas in order to replace bad habits with good ones in dependence on the Spirit of the living God. Some disciplines (e.g., playing piano scales) have no value in themselves and are totally a means to an end — learning to play beautiful music. Other disciplines (e.g., practicing your serve in tennis) are not only valuable as a means to an end when done on the tennis court, but are also intrinsically valuable for their own sake when done during the game itself.

In the same way, some spiritual disciplines (e.g., the practice of journaling, such as the habit of writing down one's prayers to God) are mere means to an end (learning to remember answers to prayer). Other disciplines (e.g., ongoing prayer) are both a means to an end when done as a discipline and intrinsically valuable in their own right when done during the actual "game" of life.

We need to center our church fellowships on fostering the regular practice of spiritual disciplines in our individual and corporate lives. Dallas Willard offers two categories of spiritual disciplines: abstinence/detachment and engagement.[7] This list is not exhaustive, but it does contain most of the classical disciplines:

disciplines of abstinence: solitude, silence, fasting, frugality, chastity, secrecy, sacrifice

disciplines of engagement: study, worship, celebration, service, prayer, fellowship, confession, submission

In disciplines of abstinence, we unhook for a period of time and to varying degrees from the satisfaction of normal, appropriate desires — food, sleep, companionship, sex, music, comfort, financial security, recognition, and so forth. These disciplines help us address sins of *commission*. In general, it is not a good idea to detach from something without filling the resulting void with attachment to something positive. Thus, disciplines of engagement go hand in hand with those of detachment, and the former help us address sins of *omission*.

In addition to classic examples of disciplines such as those listed above, any repeated practice that is fruitful for growth in Christlikeness is legitimately called a spiritual discipline; thus, the list of such disciplines is endless. To illustrate, consider evangelistic training as an example of a "nonclassic" discipline. I have trained thousands of people to share their faith. Over the years I have participated in twenty-five to thirty debates.

In March 1988 I went to the University of Mississippi to debate Kai Nielsen, a man who at that time was considered perhaps the leading intellectual atheist in the world. To be sure, I was somewhat nervous, but my nerves did not control me. In fact, the strength to do this was largely developed. When I first received Christ in 1968, I was frightened to witness. But I did not want to stay in that condition, so around five months after my conversion, I made the critical decision to become a courageous, spiritually competent witness for Christ. How was I to grow in this way? I was greatly helped by reading books on evangelism, but this was inadequate in itself. Transformation as a confident, skillful evangelist required me to practice witnessing repeatedly until the habit was formed and my character changed. If this is true in tennis and other areas of life, why should spiritual formation be any different?

After dedicating myself to the task of evangelism, I followed through by first familiarizing myself with a gospel tract, learning to give a brief testimony (which I memorized), and so on. I practiced using the tract and giving my testimony in front of the mirror repeatedly. Then I repeatedly practiced with a Christian brother, and then went witnessing around fifty times with a more experienced person. Gradually, I began to do more and more in evangelistic situations as my mentor wove me into the process gradually.

It wasn't long until I started training others how to evangelize; eventually, I ventured into the area of giving evangelistic talks in front of groups. This new area of training proceeded in the same way as my growth in one-on-one evangelism (e.g., I learned a message, gave it in front of a mirror, and so forth, all under the direction of a mentor). The rest is, as they say, history. By the time I debated the atheist in that auditorium, I had shared my faith hundreds of times and boldness had become a habit.

In light of the importance of spiritual disciplines, I offer two ideas of practical application. First, I suggest you read Dallas Willard's *Spirit of the Disciplines* and focus on cultivating the practice of specific disciplines that speak to your current need. I suspect that solitude and silence is a good place to start, but the goal is to engage in habitual practices that are tailor-made for addressing your own growth issues. Second, brainstorm with a friend or spouse some nonclassic disciplines that may be of use to you, such as the habit of driving in the slow lane, of reading for one hour three nights a week right after the evening news, of smiling and being warm to people even if you don't feel like it. Remember, the Christian life requires habit formation as a central part of transformation, and a spiritual discipline is a tool for laying aside bad habits and forming new ones more consistent with the nature of God's Kingdom.

Cultivating Emotional Sensitivity to the Movement within Your Soul

Since her beginning, one of the greatest contributions and achievements of the church is the history, literature, and people at the core of Christian spiritual formation. There is simply nothing like this tradition anywhere else, and the profundity of the development of Christian spirituality is unrivaled. Grounded in Scripture, from the Desert Fathers to Henry Nouwen and Richard Foster, we have available to us a treasure of deep, rich knowledge of the soul and its proper functioning before God.

Of central concern to this literature is the development of sensitivity to the inner affective movements of the soul, and now more than ever we need to reacquaint ourselves with this literature and the sensitivity it engenders. I say this for two reasons. First, the sociology of at least much of the white Evangelical community is one in which our visible leaders tend to be obsessive-compulsive, type A males who struggle with being split off from their emotions. Our leaders tend to be left-brained in orientation, with the result that our communities struggle to incorporate a right-brain ambiance in which the artistic, creative, affective side of the church is given its proper due.

I don't understand all the reasons for this sociology, though I suspect that two factors are central to it: our fear that emotions are too subjective to be of much value and the conviction that spiritually formative literature is Catholic, and nothing good can come from Rome. Admittedly, emotions are terrible masters. But they are wonderful servants, and they are an essential part of being human. Moreover, we Evangelicals have much in common with our Catholic friends, and central concerns and insights about spiritual formation are among them. And let's not forget that there is a rich history of Protestant literature on spiritual formation.

Second, Evangelicals on the charismatic/Pentecostal side of the family all too often develop an addiction to special experiences of the manifest presence of God as a substitute for the day-to-day process of cultivating a rich inner life as that process is captured in the church's formative literature. I am not against seeking and hungering for the manifest presence of God. Quite the contrary. In the next chapter, I will make clear that the Spirit's overt presence and power are crucial to recapturing the vitality of the church.

But rather than being a both/and, I fear that the hunger for a quick fix, coupled with plain old laziness, has created a context of abuse in churches that enjoy the manifest presence of God on a regular basis. The miraculous, manifest presence of God and his power should be seen as a supplement to the daily, ongoing processes of spiritual formation. These are not rivals, and when the latter is set aside and the former is overemphasized, a situation is created in which people get stuck in spiritual infancy and character development is substantially thwarted.

It is possible to develop a healthy, ongoing awareness of one's inner life that avoids being unduly introspective on the one hand and out of touch emotionally on the other. It is precisely a preoccupation with this sort of development that characterizes the great spiritual guides in the church's history. Luke Dysinger notes that "by the end of the fourth century there existed a well-established tradition of illustrating Christian spiritual principles through analogies based on the theory and vocabulary of classical medicine."[8] This literature is replete with detailed descriptions of the different compartments of the soul, the various movements that take place within it, a discernment of those movements, and the formation of the fruit of the Spirit within the soul as a means toward growing in the spiritual life. Great care was given to diagnosing affective movements in the soul of the world, the flesh, and the devil as well as the movement of God's Spirit in the inner life.

Similarly, the writings of Ignatius Loyola (1491–1556), especially "Rules for the Discernment of Spirits" contained in his *Spiritual Exercises*, exhibit a care, a depth of insight, and a profundity of guidance about the inner life that is completely off the radar screen among contemporary Evangelicals. We neglect this literature at the cost of our own impoverishment.

Not only is it possible to develop an inner life with a flourishing emotionality, it is imperative if we are to be the sort of people required to lead dramatic lives for the Lord Jesus. As Dallas Willard reminds us:

Feelings are a primary blessing *and* a primary problem for human life. We cannot live without them and we can hardly live with them. Hence they are also central for spiritual formation in the Christian tradition. In the restoration of the individual to God, feelings too must be renovated: old ones removed in many cases, or at least thoroughly modified, and new ones installed or at least heightened into a new prominence.[9]

We need to cultivate the ability to discern the divine, satanic, or psychological components of our emotionality. We need to learn when we are using defensive mechanisms to repress or in some other way refuse to face negative emotions of fear, anxiety, anger, and hatred. We need to learn to cultivate a background emotional tone of love, peace, and joy that is confident in God and makes it easy for people to learn that they don't have to be in control of things to be safe.

There are three things we can do to make progress in this area of the Christian life. If we make these three things more central and overt in our local churches, we will become a people about whom it can no longer be said that we are a mile wide and an inch deep. When the elders and church staff establish the church's core values and engage in yearly goal setting and the development of the church's yearly calendar, these three things need to be held before the people as central components of church identity.

First, important writings in spiritual formation should be studied and discussed, and the insights gained should be implemented. If I were going to launch out in this area, either for myself or as a leader of a church or parachurch ministry, I would invest myself in absorbing four books. First on the list is Dallas Willard's *Renovation of the Heart*. If I had one book to choose, this would be it. You cannot go wrong by developing a life strategy for cultivating spiritual sensitivity that centers around the ideas in this book. Second, Richard Foster's *Celebration of Discipline* has earned the title of a contemporary classic.[10] Third, Henri Nouwen's *The Way of the Heart* is a must-read.[11] When you read it or other things by Nouwen, the important thing is not simply the content presented but the feel, the texture, the tone of his writings. Nouwen must be read slowly and with the heart if you hope to gain from his writings. Finally, I suggest my recent book with Klaus Issler, *The Lost Virtue of Happiness*. Among other things, this book offers fresh insight for working through anxiety and depression, along with a rich discussion of the importance of friendship and how it is best cultivated.

There are, of course, many books to read in this area, but I suggest these because I believe they are at the core of our need. Multiple options can paralyze us, so it is sometimes best to focus on a limited range of alternatives so that we don't freeze. We must be proactive in this area of the spiritual life, and by reading, internalizing, and interacting with others about these four books, you will be well on the way to progress.

Second, we must bring to center stage two sorts of trained individuals who can help us in this area. There is first no substitute for solid Christian therapists and counselors. These people have given their lives to learning how to aid folks in the transition from a false to a true self, and they are experts regarding the affective movements in the soul. It goes without saying that one should be wise in the selection of a good Christian therapist. Happily, in the last two decades we have witnessed the maturation of Christian therapy, and there is a growing number of skilled practitioners who have integrated good psychology with biblical teaching. Too often, there is a stigma attached to going to a therapist, and my prayer is that we are maturing past this destructive attitude. Church ministries should do everything they can to develop mutually beneficial relationships with the Christian therapists in their area, and individual believers should take advantage of these dear brothers and sisters as opportunity and need intersect.

The other sort of trained individuals play a role with which Catholics are familiar but which is currently not on the Evangelical radar screen. There are indications that this is starting to change, but we still have a ways to go. I am speaking of the need for churches to recruit, train, and incorporate spiritual directors into their ministries. A spiritual director seeks to focus on a person's inner life in relationship to God in order to help that person identify how God is moving in one's life or how one's own inner dynamics are affecting one's relationship with God. A spiritual director is not a therapist. Whereas a therapist focuses on identifying, say, the causes of depression and finding a way to leave it behind, the spiritual director tries to help someone understand how the experience of depression is affecting his or her relationship with God or how God may be moving in or in spite of the depression.

There is little training in spiritual direction in the Evangelical community, though the ministry of Renovare is an exception to this rule.[12] Renovare offers conferences and training materials relevant to spiritual direction. Because of this lack, Evangelicals interested in this area frequently seek training in various Catholic programs. While this training can be of great value, two words of caution are in order. First, there is little quality control in training in spiritual direction, and if you are trying to find local Catholic venues for such training, you should keep in mind that you may enter a program of low quality. Second, there is little theological control over Catholic venues. Specifically, this area of training is often impacted by liberal thought, pluralistic, watered-down approaches to spirituality. Moreover, one may have to set aside certain formative teachings, such as praying to Mary, that conflict with Scripture. There is no question that Evangelicals need to recapture the importance of spiritual direction in our lives and ministries, yet we need to be wise and guided by Scripture as we seek to grow in this area.

Third, we need to gain facility in affective meditation in our hearts. We are familiar with meditation in our minds, and this is usually what we mean when we talk of meditation. So understood, we seek to ponder memorized texts, repeat themselves to ourselves, and gain insights throughout our day from what they mean. This is a good practice, and we should continue this sort of meditation. But because we already know this form of meditation, there is also an urgent need to learn meditation in one's heart.

Scripture emphasizes the nature and role of the heart in a life of peace, hope, and joy. The term "heart" has many uses in Scripture, but its basic meaning refers to the deepest core of the person. The heart is the fundamental, sometimes hidden fountain at the deepest recesses and absolute center of a person, from which spring one's more real feelings, one's most authentic thoughts, one's actual values and take on life. In this sense, it is obvious that the heart is the deepest aspect of one's soul, one's inner self, and it is not to be equated with the organ that pumps blood.

But because the soul is fully present throughout the body, one's various body parts can actually contain and/or be associated with sinful or holy tendencies to act, think, and feel in certain ways. For example, anger can reside in the stomach area and actually be felt in that region of the body. In my view, it is no accident that the term "heart" is used to represent one's deepest core, for the *physical heart area*—what C. S. Lewis called "the chest"—is the "location" where we actually experience our deepest values, feelings, attitudes, and ways of seeing the world. In some mysterious way, then, the physical heart area is an important center of meditation if it is to flow from and impact our deepest core, our metaphorical "heart."

Interestingly, a scientific strand of thought derived from recent discoveries may shed light on biblical teaching about the core of a person and its relationship to the heart organ.[13] Neuroscientists have discovered that the heart has its own independent nervous system referred to as "the brain in the heart." In a real sense the heart "thinks for itself." Some forty thousand neurons are in the heart, which is as many as are found in a number of important subregions of the brain.

The heart sends signals to different parts of the brain, including the amygdala. The amygdala specializes in strong emotional memories and is what the soul uses to process information for its emotional significance. By influencing the amygdala and other regions of the brain, scientists believe that "our heartbeats are not just the mechanical throbs of a diligent pump, but an *intelligent language* that significantly influences how we perceive and react to the world."[14] Some scientists talk about "heart intelligence," an intelligent flow of awareness and insight, an intuitive source of wisdom and clear perception that embraces both mental and emotional intelligence.

In biblical terms, the soul is the person, but the soul has two faculties of intellectual cognition and intuitive perception, and each is associated with a different body part: the brain and the heart, respectively. Thus, the brain and the heart work together to shape our thoughts, emotions, moods, and attitudes. Given that a person is just one self—not two—with one soul, it is obvious that the "I," the soul, uses both the mind (associated with the brain) and the deepest intuitive core (associated with the heart organ) to think, see, and feel about the world.

With this in mind, we should think carefully about Paul's statement: "Be anxious for nothing, but in everything by prayer and supplication with thanksgiving let your requests be made known to God. And the peace of God, which surpasses all comprehension, shall guard your *hearts and your minds* in Christ Jesus" (Phil. 4:6–7, italics added). Both the heart and mind areas of the body (the heart organ and the brain) are to be involved cooperatively in opening up to God and dispelling anxiety. Among other things, we need a strategy for developing a life-enhancing form of meditation that involves the heart. Consequently, you should consider a two-step practice.[15]

Step 1: Focus the center of your attention on your physical heart muscle. Attend to the center of your chest where your heart is and stay there for about thirty seconds. The goal is to feel the area around your heart. There are two ways to help you in this. First, pretend you are breathing in and out of your heart muscle. Second, try to "feel" and attend to the front surface of your physical heart, then the back surface, followed by the right and then the left side of your heart. When you first learn to practice this meditative activity and form it as a habit, you should take as long as necessary to focus on the heart area. At this point you may feel little emotion there or you may get in touch with a feeling of embarrassment, fear, grief, sadness, loneliness, helplessness, hurt, or some other anxiety producer.

This step is an aid in internalizing Proverbs 3:5: "Trust in the LORD with all your heart, and do not lean on your own understanding." Rather than mulling things over and over again in your mind and trying to solve your worries in the head, turn to the core of your inner life, your heart, and learn to trust God there. Step 1 is a way to practice not leaning on your own understanding. Step 2 is a way of learning to trust God in the heart.

Step 2: Using the acrostic CFAN, recall a memory emotion associated with the relevant memory and let that emotion dwell and dominate the heart area. With your attention on your physical heart area, you want to bring a new positive emotion, a healthy intuitive awareness to dwell there as a basis for meditating in your heart on God and his goodness toward you. To do this, you want to meditate on something positive in order to recall a memory emotion that is positive. CFAN stands for Compassion, Forgiveness, Appreciation, and Nonjudgmentalism. You want to recall a specific occasion you can picture in which you either gave or received compassion/love, forgiveness/removal of guilt feelings, appreciation/joy, and being nonjudgmental/accepting.[16]

The important thing is not to do all four of these, but to pick one area that is most effective for you and constantly return there. For example, recall a time when you gave real love to God, a friend, or a family member, or you received the feeling of love from God or someone important to you. Recall a time when you gave appreciation to someone—a special time of worship when you really felt God was there or a time when you gave heartfelt praise and adoration to someone—or a time when you drank in appreciation from a dear friend or from a spectacular answer to prayer or an endearing biblical truth. The goal here is not simply to recall the relevant incident, but more importantly, to have the associated emotion fill and remain in your heart area. By habitually practicing this simple two-step activity, you can train yourself to meditate in your heart on God and his goodness and to center on these emotions throughout your day.

Two legs of the Kingdom Triangle are in place: the recovery of knowledge and the renovation of the soul. But a table with only two legs is unstable, or, to change metaphors, a threefold cord is not easily broken. Chapter 7 offers guidance for putting the third leg into place.

QUESTIONS FOR PERSONAL REFLECTION OR GROUP DISCUSSION

1. Spiritual formation begins with who we are and where we are in our life stage. The "self" is viewed in American (and much of Western) culture as "empty" or is falsely presented to others (pages 141–143). Consider ways in which you may present a "false self." Is it related to making the world more safe for you? Is it used to help you be in control of situations or relationships, to gain attention, or to be ignored? How has this false self deterred you from opening up to a greater experience of authentically living as a disciple of Jesus?

   There are four traits of the empty self that undermine authentic spiritual formation: being inordinately individualistic, infantile, narcissistic, and passive (pages 142–143). Review each of these traits. Do you tend toward one trait or another? Are there true self-forming habits that can help you counter the false self-forming habits?

2. The author underscores that "Jesus is the smartest man who ever lived." Ponder Jesus' teaching in Matthew 16:24–25. How do you think Jesus' invitation (to deny ourselves and follow him) critiques the contemporary notion of happiness as pleasurable satisfaction? How does his invitation to life-giving life relate to the claim, "We were created for drama, we were meant to live dramatic lives in the thickest world one can imagine" (page 145)?

3. What does it mean to live your life in the Kingdom of God? What sorts of ideas or images come to mind? Do you have a thick or a thin notion of life in the Kingdom of God? According to Matthew 16:24–27, the invitation to "self-denial," "taking up one's cross," and "losing yourself" are crucial ways that commend themselves to healthy, Kingdom life. How are they an anathema to the empty self? How can self-denial be hard in one sense and yet an "easy yoke" in another sense?

4. Spiritual disciplines are effective tools that assist in achieving healthy, biblically informed self-denial. They permit room for appropriate self-interest without being dominated by an obsessive quest for your own happiness. Reflect on Romans 12:1 in light of 6:12–13, 19. What

stands out to you? What role does the body and its members have for spiritual transformation? Now consider the message of these passages in light of other Pauline directives found in Colossians 3:5 and 1 Timothy 4:7–8. Again, what do you notice?

5. Does Paul's vision of "getting good at life" make sense to you? How is it related to character development? Why is this getting good at life more than just skill acquisition?

What parts of your body have good and bad habits or ingrained tendencies? What must be done in order to develop good habits to replace bad ones? What kind of Christian spiritual disciplines facilitate repeated bodily transformation in the relevant members of your body? Do you have a trustworthy mentor to help you practice righteousness in place of unrighteousness?

6. Dallas Willard distinguishes between "disciplines of abstinence" and "disciplines of engagement" (pages 153–154). Compare and contrast these two categories. Is there one discipline from each category that you would like to especially practice? Why?

Evangelistic training is one example of a "nonclassic" discipline. What are other "nonclassic" spiritual disciplines? Be creative, innovative, and attentive to your life and the life of those closest to you (e.g., the habit of driving in the slow lane, of reading for one hour three nights a week of smiling and being warm to people, of giving your eyes an internet fast, etc).

7. Neglecting emotional growth is one sure way to be malformed in our interior life (pages 156–157). How do you cultivate being emotionally sensitive to the movement of affection within your soul? What is holding you back? What good habits need to be formed in order to empower you to be more mindful, attentive, and careful with yourself, interiorly? Does your life have a background emotional tone of love, peace, and joy that is confident in God and makes it easy for people to learn that they don't have to be in control of things in order to be safe? Do you have a mellowness of heart?

8. The author presents three important areas where progress in spiritual formation can be made for an individual or for a local church (pages 157–160).

   a. The first includes reading, studying, and discussing the writings of those well-practiced in this area. Have you read any books by Dallas Willard, Richard Foster, or Henri Nouwen? If not, then over the course of your lifetime commit yourself to researching, studying, and implementing insights from men like these.

   b. The second is to incorporate the gifting and experience of well-trained Christian therapists and counselors along with spiritual directors into your life and the life of your local church. Have you ever received counsel from a Christian therapist or a trustworthy spiritual director? How did that benefit you? How have you implemented their advice or direction?

   c. The final area is to learn how to effectively gain facility in affective meditation. How does such meditation make sense in light of Paul's encouragement to have the peace of God "guard your hearts and minds in Christ Jesus"? How have contemporary discoveries in neuroscience contributed to this discussion?

9. The author develops a two-step practice for facilitating affective meditation in our hearts (pages 160–161). With Step 1, do you "feel" a little emotion where your heart is, or can you get in touch with a feeling of embarrassment, fear, grief, sadness, loneliness, helplessness, hurt, or some other anxiety producer? With Step 2, can you bring a new positive emotion, a healthy intuitive awareness to dwell there as a basis for meditating in your heart on God and his goodness toward you? To do this, you want to meditate on something positive in order to recall a memory emotion that is positive.

CHAPTER 7

RESTORATION OF THE KINGDOM'S
MIRACULOUS POWER

The Sunday evening service on February 20, 2005, had just ended and I wanted to get home. I was frustrated. I had been distracted during the entire service and now had to decide what I was going to do. The previous Thursday a virus landed in my chest and throat, and in a period of less than three hours I went from being normal to having the worst case of laryngitis in the thirty-five years since college. On Friday I went to our walk-in clinic and received the bad news. The doctor warned that this virus was going around, she had seen several cases of it in the last few weeks, and there was nothing that could be done about it. I just had to wait it out. The laryngitis would last seven to ten days.

This couldn't be, I whispered to her. My main day of teaching at the university was Monday, and I was looking at a full day of lecturing. I couldn't afford to cancel classes because I had already missed my limit of canceled classes for that semester. To make matters worse, I was scheduled to deliver a three-hour lecture at a nearby church that Tuesday evening, and I didn't want to let the church down.

It made no difference. The doctor said I wasn't going to be able to speak either day, so I had to make other plans. My throat felt as if it had broken glass in it, and I was reduced to whispering. On Sunday evening I whispered a few greetings to various church friends; I tried to speak normally, but it hurt too much. After the service I had to get home, try to contact our department secretary that night (I didn't have her home phone number), and cancel my classes for Monday. I could cancel with the church the next day.

As I was walking out of the sanctuary, two lay elders intercepted me. "Hey, J. P.," one yelled, "you can't leave yet. Hope (my wife) just told us you have laryngitis, and we can't let you get outta here without loving on you a bit and praying for your throat!" So one elder laid hands on my shoulders and the other placed his hand on my lower throat area and started praying.

To be honest, I wasn't listening to a word they said. I had already left the church emotionally and wanted to get home to make my phone call. But something happened. As the two men prayed gently for me, I began to feel heat pour into my throat and chest from one elder's hand. *After two or three minutes of prayer, I was completely and irreversibly healed!* I started talking to the brothers normally with no pain, no effort, no trace that anything had been wrong. I never had to make that call to my secretary. The laryngitis never returned.

This may sound like a small thing to you, and in a sense it is. Laryngitis is not at the level of being blind, lame, or terminally ill with cancer. As you will discover in the pages to follow, we have seen all these maladies healed through prayer in the last few months, and we have seen with our own eyes and heard eyewitness testimony of much, much more. But in another sense, the healing of my laryngitis is a big deal indeed. For one thing, it's big because the wonderful, tender, Triune God actually cares about the "little" things of life. Life is basically made of a series of "little" things, and our dear Lord Jesus walks with us in all things big and small.

But there's something else looming in the shadows of my healed throat, and it is so wonderful, so powerful, so real, that nothing can contain or stop it. According to every credible statistic available, it is bursting forth at a breathtaking rate all over the world. If we Western Christians want to be a part of it, we will discover in a fresh, new way that it is a main part of the solution for the crisis of our age.

WHAT IN THE WORLD IS GOING ON WITH THE SPREAD OF THE KINGDOM OF GOD?

In his 2002 book entitled *The Next Christendom: The Coming of Global Christianity*, Philip Jenkins, Distinguished Professor of History at Penn State, notes that the most significant changes in the world during the last portion of the twentieth century were not secular trends like fascism, communism, feminism, or environmentalism.[1] Rather, "it is precisely religious changes that are the most significant, and even the most revolutionary, in the contemporary world.... We are currently living through one of the transforming movements in the history of religion worldwide."[2] The church is exploding at unprecedented rates in the so-called Third World.

Jenkins is not alone in this assessment, and it has become evident to all who know the facts that in the last fifty years or so, and especially since 1980, there is religious revival breaking out all over the world. The best-kept secret of the era is the explosion of the Kingdom of God and a harvest of converts and disciples greater than anything the world has ever seen. In fact, the single most explosive movement of any kind—political, military, whatever—is the spread of the gospel and the advance of the Kingdom in the last fifty years.

Consider the following:[3] Some estimate that in 1970, there were around 71,000,000 born-again Christians with a vision to reach out to the entire world for Christ. By 2000, there were 707,000,000, roughly 11 percent of the earth's population! Up until 1960, Western Evangelicals outnumbered non-Western Evangelicals by two to one, but by 2000 non-Westerners (mostly Latinos, Africans, and Asians) lead by four to one, and the figure will be seven to one by 2010. Today more missionaries are sent from non-Western than Western nations. At a church planting congress in 1998, representatives from Latin American countries set a staggering goal of planting 500,000 new churches by 2010 and—get this—progress up to 2005 indicates that the target will be reached! In fact, five nations have already reached their target goals and have set new ones!

If things continue this way for the next twenty years, a transformation of epic proportions will characterize the global scene. Keep in mind that these numbers do not just represent nominal converts. There is a transformation of social, cultural, religious, and even economic conditions that often accompany these conversions.[4] While we should never rest on today's laurels, we should be absolutely thrilled at the revivals breaking out today all over the world. Something is afoot, and we need to take note of it and learn from it.

But therein lies the rub for many of us Western believers. To see why, consider the following parable recorded by Jenkins:

> Imagin[e] a brilliant African student going off to a European seminary. Here he "learns German, French, Greek, Latin, Hebrew, in addition to English, church history, systematics, homiletics, exegesis and pastoralia." He reads all the great European Bible critics, such as Rudolf Bultmann. Returning home to his native village, the student is welcomed joyfully by his extended family but, suddenly, his sister falls dangerously ill. With his Western training, he knows that her illness requires scientific medicine, but everyone present knows with equal certainty that the girl is troubled by the spirit of her dead great-aunt. Since this fine student has so much theological training, the family

knows that it is obviously up to him to cure her. The debate between the student and his family rages until the people shout "Help your sister, she is possessed." He shouts back, "But Bultmann has demythologized demon possession!" The family is not impressed.[5]

A major factor in the current revival in the Third World—by some estimates, up to 70 percent of it—is intimately connected to signs and wonders as expressions of the love of the Christian Father-God, the lordship of his Son, and the power of his Spirit and his Kingdom. A manifestation of the supernatural power of God through healings, demonic deliverances, and the prophetic are central to what is going on today. Jenkins goes so far as to say that for Third World Christians and the explosive growth of the church in their communities, the heart of the matter is "the critical idea that God intervenes daily in everyday life," an intervention that is an expression of the power of God's Kingdom.[6]

Just two weeks prior to my writing this, *The Washington Times* featured a story on the explosion of Christianity in China.[7] According to the article, the underground church alone contains at least 100,000,000 believers compared to 70,000,000 members of the Communist Party. Christianity is a social revolution of staggering proportions.

Why is Christianity growing like this? Here's the answer given in the article: "One of the driving forces of Christianity's growth in China has been its association with healing powers, particularly in rural areas where basic health services are lacking." To illustrate this, the article cites the case of a young woman who had contracted a virus doctors had never seen before. She was on a ventilator and everyone had lost hope for her recovery. But following prayer, she was healed and fully recovered. As a result, "now her family follows Christ, too."

In 1996, while Thai missionary Lun Poobuanak was conducting a Sunday service for a small band of Christians in a predominantly Buddhist village in Kalasin province, he was interrupted by the village leader. The leader shouted to Lun that because the monsoon rains had not come, their crops were almost ruined, and that if he would ask his God for rain that month, if he answered, all 134 families in the village would become Christians. The believers prayed and fasted for three days. On the fourth day, a cloudburst came that solved the problem, and all 134 families became Christians.[8]

Consider this report from Paul Eshleman, director of Campus Crusade's *Jesus* film project, in April, 1997:[9]

In the state of Bihar, India, there is a notoriously anti-Christian tribe called the Malto. When a crew with Campus Crusade's *Jesus* film attempted to schedule a showing there in 1998, they were strongly rebuffed. A few days later, a 16-year-old Malto girl died. But that evening, just as her parents were about to bury her, she came back to life. As an awed crowd gathered around her, she told them that the God of the film crew had sent her back for several days "to tell as many people as I can that He is real." The girl and her mother went searching, and the next day, they found the crew in a nearby village and invited them back for a showing. For seven days she told her story in every village they could get to, drawing large crowds for the film. Hundreds of people became Christians and started churches. After seven days the girl still looked fine, but she collapsed and died once again.

Because we Western Christians have absorbed more of a secular worldview than we may like to admit, we may find these stories hard to believe. Christian anthropologist Charles Kraft observes:

> In comparison to other societies, Americans and other North Atlantic peoples are *naturalistic*. Non-Western peoples are frequently concerned about the activities of supernatural beings. Though many Westerners retain a vague belief in God, most deny that other supernatural beings even exist. The wide-ranging supernaturalism of most of the societies of the world is absent for most of our people.... Our focus is on the natural world, with little or no attention paid to the supernatural world.[10]

Kraft goes on:

> In the present day, Evangelicals tend to believe that God has stopped talking and doing the incredible things we read about in scripture. Now we see God limiting himself to working through the Bible ... plus an occasional contemporary "interference" in the natural course of events. What we usually call a miracle—the power God used to manifest in healing—has been largely replaced by secular medicine. The speaking he used to do now comes indirectly through rationalistic reasoning in books, lectures, and sermons—similar to the process used by secular scientists.[11]

Kraft may be overstating matters to make a point, but the truth is that his claims are too close to home for American Evangelicals to dismiss them as extreme. I fear Kraft's assertions largely characterized my own

Christian journey until a few years ago when I began looking into, hearing firsthand, and even experiencing things of this sort myself. Recently, I talked to a missionary couple working in Nepal, one of the hardest Buddhist areas in the world to evangelize. They related to me that they had recently led a poor Buddhist woman to Christ. Shortly thereafter, her main source of economic hope, a little calf, took deathly ill and lay listlessly in a field near her little shack for a day and a half. Being a new Christian who was just becoming familiar with the miracles of Jesus in the gospels, she gathered several of her Buddhist friends around the calf and announced that she was going to ask Jesus to heal it. He did! Instantly the calf arose in full health and her Buddhist friends became Christians.

As I write this, just a few months ago I was talking to an American teacher in Brazil with the Association of Christian Schools International. He told me that two of his missionary friends had recently been called into a village to pray for a desperately sick little boy with a softball-sized hernia protruding from his abdomen. They laid hands on the boy and prayed, and before their very eyes, the hernia disappeared and the boy was healed. This event was not tied to evangelism. It was just an act of God's love for a family in need.

Recently at church I met a missionary to the Congo who was home on furlough. He told me that he and others have seen numerous miraculous healings in recent months, as well as supernatural prophetic words of great help to the local believers. He also testified to seeing demonic deliverances in significant numbers. As I write this, three days ago I had lunch with a world-renowned American New Testament scholar. He had just taught a course for around twenty missionaries, and he heard story after story of the supernatural power of the Kingdom from these missionaries. One man told him that in several years, every one of the many conversions to Christ he had witnessed came by way of the Lord speaking or appearing to the person in a dream or vision.

Just a few weeks ago I had an amazing conversation with Nathan, one of my philosophy graduate students. Before coming to Biola University, Nathan and a friend were on the Long Beach State debate team and were ranked fifth in the country, having beaten Harvard and other top schools in debate competitions. Needless to say, Nathan is a very rational person not prone to being gullible. Nathan relayed that when he was thirteen, he was diagnosed with GERDS (Gastroesophageal Reflux Disease), in which the valve between his esophagus and stomach did not work properly. He would wake up at night not being able to breath because of the stomach acid gathering in his chest and the severe pain that followed. Nathan developed insomnia—he had to sleep sitting up and did not sleep through the night for nine years. In 2002, Nathan got married and his wife made him go to a doctor to investigate surgery. When he did, he was told that he would need a series of five surgeries and would be on medication the rest of his life.

The next day, Nathan and his wife attended a small group Bible study at which a missionary couple from Thailand was going to share about their ministry overseas, a ministry that included miraculous healings. No one at the Bible study knew of Nathan's illness. While there, something shocking happened to him. In Nathan's own words, "During the Bible study, out of the blue, the speaker stopped praying for another person, turned and said, 'Someone in the room is suffering from Gastroesophageal Reflux disease.' This man had never met me nor could he have known the disease name."

Nathan went on to say that the missionary described a painful event that had happened between the person with GERDS (Nathan had not yet identified himself as the person) and his father when he was diagnosed with the disease as a young boy (all details of which were unknown to anyone, including Nathan's wife, and were accurately described). Nathan identified himself as the person with GERDS, the missionary laid hands on him and prayed for his healing, and he was instantly and completely healed! From that night until the present (about three full years), Nathan has never had an incident, he has slept through every night since that Bible study, and the doctor cleared Nathan shortly thereafter of the diagnosis. Skeptics who say Christianity is superstition and that miracles don't happen have not looked sincerely for their presence.

I could repeat such stories over and over again, but enough has been said to make an important point. As Jim Rutz notes, "Since about the mid-1980s, a tide of miracles has begun to engulf the entire planet. As time goes on, miracles are multiplying like loaves and fishes."[12] Jenkins notes that Third World churches "are quite at home with biblical notions of the supernatural, with ideas like dreams and prophecy."[13] I would add, "and ideas like healing and demonic deliverance."

It may well be that the explosion of such phenomena is of recent vintage, but even if this is true, it would be wrong to think that miraculous manifestations of the Kingdom's power have not been part of the church's life ever since her inception, especially during the first four centuries. Michael Green makes a crucial observation in this regard. Though he begins by speaking of the early church's emphasis on the power of the Spirit in its mission, he draws a penetrating and urgent mandate for the contemporary Western church:

> In particular, the Spirit was valued for two great reasons. He it was who so worked within the lives of the Christians individually and the Church corporately that they began to be conformed more and more to the character of Jesus. And it was the Spirit who gave his followers remarkable spiritual gifts. Prophecy, tongues (and interpretation), healing and exorcism were the most prominent in apostolic and sub-apostolic days alike. People did not merely hear the gospel; they saw it in action, and were moved to respond. The Western Church has grown too dependent on words, and not nearly dependent enough on the power of the Holy Spirit. The Enlightenment induced much embarrassment about divine activity in today's world, and this tendency has outlived the demise of the Enlightenment. Instead of being a community demonstrating the Lord's power, we have become one which talks incessantly. We need to remember that "the kingdom of God is not talk, but power." Where churches have regained dependence on God's Spirit, where they have believed that God is active among his people today, where they have prayerfully asked him to give them not only qualities of character but spiritual power, then those same gifts which we see in the New Testament have appeared today. By far the fastest growing Christian communion in the world is the Pentecostal. They have some weaknesses, to be sure, but they expect to see God at work among them. They expect to see healing. They experience God speaking through them in prophetic clarity that is hard to decry. And they find that when they come against spiritual forces which hold men and women in bondage, these are cast out by God's Spirit and the result is a new liberation; indeed, what the New Testament calls a new creation. It has long been fashionable for us to dismiss these gifts as unnecessary or unattainable today. We would be unwise to do so. They are part of God's equipping of his church for Evangelism.[14]

However unwise, we Evangelicals are often too quick to dismiss healing, demonic deliverance, miracles, and prophetic words of knowledge and wisdom. Fortunately, there has been a growing consensus among Evangelical New Testament scholars that certain biblical themes provide a mandate for the Spirit's miraculous power that makes such a dismissal unnecessary and unbiblical.

THREE LINES OF NEW TESTAMENT EVIDENCE IN SUPPORT OF MIRACULOUS MINISTRY

The Gospel of the Kingdom of God

While justification by faith is essential to any understanding of the gospel, in the last forty years there has been a recovery of a broader gospel that Jesus and his apostles preached, a gospel within which justification is embedded: "Jesus was going throughout all Galilee, teaching in their synagogues and proclaiming the gospel of the kingdom, and healing every kind of disease and every kind of sickness among the people" (Matt. 4:23). If one compares the Great Commission (28:18–20) with Jesus' words in 24:14 ("This gospel of the kingdom shall be preached in the whole world as a testimony to all the nations, and then the end will come"), it is clear that proclamation and extending the influence of the Kingdom is the church's primary mandate.

Indeed, the book of Acts makes clear that the activity of the early church centered on proclaiming and extending the Kingdom, with justification by faith at the core of their agenda (cf. Acts 8:12; 19:8; 20:25; 28:30–31). Though I believe that there is a unique form of God's Kingdom that will be manifested in the future, the Kingdom is here now, and learning to live according to its nature and from its power and to proclaim and extend that Kingdom is our primary business.

The Kingdom of God is primarily the reign, rule, or authority of God himself; secondarily, it is the realm in which that rule is directly exercised, consisting largely in the laws governing the natural world and, more importantly, the individual and collective hearts of those who have bowed to God's rule.[15] The gospel of the Kingdom is the idea that the direct rule of God is now available to all in and through Jesus Christ, and that one may live from the power of that rule in the realm of the Kingdom.

Among other things, the concept of the Kingdom brings to center stage the supernatural power of God over disease, death, and the kingdom of darkness. As we saw above, Jesus' proclamation of the Kingdom was accompanied by a manifestation of miraculous power as an accurate expression of the nature of that Kingdom and as an extension of its rule and victory over Satan's kingdom. Paul flatly states that "the kingdom of God does not consist in words but in power" (1 Cor. 4:20). An important arena in which this power is manifested is in healing, demonic deliverance, and divine interaction through dreams, visions, words of knowledge/wisdom, and prophetic utterances.

A faculty colleague of mine who teaches in the School of Intercultural Studies at Biola University assigns summer internships to his doctoral students in which they go to various places around the globe and interview pastors and other Christian leaders about the impact of their ministries. I have read some of their reports, and it is clear that the power of the Kingdom of God over disease and the devil and supernatural revelation are at the core of the expansion of the church in the Third World.[16]

Jesus' Ministry and the Holy Spirit

When I was saved in the late 1960s, I was taught that Jesus' miracles proved he was God because he did them from his divine nature. It has become clear to me, however, that this was wrong, for Jesus' public ministry was done as he, a perfect man, did what he saw his Father doing in dependence on the filling of the Holy Spirit. Thomas Oden notes:

> As a man, Jesus walked day by day in radical dependence upon God the Spirit, prayed, and spoke by the power of the Spirit. In portraying Jesus as constantly dependent upon the Spirit, the Gospels were not challenging or questioning his deity or divine Sonship. Rather, as eternal Son the theandric person already was truly God, while as a man, Jesus was truly human, bone of our bone, flesh of our flesh, seed of Abraham, whose humanity was continually replenished by the Spirit (Luke 4:14; Heb. 2:14–17). He did not walk or speak by his own independent human power, but by the power of the Spirit. Every gift requisite to the Son's mission was provided by the Spirit.[17]

The implications of this understanding of Jesus' ministry are remarkable: "Jesus is living proof of how those who are his followers may exceed the limitations of their humanness in order that they, like him, might carry to completion against all odds their God-given mission in life—by the Holy Spirit."[18] It is becoming clear that when Jesus said that "greater works than these he [i.e., the one who believes in Jesus] will do, because I go to the Father" (John 14:12), he meant it in the ordinary way these words would be interpreted.

In imitation of Jesus' ministry, the church is invited to exercise the miraculous power of the Spirit in the service of the Kingdom. In an interview about his book *Jesus the Miracle Worker* with InterVarsity Press editor Dan Reid, New Testament scholar Graham Twelftree acknowledged that at the beginning of his research regarding the credibility and centrality of miracles to Jesus' life and mission, he was skeptical of what he would find. However, to his surprise, Twelftree discovered that not only are the miracle stories credible, but they play a much more central role in displaying the presence of the Kingdom of God in Jesus' ministry than he had previously imagined. Twelftree then calls for a revolution in our understanding of contemporary ministry:

> It seems to me that nothing less than a revolution will need to take place in our understanding of what constitutes a Christianity that proposes to be on a trajectory with or that is faithful to what is disclosed about Jesus in the Gospels. What I mean is that what is now seen as Christianity, at least in Western traditional churches, as primarily words and propositions to which we are expected to give assent and then further propagate will surely have to be replaced by a Christianity that involves and—I would go so far as to say—is dominated by understanding God's numinous power not only to be born uniquely in Jesus but also expected and experienced in his followers in the performing of miracles, certainly a lot more frequently than is presently reported. Put simply, Christian ministry that is faithful to the perspective of Jesus and the Gospels will be a show and tell activity that involves not [merely] the news that God was reconciling us to himself in what Jesus said and did in the Easter event but that reconciliation is God's being powerfully present to forgive, heal, win over the demonic and deliver from danger so that he can have an intimate and whole relationship with his people.[19]

The Abandonment of Cessationism

Cessationism is the idea that the miraculous gifts of the Spirit, such as prophecy, healing, miracles, and tongues (see 1 Cor. 12:8–10; 13:8–10), ceased with the death of the apostles and, thus, are no longer available today. Fewer and fewer Christian scholars hold to cessationism, and it may fairly be called an increasingly marginalized viewpoint. This shift in scholarly opinion has been partly responsible for the renewal of miraculous ministry in the Western church (non-Western Christians are almost never cessationist in orientation).

If you are a cessationist, please do not misunderstand my point. I was trained in a cessationist seminary and have great respect and love for my cessationist friends. Cessationists have tirelessly and faithfully called the church back to the Bible as the final authority for ministry and practice.

The church owes their cessationist brothers and sisters an incredible debt for this, even if not for their cessationist conclusions.

Moreover, the simple fact that cessationism is an increasingly minority position does not prove it is wrong. However, this observation is of limited value. If a viewpoint is an increasingly minority position among learned folk and yet one continues to accept that viewpoint, one needs to be able to explain why it is losing favor in such a way that one can continue to accept the position with intellectual integrity. For example, if one can show that for historical, sociological, or spiritual reasons, people have a vested interest in retaining a majority viewpoint even though it is false and, perhaps, less rational than the marginalized position, then this carries weight.

Precisely this strategy is what critics of evolution use in arguing that, while in the minority, Intelligent Design and various creationist theories are better justified than evolutionary alternatives. But this strategy is a hard sell regarding the waning of cessationism. Indeed, a growing number of noncessationists have come from cessationist camps, and they have a solid understanding of the case for cessationism. Moreover, it is hard to find sociological, historical, or spiritual reasons that adequately explain the growing and widespread acceptance of noncessationism among Evangelical scholars and pastors.

Because of this, I urge my cessationist brothers and sisters to reconsider their viewpoint. At the very least, the direction of Evangelical thought on these matters should cause cessationists to lower the degree of strength they take themselves to have regarding the truth of their position. In other words, even if one continues to assert cessationism, one should be far less confident that it is true than was possible, say, forty years ago. This means that the harshness and rigidity that sometimes characterized cessationist advocates should be tempered, not merely because all of us need to dialog about our differences in a gracious manner, but because it may well be intellectually irresponsible to embody the sort of certainty with respect to cessationism that sometimes fuels such harshness and rigidity.

Even if you remain a solidly convinced cessationist, however, there is still plenty of room in your theology to increase your passion for and expectation of the supernatural, miraculous aspect of new covenant life and ministry. To illustrate, a well-known cessationist professor told me that a few years ago she went through a period of several months in which she grappled with an important decision to no avail. Knowing that she had to decide the matter on Monday, she went into the weekend a bit frustrated with what she perceived as the Lord's lack of concern to provide guidance on this crucial matter. On Sunday, as she was leaving church, a fellow parishioner with whom she was modestly acquainted approached her somewhat sheepishly and said, "I don't know you very well, but you are grappling with making a decision about such and such, aren't you? Well, I almost never dream, but last night I had a vivid dream about you and your decision, and I have to tell you what I saw."

This professor went on to tell me that the woman described in incredible detail the nature of the decision, the options, and the direction she saw in the dream. Keep in mind that no one knew about the professor's decision. The event was simply supernatural, and while she responsibly weighed it with her own sense of God's leading, it played an important role in giving her direction. She finished our conversation with this remark: "I don't believe in gifts of healing, prophecy, and so forth, but I believe that God still heals, speaks in various ways, and performs miracles. The only difference between me and noncessationists is that they expect these things to happen more than I do, and I want to grow in my experience of God's supernatural Kingdom."

In a recently published ground-breaking book, cessationist scholars Daniel Wallace and M. James Sawyer bring together a team of writers to rethink the role of the Holy Spirit within that tradition.[20] Partly seeking to correct the sterility in that tradition, Wallace and Sawyer identify their view as *pneumatic Christianity* and argue that traditional cessationism is reductionistic and reactionary regarding charismatic, Pentecostal, and Third Wave excesses with respect to the Spirit, and that cessationism is too often rooted in a desire to be in control—a desire particularly attractive to that branch of the church largely lead by white, obsessive-compulsive males. The Holy Spirit did not die in the first century even if certain gifts did, they note, and cessationists need to allow for a greater role for the Spirit in guiding believers, in fostering an experiential relationship with God, and in healing and performing miracles. Their book is an encouraging sign that even among cessationists, there is much room for growth in Spirit-empowered Kingdom works.

FOUR SUBGROUPS IN THE CHRISTIAN COMMUNITY

While labels can be misleading and even demeaning, they can be helpful if employed with the right spirit and with allowances for nonrigid application.

Statements like "All Democrats or Republicans think thus and so" are usually wrong, but it is still the case that tendencies can be observed among Democrats and Republicans, and knowing such tendencies can be useful for a number of purposes. In an important book edited by Wayne Grudem, four positions are identified regarding miraculous gifts; in my judgment, Grudem's identification of these viewpoints is both accurate and helpful for facilitating understanding and unity among Jesus' apprentices.[21] Here they are:

- *cessationist*: there are no miraculous gifts today; gifts such as prophecy, healings, and tongues ceased with the death of the apostles because their function of establishing the church was complete.
- *open but cautious*: cessationist arguments fail; miraculous gifts are, indeed, possible today, but the teachings and practices associated with the current use of such gifts are unimpressive, frequently characterized by abuses, and not important for evangelism and discipleship compared to Bible study, obedience, and allegedly more traditional forms of spiritual growth.
- *Third Wave*: all Christians are baptized by the Holy Spirit at conversion, subsequent fillings and anointings of the Spirit are achieved through yielding and faith; while the gift of tongues is for today, tongues is not emphasized nor is it seen as evidence of the Spirit's filling; miraculous gifts, especially those associated with healing, deliverance, and words of knowledge and prophecy, are important for the life of the church.
- *Pentecostal/charismatic*: while these two groups are different in some ways, they may be collectively understood as accepting the current availability of the miraculous gifts; they often hold to a baptism of the Holy Spirit subsequent to salvation and evidenced by speaking in tongues, and if they do not embrace such a second baptism, there is, in any case, greater emphasis on speaking in tongues than advocated by Third Wave believers.

Grudem lays out areas of agreement and disagreement among these four groups.[22]

- *areas of agreement*: commitment to Scripture, fellowship, experiencing a personal relationship with God, and a measure of agreement on some details about miracles and the work of the Spirit, including the idea that God does heal and work miracles today, God guides believers, the Holy Spirit empowers us for life and ministry, and the Spirit speaks to people today by bringing the words of Scripture to mind in a time of need, by giving us insight into the application of Scripture, by influencing our feelings and emotions, and by giving us specific information about real life situations that we did not acquire through ordinary means

- *areas of disagreement:* degree of expectation for seeing the Spirit work in miraculous ways, degree to which we should encourage people to seek miraculous works today, the extent to which we see church life in the New Testament as a pattern to seek to imitate today, and the degree to which "space" is provided during services for the miraculous work of the Spirit as understood in the context of our discussion to take place[23]

I believe we can achieve greater unity among these four groups than ever before, and I also believe the time is ripe for all of us, regardless of our position on the spectrum, to seek with greater intensity to believe God for more of his supernatural, miraculous power in and through our lives and ministries. When you look carefully at the areas of disagreement among us, it becomes obvious that much of it, though admittedly not all, turns on the degree to which healing, deliverance, and divine speaking outside scriptural exegesis is expected and practiced. I am going to provide a challenge to all of us to increase our intensity in these areas shortly, but three preliminaries should be put on the table before I do this.

First, I suggest that you look at these four views as overlapping segments on a continuum and that you try to locate where you and your church are on that continuum.

Second, we can all seek to live more explicitly supernatural lives without denying where we are on this continuum and while remaining respectful of those at different places. By using "explicitly supernatural lives" in connection with healing, deliverance, and learning to hear God speaking today, I do not mean to communicate that conversion and sanctification are not supernatural. I limit my focus because we all agree on that point.

I am a bit uncomfortable making the third point because it can appear to be negative and critical. I do not intend it that way. The facts are that we are in a dramatic conflict with the world, the flesh, and the devil that is raging out of control today, and God's Kingdom is exploding in unprecedented ways around the world. This is not about you or me, and we all need to hear admonishment from each other because the stakes are high. That said, as my third point I want to get some ideas on the table for those at each end of the spectrum.

Let me begin with a word to my cessationist friends. As already stated, I was raised a cessationist and attended a cessationist seminary. I planted two "open but cautious" churches, pastored in two others, attended them for thirty years, and have spoken in around three hundred churches from these two groups in thirty-five years. Your emphasis on Scripture and theology is critically needed today, and I urge you to continue to champion these themes and the life of the mind as essential to discipleship. But frequently, you are too cautious and too concerned about "being in control" to allow things to get messy and to take risks where you may look foolish if God's manifest presence does not show up. Too often, there is a rigid, controlling, fearful spirit among you. Too often, you are defensive and stuck in tradition for its own sake. There is too little power in your churches, too little extravagant worship in which your people pour out their hearts to God on Sunday. Too much of your church's accomplishments can be explained without there needing to be a God to explain them. Things are too predictable and too, well, American.

I know whereof I speak. I have been in these churches for thirty-five years, I love this branch of the church dearly, and for this reason I want your churches to lose their sterility. I believe you are going to have to be more passionate and intentional in seeking facility with supernatural ministry. I urge you to read with an open mind and a hungry heart Sam Storms' *Convergence: Spiritual Journeys of a Charismatic Calvinist*.[24] Storms does a masterful job of combining a theologically sophisticated, biblically grounded approach to life with a warm-hearted, supernatural, experientially rich relationship to God's Spirit and Kingdom power.

Now a word to those on the more Pentecostal/charismatic end of the spectrum. I attend a Third Wave church, and I have spoken in several churches at this end of the spectrum. In my view, you have led the way in Spirit-filled worship, you have brought healing, deliverance, and the prophetic back to the Evangelical community, and your message is dominating the missionary spread of the gospel worldwide. But you need to be careful about two things. First, you are too anti-intellectual. If I hear another Third Wave or Pentecostal/charismatic speaker say "God offends the mind to reveal the heart," I think I'll scream. In context, the remark is true enough, but why don't we also hear you say that God offends the heart to reveal the mind. I fear that this statement is often an excuse for intellectual laziness.

As "signs and wonders" continue to increase worldwide, there will be satanic counterfeits, and it may well be that the caution and biblical fidelity emphasized by those at the Word end of the spectrum will become more important than ever. I urge you to read Rick Nañez's *Full Gospel, Fractured Minds?*[25] — a book that specifically addresses Pentecostals/charismatics and calls you to recapture the life of the mind in a way distinctive to your community.

Second, I see too many of your people addicted to seeking experiences of the prophetic, the Spirit's power, and so forth as a substitute for the day-in and day-out processes of faithful discipleship and spiritual formation. I don't know what it means to know and love someone, including God, if that does not include experiences of the other person and an interactive relationship with them. I don't know what the fruit of the Spirit means if it does not include experiences of love, joy, peace, and so forth. Experiences are crucial to the Christian life. But one can become so focused on and addicted to them that one's strategy for sanctification centers on constant refillings of power, anointings of the Spirit, reception of words of knowledge/wisdom that one becomes bored with less "dramatic," faithful processes of spiritual growth. It should be a "both/and," but too often in your circles, Christian counseling, the life of the mind, study, memorizing Scripture, and other such things are not given their due. You are not careful enough in expecting providers of words of knowledge and their kin to provide credentials for why people should believe them. Absent such care, these words can harm people or become so commonplace that no one listens to them anymore.[26]

I want these remarks to help spark constructive growth and vitality in you and your church. I don't want them to sound self-righteous and fall on deaf ears accordingly. I need admonishment and help as much as the next person, as my wife never tires of reminding me!

Here's an idea: Why not gather with others in your church that share your location on the spectrum and ask together what you can learn from those who admonish you from other positions on the spectrum. In what follows, my focus will be on facilitating supernatural ministry, so I will center my advice on growing in the use of the supernatural, not on abuses sometimes associated with healing, deliverance, and the prophetic. I am painfully aware of those abuses, but I think the need is sufficiently great for North American Christians to join their brothers and sisters worldwide in engaging in the supernatural works of God's Spirit and Kingdom, that such an emphasis is warranted.

BECOMING NATURALLY SUPERNATURAL

While I still have much to learn about the Kingdom's supernatural power, I have changed dramatically in recent years regarding what I have seen, heard, and done. I began as a cessationist, lived for years as an open but cautious Evangelical, and would now be considered a Third Wave Evangelical. Next to the early years after my conversion in 1968, this period of growth has been the most moving, wonderful, impact-full time in my thirty-seven years of being a Christian. If you hunger as I do to become more "naturally supernatural," as a friend calls it, then I want to share some things that have greatly helped me in my own development.

Fundamentally, you need to develop a plan to learn more about this area, to believe more strongly in it, and to learn to step out, take risks, and see God's Spirit work in and around your life. You must be intentional about this. Growth doesn't happen by osmosis. Dallas Willard says that we should come to a point that we expect to see the miraculous outbreak of the Kingdom take place as an "ordinary" part of our "extraordinary" Christian lives.

Should we seek signs and wonders? Yes and no. Our main concern is to bring fame and respect to our God by learning to live in and on behalf of his Kingdom and to become like Jesus. It is not signs and wonders. However, Scripture itself says we should desire earnestly to prophesy (1 Cor. 14:39), and if we need to hear from God or if someone is sick, we should seek to meet the need of the moment as best we can. And if that need seems to involve a miracle, then we should wisely and unpresumptuously seek to bring God's supernatural power to bear on the need. Moreover, when one is trying to get good at something, one needs to be intentional about growth in excellence and effectiveness, and this clearly involves seeking certain things as a means to progress.

Before I offer some specifics, three things must be kept in mind. First, never try to make something happen. If you have to crank something up or act like God is doing something when it is fairly clear he isn't, then you are feeling a pressure to make things happen that is inauthentic and contrary to the nature of God's Kingdom.

Second, be gentle, humble, and patient with yourself and others as you grow in the miraculous. Few topics are more divisive than this one, and as one grows in power the temptation of pride and arrogance surfaces. It is an ugly distortion of the Kingdom for one to look down on others because they are not as far along in the Christian life, and nowhere is this more prominent than in growth in signs and wonders. At the end of the day, this is not about us. It's about becoming more effective colaborers with God in the Great Commission enterprise.

Third, you cannot create faith by simply trying directly to believe something more strongly than you do. If someone offered you money if you would believe a pink elephant was standing in front of you, you couldn't really believe this even though you might say you did. Beliefs are not subject to the direct control of the will, so one cannot simply will to believe something and have it happen on the spot. This is why merely exhorting people to believe things is ineffective. Thankfully, we can change our beliefs or their degree of strength indirectly. By study, meditation, risk, learning from successes and failures, and in related ways, one can grow in faith. The specifics that follow are largely intended to help your faith increase in this area of the Christian life.

Read in This Area of Ministry

Develop a reading plan in this area with two things in mind. First, gain knowledge about hearing from God, praying for the sick, and engaging in demonic deliverance. Second, read to grow in faith from the testimonies of others as they bear witness to the things they have seen and heard. Be thoughtful and hungry as you read.

Regarding demonization, there is much confusion about this topic among Christians. First, the New Testament does not talk in terms of "demon possession" or distinguish it from demonic oppression. Scripture simply talks about being demonized or having a demon. And while demons cannot own or completely control believers, they can inhabit and exert considerable influence on them. Second, demons are best thought of as rats—they feed on garbage. Thus, if one fails to deal with anger, bitterness, fear, and the like, one gives the devil greater opportunity to influence one's life. Among other things, this means that dealing with a demon is usually not the only thing needed for relief; there is also a need to deal with the garbage through therapy, discipleship, and so forth.

Some time ago, I was speaking to a group of students at Talbot School of Theology on a Tuesday night and, as the meeting ended, I had a sense of darkness and oppression in the room. As I closed the meeting, I prayed for deliverance for anyone in the room being demonized. The next morning during my office hours, a student I'll call Frank came to see me. Unknown to me, he had been undergoing immense internal struggles for about six weeks, to the point that the Sunday before the meeting, he almost checked himself into a psychiatric hospital. He had not slept well in weeks. However, when I prayed for deliverance, he felt a dark presence leave him, and heat began to pour into his body, starting at his head and moving slowly to his feet. He felt completely healed and had slept well for the first time in weeks. That was two years ago and the problem never came back. He was irreversibly delivered that night.

Less than thirty minutes after he left, there was a knock on my office door, and a student I'll call Fred came in. With no knowledge of Franks' story, he told me that for weeks he had been suffering emotional and internal torment, but while I was praying, he felt an evil presence leave his body and heat poured into him from his head down to his feet. He testified that in all his Christian life, he had never more strongly sensed God's intimate love for him. The torment has never returned to this student either.

Two books have helped me greatly in this area of ministry. In my view, the place to start is with Charles Kraft's book *Defeating Dark Angels*.[27] This is the single best source I have read on this topic. Second, I would read Clinton Arnold's *Three Crucial Questions about Spiritual Warfare*.[28]

Regarding healing and praying for the sick, I suggest three key books. I would begin with Jack Deere's *Surprised by the Power of the Spirit* because it gives a powerful overview of supernatural Kingdom ministry and locates healing against that backdrop.[29] Two sources that provide the best practical advice on learning to pray effectively for the sick are John Wimber's *Power Healing* and Francis MacNutt's *Healing*.[30]

Last week, my wife and I attended a small group fellowship that is part of our church. We talked at length with a dear twenty-year-old named Mindy. She works in a Christian clothing store called "C28" at Main Place Mall in Santa Ana, California. Part of her job description is to offer prayer to shoppers. A few months ago, a woman entered the store, and Mindy sensed a burning need to pray for her; but when she offered to do so, the woman said that she wasn't interested. About ten minutes later, while Mindy was at the cash register totaling up the woman's bill, the Lord spoke to Mindy and told her that the woman was seriously ill and she was to pray for her. So Mindy asked the woman if she had a serious illness, and the woman began to weep and told her that she had a serious form of cancer; while she had recently started chemotherapy, the doctor's told her that there was only a slight chance the therapy would work.

In response to the woman's change of heart, Mindy laid hands on her and prayed for healing. Two weeks later, the woman returned to the store looking for Mindy. She had brought her entire family with her. The week after receiving prayer, the woman's doctor performed a scheduled test on her, and to his amazement he found that the cancer was completely gone! The woman had been healed, and she had brought her entire family to the store for Mindy to pray for them.

When you pray for the sick, your goal is to love and bless that person and leave the results to God. Still, I want to see an atmosphere of appropriate expectation created in our churches so that folks like Mindy have the courage to step out and pray for the sick with growing confidence and skill.

Regarding learning to hear God's voice, I suggest two books: Dallas Willard's *Hearing God* and Jack Deere's *Surprised by the Voice of God*.[31] I could tell many stories of my own experience of guidance, words of knowledge, and the prophetic, but I will leave that for another time. Mindy's story nicely illustrates the role of guidance in supernatural ministry.

At this point I should say a word about assessing the credibility of miracle stories. In the fall of 2004 I debated Eddie Tabash on Lee Strobel's *Faith under Fire*, aired on PAX television. The topic was "Is the Supernatural Real?" and during the dialog, Tabash, an influential humanist and a prominent California attorney, asserted that there was no scientific evidence for miracles and that unless such were forthcoming, no one should believe in such things.

Limiting our focus to assessing the credibility of contemporary miracles, I have two things to say. First, it is simply not true that there is no medical evidence for miracles, so Tabash's claim is mistaken.[32] But second and more importantly, this standard of evidence is too high to guide the belief selection of a rational person because it would justify rejecting beliefs that have enough rational support to make them intellectually obligatory to believe. Tabash's remark was curious in light of the fact that he is a lawyer. The practice of law would be distorted beyond all recognition if courts followed Tabash's advice. While scientific information is one source of evidence, court decisions are rightly reached all the time without it. Specifically, juries regularly make the right decision on the basis of eye-witness testimony without the presence of scientific evidence, and while they might be wrong (and "scientific evidence" can go wrong, too), such testimony is an appropriate rational basis for belief.

In my experience, when people are healed, folks related to the event usually don't take the time to gather scientific evidence for the healing even though it is available. By way of application, if there is credible eye-witness testimony for an event, including a miracle, then, all things being equal, one ought to believe the event even if there is no "medical proof." And there is widespread credible evidence for miracles today, which is what you would expect if they were taking place in the lives of busy people who were not interested in medical documentation.[33] If you adopt Tabash's standard of evidence, you will miss the opportunity to believe a number of rationally justified truths that can transform your life.

Three Other Ideas

Besides reading, there are at least three other ways to grow in this area. First, find credible people in your area who have moved in these things and invite them to your church or small group to teach and share about these matters. All churches are not created equal in this area, and we should learn from those more at home in the miraculous than our own Christian circle. You may not agree with all that is said, but you can still learn from others in your area. Ask lots of questions and be honest with your doubts or needs.

Second, start providing opportunities for people in your small group or church to share their own experiences of answers to prayer or other miracles. You would probably be shocked at how many people in your church have seen but are either reluctant to share or are not given natural occasions to do so. Such sharing can be an incredible faith builder.

Finally, make growth in the miraculous one component of the mission-ary aspect of your church. When you or someone else goes on a mission trip, part of their assignment should be to gather credible reports of what God is doing miraculously in other parts of the world. If a missionary returns on furlough, ask him or her questions about miracles in his region of the world. We should take advantage of what God is doing around the world in strengthening our faith in God's miraculous power and in gain-ing knowledge of how our brothers and sisters in other places are engaging in Kingdom works of this sort.

I close this chapter with a final word of perspective about supernatural ministry. In the last three chapters I have been at pains to develop three aspects of what I call the Kingdom Triangle — three legs that, given the current status of American Evangelicalism, we must put in place to provide a balanced, healthy way forward: recovery of knowledge and the Christian mind, renovation of the heart and spiritual formation, and restoration of miraculous power. All three are crucial if we are to meet the needs surfaced by the crisis of our age.

However, there is one aspect of the restoration of miraculous power that I want to plant in the center of your attention. The Vineyard is a rapidly growing movement of Third Wave churches established in the early 1980s by John Wimber. A few years ago Dallas Willard gave an admonition to the Vineyard movement that I believe applies to the entire Evangelical church:

> You must ensure that Vineyard churches maintain the visible signs of the Holy Spirit and the kingdom of God, or else Vineyard churches will never maintain the faith for discipleship or evangelism or anything else.... I go to churches all the time where the people's hunger for piety is enormously high, but they live in constant frustration because they don't have the accompanying faith that God really could change who they are — because they never see signs of God doing things. If you want your pastors to have the faith for evangelism, if you want them to have the faith for changed lives, you have to maintain the visible signs of the Holy Spirit.[34]

Questions for Personal Reflection or Group Discussion

1. Michael Green observes the early church's emphasis on the power of the Spirit in its mission (page 172). What stands out to you in his comments? Are you generally quick to dismiss the possibility of healing, demonic deliverance, miracles, and prophetic words of knowledge and wisdom? If so, why? What motivates this dismissal? How can you grow in overcoming a fear of risk or failure in learning to practice being more naturally supernatural?

2. Three important lines of New Testament evidence support miraculous ministry: the gospel and the Kingdom of God, Jesus' ministry as dependent on the person and work of the Holy Spirit, and the abandonment of cessationism (pages 173–177). Were you familiar with these reasons prior to reading them in this book? If not, how have your own beliefs grown?

3. How does the author define the "Kingdom of God" (page 173)? In what sense does the New Testament concept of the Kingdom bring to center stage the supernatural power of God over disease, death, and the kingdom of darkness? Did Jesus' miracles prove that he was God because he did them from his nature? Or did Jesus exercise the full capacity of his public ministry because he, the perfect man, did what he saw his Father doing in dependence on the filling of the Holy Spirit?

4. Would you characterize yourself as a cessationist? If so, why? Do you tend to view God as transcendent rather than immanent in his activity? If someone claims to "experience God," does this make you suspicious? What do you think are the merits or demerits of Daniel Wallace and M. James Sawyer's "pneumatic Christianity"? Do you agree with their judgment that traditional cessationism is "reductionistic and reactionary" and is "too often rooted in a desire to be in control"?

5. Regarding the four groups in the Christian community (cessationist, open but cautious, Third Wave, and Pentecostal/charismatic, did you know that there were these positions related to whether "miraculous gifts

are for today"? Which of the four do you presently agree with? Is this the same position of your local church? How has your experience with God and/or the church affected why you believe what you believe now?

6. The author makes some important comments both to cessationists and to Pentecostals/charismatics (pages 180–182).

   a. What stands out to you in the comments to cessationists? Do they ring true? How do they help you assess the strengths and weaknesses of cessationism? How would Jesus or the apostles react to this position?

   b. The Pentecostal/charismatic end of the spectrum have a tendency to be anti-intellectual and addicted to seeking experiences of the prophetic and power encounters as a substitute for the day-in and day-out processes of faith discipleship and spiritual formation. Do these comments ring true? How do they help you assess the strengths and weaknesses of Pentecostals/charismatics? How would Jesus or the apostles react to this position?

7. The author encourages us to get good at becoming "naturally supernatural" by being intentional about our growth (pages 182–183). What three things must you keep in mind? How can you have a sense of ease as you grow in awareness and activity of the miraculous?

   a. If you are in a Third Wave or a Pentecostal/charismatic church, do you feel as if you need to somehow supernaturally perform for God or for others in order to be validated? Why is that unhealthy to your growth?

   b. If you are in a cessationist or an open but cautious church, do you feel as if you cannot be yourself when seeking God's presence and power in your life? How might you grow (and encourage others around you) to just be yourself, naturally supernatural?

8. How does the author clarify the discussion of demonization among Christians? Recall the stories of the Talbot students delivered from a demonic presence. How do you respond to such stories? Do you think something supernatural happened when the author prayed for deliverance?

9. When praying for the sick, the author encourages that our goal is to love and bless people and leave the results to God (pages 184–185). Does this perspective make you feel less pressure or awkwardness to pray for the sick? What is the single, greatest obstacle you experience when attempting to simply open up yourself to give healing prayers for the sick?

10. How does the author respond to the claim that "there is no scientific evidence for miracles, and unless such were forthcoming, no one should believe in such things" (pages 185–186)? What can you learn by the manner in which the author responds to this claim?

When you hear of miraculous happenings, do you get a sense of the missional heart of God around the world and at home? How does this impact what you pray for and the manner in which you pray? How is being missionally minded intimately related to our expectations for God to show up, to demonstrate his power and presence in our midst, and to make his name famous?

CONCLUSION

CONFRONTING THE CRISIS OF OUR AGE

We began our journey with the story of Helen Roseveare, the medical missionary in Zaire, Africa, and the miracle of the hot water bottle. I begin our final moments together with another story. Consider this stunning answer to prayer that comes, in his own words, from a well-known and highly respected Christian doctor whom I know well:

> Our daughter, Ashley, who was probably about ten years old at the time, had two parakeets. One of them had just died. She told her mother that she wanted to get another one so that she would have a couple again. Mother, however, had had enough pets for the time being and told Ashley that we weren't going to get another parakeet at this time. Ashley, however, had a mind of her own. She said that she was going to pray to God for another parakeet, which she did. The next day, Ashley was playing outside with her friends when one of the kids saw that there was a bird in the tree. They all knew that Ashley had just lost her pet. It was a parakeet, the same color as the one she had just lost! (To this point, no one could remember ever having found a parakeet in the neighborhood before — and this occurred just the next day.) You can imagine her sense of triumph as she brought the bird home and announced that God had answered her prayer.

The doctor went on to share the sense of shock he and his wife experienced as Ashley brought a duplicate of her lost parakeet into the house the next day on her finger! Stop and think about this for a moment. How in the world would a naturalist or postmodern relativist explain this? I have no idea what it would mean to say that this incident was the doctor's truth but not something true for everyone. The event actually happened, period. Moreover, it stretches all credulity to say it was just a lucky coincidence. When was the last time you saw a parakeet flying around in your backyard, one that looked exactly like your deceased pet, one that came the very next day after your pet died, one that came the very next day after a family member specifically asked God for a new parakeet, and one that allowed a little girl to capture and bring it into the house!

The worldview that allows for and explains — no, *expects* — things like this is the only worldview thick enough to make sense out of the human search for drama and meaning to life. And that worldview is the one Jesus believed, preached, demonstrated, and brought. It is the vision of human life caught up in that divine conspiracy constituted by the progressive spread of the Kingdom of God and the gathering of a community under and around the Triune Being who stands in the middle of that Kingdom.

Make no mistake about it, this drama and this Kingdom's agenda is at the center of the meaning of cosmic history and your own individual story. Like a grand conductor who calls in the flutes at just the right time, your Father has brought you into the Cosmic Symphony at your unique place in time and space so you can be a vibrant outpost of the Kingdom in your sphere of influence. In short, you are here to be an apprentice of the Lord Jesus to learn how to live your life well as part of God's broader purposes. This is your calling, this is your destiny, this is your only chance to have a life of genuine, full human flourishing.

Take heart. The Kingdom is exploding today in a way that has not happened in the two thousand years since King Jesus inaugurated its most mature form to date. Don't let the secularization of prime time news coverage of world events fool you. Aslan is afoot! To take one "small" example of this, listen to Jim Rutz describe Kingdom advances among Muslims:

> The whole [Islamic] religion is heading towards collapse.... Since 1997, by our count, 522,000 Bangladeshi Muslims have turned to Isa, the No. 2 Islamic prophet we know as Jesus. This is often a difficult step to take in a highly repressive Muslim culture. Currently, about 10,000 a month in Bangladesh are becoming Christians. That doesn't sound like a lot in a nation of 144 million, but it's a rising number, multiplying geometrically. Also: Just in the last year, 50,000 Pakistani Muslims have recognized Isa as Lord and become His followers.... If you lack a reference point for these numbers, consider that until now, three or four Muslim converts a year was par for the course for most missionaries.[1]

The drama of the struggle of the Kingdom of God and the kingdom of Satan, the deeply meaningful call to get good at life as an apprentice of Jesus in his Kingdom, and the vision of locating one's individual gifts, circumstances of life, and resources toward advancing that Kingdom throughout every sphere of culture is exactly what people are hungering for even if they don't know it. I have shown how the combined world-views of naturalism and postmodernism fail to provide the resources for embracing a thick worldview that is true and can be a source of knowledge apt for a life of human flourishing.

However, irrespective of whether or not these worldviews can make sense of the deep-seated hunger for meaning in life and objective human flourishing, this is, in fact, our Father's world. People were made for happiness understood in the classic sense of living a flourishing life of wisdom and virtue the way we were made to live. This is why the most popular class at Harvard is one that focuses on the pursuit of happiness.[2]

But secular approaches to life simply cannot provide what is needed to make sense of this hunger, much less offer a satisfying solution to it. In fact, a secular approach to life may not even be able to make sense out of the notion of happiness itself. This is the conclusion of philosopher Nicholas White in his book *A Brief History of Happiness*, a book that is arguably the most authoritative treatment of the secular notion of happiness to date.[3] White writes:

> The various aims—and enjoyments, desires, judgments about what's worthwhile, etc.—all of which the notion of happiness is taken to include, seem often to conflict with each other.... Accordingly there might be no non-arbitrary way of constructing a coherent concept of them. The concept of happiness may simply be the expression of a firm but unrealizable hope for some kind of coherence of aims.[4]

White concludes:

> For the most part, we build up a conception of what happiness would be out of the aims we have [presumably, not Hitler's aims]. But we never have or try for a *completely and consistently articulated* concept of happiness, or even suppose that there might be such a thing.... If that's right, then in an important sense the history of the concept of happiness has been a search for something that's unobtainable.[5]

White makes no serious attempt to include in his study a Christian conception of happiness and, inexcusably, there is no reference to, much less interaction with, Jesus' teaching on the matter. As a result, White is correct about what secularism can offer regarding happiness—there is no coherent conception of it because there is no reason to think a harmony of the various components of happiness can be woven together.

As we saw in chapter 3, without (especially Christian) monotheism, our uni-versities have degenerated into plural-versities. And whether or not he knows it, White is saying the same thing about our individual lives: Happiness requires a unified life that consistently moves towards its unifying *telos* (end or purpose) in God, and neither naturalism nor postmodernism can provide any sense out of such a unified life. And with a unified life gone, a coherent notion of happiness goes with it. This is why liberal secularists devote themselves to socialist, collectivist political activism, hoping that such will provide the unifying *telos* needed for their own happiness. But such an attempt is like raising funds to support the orchestra as the Titanic sinks. In such a context, sooner or later it will be every person for himself or herself, and the orchestra will be set aside as each one fights to get on a lifeboat. Social anarchy is the inevitable outcome of a secular collectivism that tries to fill the void left by the death of God.

The more obvious route to take when hope is lost for a coherent and reachable notion of objective happiness is individual pleasure. But this won't work either. In a widely published editorial, University of Colorado professor Paul Campos reports on the findings of several studies about happiness and American life.[6]

> Americans today are on average twice as rich, and far healthier, more youthful and safer than our predecessors were a half century ago.... In other words, what is conventionally thought of as the American dream—that you will be better off than your parents, and that your children will in turn be better off than yourself—seems to keep coming true. There's just one little problem with this rosy scenario ... all this "progress" doesn't seem to have made Americans any happier.

Campos concludes that American life is organized around a completely false principle—that ever-increasing levels of wealth, health, and liberty will produce ever-increasing levels of happiness. What people really need instead, he notes, is to acquire meaning in life. Indeed. But how could there be such a thing, where does it come from, and why think we can find it? Campos never tells us. Such is the tragedy of our secular cul-de-sac.

Similarly, columnist George F. Will recently wrote of social science research that shows that political conservatives are typically happier than liberals.[7] Why? Will's answer is that conservatives are more pessimistic about human life than are liberals, they are usually right about the course of human events, and thus they are happy to be wrong. Moreover, conservatives reject statism (a commitment to the state as the supreme absolute) and a victim mentality, preferring to take responsibility for their own happiness. Among other things, Will concludes, this allows them to enjoy the fruits of their labor without guilt.

George Will is one of my favorite commentators, but I have to part company with what I believe is his uncharacteristically shallow analysis of the situation. What escapes his notice is that survey after survey proves that political conservatives tend strongly to be more religious and tend to get their meaning in life from a transcendent God and his commands, far more than do political liberals, who tend more toward secularism.

Dear fellow sojourner in the Way of Jesus, these are unprecedented times for the church to fill the huge void in our culture that has resulted from decades of secularization. We actually have "the way, and the truth, and the life" (John 14:6). There is, however, a problem. Pollster George Barna warns that there is a growing sense of boredom with playing church, with the encrusted practices of the traditional church whose only rationale is that they are the way we have always done church. Eight out of ten believers do not sense they have entered into the presence of God during a typical worship service. Half of all believers do not believe they have entered into God's presence or connected with him in an intimate way during the past year. Only 9 percent of Christian adults have a biblical worldview. Fewer than one out of every six hundred churched believers has a relationship with another believer through which spiritual accountability is provided.[8]

I am neither a social scientist nor the son of one, so I cannot vouch for Barna's research. But it does fit my own experience of contemporary church practice, and Barna is, after all, a highly respected researcher. But Barna's basic point is not bad news. It's really hopeful: There is a growing hunger among believers (and nonbelievers) to have intimate worship, to have an authentic relationship with the Triune God, to be a real disciple, and to experience community the way the New Testament describes it.

I believe Barna is right and, in fact, I have offered a worldview analysis of why this hunger is growing as a result of the emergence of naturalism and postmodernism in place of a Christian worldview. These alternatives are not sufficient, and more and more people hunger for what Christianity offers whether they know it at the moment or not. The time is right for us to shine. And while Barna offers good advice for where to go from here, I believe that the Kingdom Triangle must be at the very heart of the new revolutionary movement gaining momentum day by day. This Triangle must become part of your day-to-day life, and the structures of the local church must find new ways to integrate them into its strategy to produce revolutionary individuals and communities that have not bowed the knee to the secular Baals all around us.

In this book I have been at pains to show that this Triangle—namely,

- the development of the life of the mind, learning what and why one believes, acquiring a thoughtful Christian worldview
- the cultivation of an inner life, developing emotional intimacy with God, engaging in classic spiritual formation practices, absorbing the great formative literature in the history of the church
- learning to live in and use the Spirit's power and the authority of the Kingdom of God, developing a supernatural lifestyle, receiving answers to prayer, learning to effectively pray for healing and demonic deliverance, growing in hearing God's voice through impressions, prophetic words of knowledge and wisdom, dreams and visions—

is central to Jesus' ministry in the Gospels, in Acts, and in the first four centuries of the church. I refuse to believe it has to be an either/or. Why can't one be intellectually careful, emotionally together, and comfortable with a life of intimacy with God and a vibrant inner life, and one who is learning to be naturally supernatural? This threefold cord is the way forward, and I pray for a revolution in which an increasing number of individuals and Christian communities and churches corporately will be aggressive in developing all three aspects of holistic discipleship.

Over the last several years, whatever reputation I have acquired has been associated with scholarship and the life of the Christian mind. So my emphasis on the first leg of the Triangle will come as no surprise. The second leg (the inner life and spiritual formation) should not be much of a stretch either. Admittedly, it is too often the case that visible Christian scholars live in their heads too much and give little evidence of being concerned to develop emotionally or to get their interior castle in order. Still, I suspect that you, my reader, will not take the first two legs of the Triangle as hard pills to swallow. It is the third leg that may come as a shock to many of my readers. So let me close with a final word about the supernatural power of the Kingdom and contemporary miraculous manifestations of the Spirit's power.

Unfortunately, many believers are suspicious, even downright skeptical of such things. In fact, many would refrain from labeling something as a supernatural manifestation of God, an angel, or a demon even if they saw it with their own eyes. As a result, their faith may easily degenerate into a mild form of mental assent coupled with repeated attempts to be more committed. But raw, brute exercises of will to be more committed seldom do much for folks, unless they are combined with a growing confidence and trust in God and his Word. By themselves, such acts seldom last long, and when they taper off, guilt and shame arise and people go into hiding to protect themselves from being "exposed" for what they really (do not) believe. What's worse, when a believer sees a miracle, he or she is afraid of sharing it because they don't want to appear weird or gullible.

Let me ask you a question. Did the authentic stories of God's supernatural activity shared in this book encourage your faith in and love for God? I am certain they did. Whenever I hear of an answer to prayer, a miraculous healing, or some other supernatural act of God, it increases my faith and draws me into deeper intimacy with a loving Father who acts on behalf of his children. It is a wonderful thing to testify to and hear of God's actions on behalf of his people and for the honor of his name. We need to get over our fear of appearing gullible or weird. After all, we are *supernaturalists*; we believe in a *living* God who is always on the go. We need to provide opportunities for credible testimonials to be given to each other on a regular basis, because they strengthen people's confidence in God and his Word.

Still, many remain skeptical and hesitant. There are many reasons for this skepticism, but here are two main ones.[9]

1. *We have a stereotype that people involved in these things are weird, uneducated, and in extreme cases, frauds.* I empathize with this concern, but if you are not careful, adherence to it can throw the proverbial baby out with the bathwater. The result will be a missed opportunity to strengthen your faith. I offer these two points for you to ponder.

First, God sometimes asks his children to do some pretty weird things: Joshua and his band to walk around Jericho, Isaiah to go naked for three years, Hosea to marry a practicing prostitute. We must be careful in labeling something weird. This caution is especially important for type A people who like to control things. Of course, weirdness for weirdness' sake is wrong. And while we must always approach things with wisdom and discernment, this admission must not become an excuse to become a naysayer. We should adopt a spirit of wise, gracious, seeking hunger for God and his glory.

Second, I admit that there is truth to the stereotype and, indeed, many of the things done in the name of the Spirit are just plain wrong, stupid, and distracting. In some cases, they are fraudulent. But one does not determine the proper use of the real thing (e.g., how to use real money) by focusing on the abuse of a counterfeit. Proper caution is not the same thing as unbelief or a stiff-necked legalistic form of control that is afraid of risking.

2. *We have a fear of risking and looking foolish if we pray for the sick and nothing happens.* A major purpose for hearing and giving testimony to God's acts on our behalf is that such testimony builds faith so that people have more confidence to step out and trust God in new ways. This always involves some sort of risk. But ask yourself this question: Would you rather play it safe and never see much happen in the spiritual realm, or would you rather step out, take some faith risks, "fail" from time to time, see God "not show up" as you had hoped, but still see genuine faith, inducing answers to prayer and other miracles?

I have opted for the latter alternative. I would rather pray for two hundred sick people and see five healed than pray for ten and see nothing happen. In fact, this is exactly what I have done. For two years I have devoted more time to praying for the sick than ever before in my Christian life. Months ago, I was speaking at a conference in which a young lady who had a damaged knee received healing prayer. She had been on crutches for about a month and walked with a serious limp, and she had not exercised for two full months. After receiving prayer, she was completely healed. She shed her crutches, began walking normally to this very day, and returned the next morning to her daily routine of jogging, all with no pain at all. I could share numerous similar stories with you, but I have shared some of them earlier in this book and this is probably adequate to make the point.

Two weeks ago I met with George Otis Jr. George is a missiological, anthropological researcher who has traveled to over fifty countries in the last several years to document the miraculous movement of God's Kingdom and the strategies of the kingdom of darkness.[10] I asked what the main thing was that all of this research into signs and wonders had done for him. He answered without a moment's hesitation. "My faith," he said, "in the reality of God and his presence in my life have soared." That was already obvious to me. When you are around someone, you get a sense of who they are. George's sense of peace, his obvious tender love and excitement for the Lord Jesus, and his confidence in God were evident.

I agree with Otis. Learning to be naturally supernatural as I mean that in the present context is not primarily a matter of one's view of spiritual gifts. As I have already said, it is a matter of learning about the presence and power of the Kingdom of God, and recovering the implications of viewing Jesus' activities as flowing from his life of dependence on the Spirit, doing what he saw the Father doing, and providing a human model of what we should be doing.

If you want to lead a rich, vibrant life during the remainder of your years, you must develop and live according to a rational life plan—an approach to life that takes into account your values, priorities, use of resources, gifting, and calling and which is rationally justifiable to take as true. I have argued that the only sensible rational life plan is to enlist as an apprentice of the Lord Jesus. There is simply no other game in town that comes close to rivaling this approach.

As you enter more and more deeply into progress in the way of Jesus, the Kingdom Triangle must be at the core of your life and (your church's) strategy. The first leg provides a thoughtful sense of truth, knowledge, and direction to this approach to life; the second leg gives passion to the journey and allows one to lay aside baggage that gets in the way; the third leg provides the faith and confidence to risk more and more for God and expect him to actually be a coworker in the only sensible life plan available.

This is what our culture needs. This is what you have to give. This is the thick drama for which you long. Don't waste your life being preoccupied with things that don't really matter. Join me in the revolution. This is your opportunity. Seize it and rejoice in it.

POSTSCRIPT

MAKING NEW FRIENDS

In the pages that follow, I have provided you with a solid and, I hope, helpful bibliography. But I want to do more than that. My passion in writing this book is to foment a revolution in how we do church and how we conceive of our presence in the world as Jesus' apprentices and representatives. If my reflections have been of value to you, then I am deeply encouraged. If you have grasped the nature and importance of this revolution, then you also recognize that you cannot rest content with having read a helpful book. You need to become an activist to spread this revolution as effectively and earnestly as you can.

Part of your activism must be the dedication of your time to read more about these matters so you can live more effectively according to the revolution's values and be more informed in spreading these ideas to others. I hope you will encourage others to read this book and engage in the discussion, debate, and application of these ideas. I also want to give you my take on where I would go from here if you want to read further. A good book is like a good friend—you should treasure it and spend regular time together. With that in mind, let me introduce you to a select group of friends I would get to know if I were in your shoes.

Nancy Pearcey's *Total Truth* (Wheaton, IL: Crossway, 2004) is the book to read for further analysis of the issues presented in chapters 1 to 3. My book with Klaus Issler (*The Lost Virtue of Happiness* [Colorado Springs, CO: NavPress, 2006]) provides further analysis of some of the key shifts mentioned in chapter 4; more importantly, it offers a personal strategy for learning to march to a different drummer than the one leading the march toward secularism.

Regarding the Kingdom Triangle, if I had to pick one book to encourage and equip believers to recapture knowledge and the life of the mind, it would be Lee Strobel's *The Case for Christ* (Grand Rapids: Zondervan, 1998). Similarly, my first choice for additional insight on spiritual formation is Dallas Willard's *Renovation of the Heart* (Colorado Springs, CO: NavPress, 2002). For books that provide a thoughtful, balanced treatment of Kingdom power that is must reading for all sides of this dispute, two books are crucial: Rich Nathan and Ken Wilson, *Empowered Evangelicals* (Ann Arbor, MI: Servant, 1995), and Sam Storms, *Convergence: Spiritual Journeys of a Charismatic Calvinist* (Kansas City, MO: Enjoying God Ministries, 2005). Finally, for learning to make progress in Kingdom power, you can't do better than Jack Deere's two books with Zondervan entitled *Surprised by the Power of the Spirit* (1993) and *Surprised by the Voice of God* (1996).

If you forced me to narrow this list to four, I would select Willard, the book by Nathan and Wilson, and the two by Deere. If you were going to read only one book, then I would recommend Willard's.

A Selectively Annotated Bibliography

Some of these sources are drawn from the endnotes and some of these sources are supplemental to those already identified in the notes. All sources are alphabetized and organized according to the chapter in which they appear and classified in association with their level of readership. The "beginner" level is intended for anyone with at least a high school background. "Intermediate" is intended for both high school and undergraduate readers. "Advanced" is intended for individuals in graduate or postgraduate work.

Chapter 1: The Hunger for Drama in a Thin World

Beginner

Pearcey, Nancy. *Total Truth: Liberating Christianity from Its Cultural Captivity.* Wheaton, IL: Crossway, 2004. Awarded a Gold Medallion award, this is a helpful book for further analysis of the issues presented in chapters 1–3.

Russell, Bertrand. "A Free Man's Worship." Pages 104–16 in *Why I Am Not a Christian*, ed. Paul Edwards (New York: Simon & Schuster, 1957). Regarding the existence of intrinsic value, recall that Bertrand Russell's depiction of the universe cited in chapter 1 is the most consistent one for a naturalist to adopt.

Shalit, Wendy. *A Return to Modesty: Discovering the Lost Virtue.* New York: Free Press, 1999.

Shapiro, Ben. *Porn Generation: How Social Liberalism Is Corrupting Our Future.* Washington, D.C.: Regnery, 2005. Shapiro provides documentation of the widespread celebration of and addiction to sexual perversion and pornography in Western culture, especially on college campuses. What Shapiro fails to see, however, is that the ultimate locus of responsibility for the ethics of sexual perversion is the shift in understanding regarding ethical and, ultimately, theological knowledge in those institutions.

Sire, James. *The Universe Next Door: A Basic Worldview Catalog.* 4th ed. Downers Grove, IL: InterVarsity Press, 2004. A handy compare/contrast catalog of prominent Western and Eastern worldviews, including Christianity, naturalism, and postmodernism.

Intermediate

Carter, Stephen L. *The Culture of Disbelief: How American Law and Politics Trivialize Religious Devotion*. New York: Basic Books, 1993. Carter is a Yale professor of law and has become one of America's foremost "public intellectuals" concerning the role of religion in the marketplace.

Cushman, Philip. "Why the Self is Empty: Toward a Historically Situated Psychology." *American Psychologist* 45 (May 1990): 599–611. Cushman is a professor at the California School of Professional Psychology. The thesis of this piece becomes more developed in later works, including a coauthored article with Peter Gilford titled, "From Emptiness to Multiplicity: The Self at the Year 2000," *Psychohistory Review* 27, 2 (1999): 15–31; also see P. Cushman, "How Psychology Erodes Personhood," *Journal of Theoretical and Philosophical Psychology* 22, 2 (2002): 103–13.

Hartwig, Mark, and P. A. Nelson. *Invitation to Conflict: A Retrospective Look at the California Science Framework*. Colorado Springs, CO: Access Research Network, 1992. For more information on the Access Research Network, which produced this study, see their website: http://www.arn.org/.

Sorokin, Pitirim. *The Crisis of Our Age: The Social and Cultural Outlook*. New York: Dutton, 1941. A renowned Harvard sociologist who divided cultures into two major types: *sensate* and *ideational*.

Advanced

Mavrodes, George. "Religion and the Queerness of Morality." Pages 213–26 in *Rationality, Religious Belief, and Moral Commitment*, ed. Robert Audi and William Wainwright. Ithaca, NY: Cornell Univ. Press, 1986. Mavrodes is professor emeritus in the philosophy department at the University of Michigan.

Rachels, James. *The End of Life*. Oxford: Oxford Univ. Press, 1986. I offer a critique of Rachels in my "James Rachels and the Active Euthanasia Debate," *Journal of the Evangelical Theological Society* 31 (March 1988): 81–90. (This is reprinted in Francis Beckwith, ed., *Do the Right Thing* [Boston: Jones & Bartlett, 1996], 239–46; David K. Clark and Robert V. Rakestraw, eds., *Readings in Christian Ethics; Vol. 2: Issues and Applications* [Grand Rapids: Baker, 1996], 102–8.)

CHAPTER 2: THE NATURALIST STORY

Beginner

"Address delivered on September 20, 1912, at the opening of the 101st session of Princeton Theological Seminary." Reprinted in J. Gresham Machen, *What Is Christianity? and Other Addresses*. Grand Rapids: Eerdmans, 1951.

Barlow, N., ed. *The Autobiography of Charles Darwin*. New York: Harcourt Brace, 1959.

Dembski, William A. *Darwin's Nemesis: Phillip Johnson and the Intelligent Design Movement.* Downers Grove, IL: InterVarsity Press, 2006.

Gould, Stephen Jay. "The Meaning of Life." *Life* (December 1988), 84.

Johnson, Phillip E. *The Right Questions.* Downers Grove, IL: InterVarsity Press, 2002.

_____. *Darwin on Trial.* Downers Grove, IL: InterVarsity Press, 1991.

Kinsley, Michael. "If You Believe Embryos Are Humans ... Then Curbing Research on Stem Cells Is an Odd Place to Start Protecting Them." *Time* (June 25, 2001), 80.

Wells, Jonathan. *Icons of Evolution.* Washington, D.C.: Regnery, 2000.

Willard, Dallas. *The Divine Conspiracy.* San Francisco: HarperSanFrancisco, 1998.

Intermediate

Dembski, William A. *The Design Inference: Eliminating Chance through Small Probabilities.* Cambridge: Cambridge Univ. Press, 1998. Examines the design argument in a post-Darwinian context and analyzes the connections linking chance, probability, and intelligent causation.

Kuhse, Helga, and Peter Singer. *Should the Baby Live?* Oxford: Oxford Univ. Press, 1985.

Moreland, J. P. *Scaling the Secular City: A Defense of Christianity.* Grand Rapids: Baker, 1987.

Moreland, J. P., and Kai Nielsen. *Does God Exist? The Debate between Theists and Atheists.* Buffalo, NY: Prometheus, 1993.

Pojman, Louis. *Ethics: Discovering Right and Wrong.* Belmont, CA: Wadsworth, 1990.

Advanced

Barrow, John, and Frank Tipler. *The Anthropic Cosmological Principle.* Oxford: Clarendon, 1986.

Bishop, John. *Natural Agency.* Cambridge: Cambridge Univ. Press, 1989.

Callahan, Daniel. "Minimalist Ethics." *The Hastings Center Report* 11 (October 1981): 19–25. The main intellectual factor left out of Callahan's analysis is a loss of belief among cultural elites in particular, and the broader public in general, in the existence of nonempirical, nonscientific knowledge, especially of moral and religious knowledge.

Churchland, Paul. *Matter and Consciousness: A Contemporary Introduction to the Philosophy of Mind.* Cambridge, MA: MIT Press, 1984.

Dennett, Daniel. *Elbow Room: The Varieties of Free Will Worth Wanting.* Cambridge, MA: MIT Press, 1984.

Hoffman, Joshua, and Gary S. Rosenkrantz. *Substance: Its Nature and Existence.* London: Routledge, 1997.

MacIntyre, Alasdair. *After Virtue: A Study in Moral Theory.* 2nd ed. Notre Dame, IN: Univ. of Notre Dame Press, 1984.

Mackie, J. L. *Ethics: Inventing Right and Wrong.* New York: Penguin, 1977.

_____. *The Miracle of Theism: Arguments for and against the Existence of God.* Oxford: Clarendon, 1982.

Moreland, J. P., ed. *The Creation Hypothesis: Scientific Evidence for a Designer.* Downers Grove, IL: InterVarsity Press, 1994.

Moreland, J. P., and William Lane Craig, eds. *Naturalism: A Critical Analysis.* London: Routledge, 2000.

Papineau, David. *Philosophical Naturalism.* Oxford: Blackwell, 1993.

Post, John. *Metaphysics: A Contemporary Introduction.* New York: Paragon, 1991.

Ruse, Michael. "Evolutionary Theory and Christian Ethics." Pages 262–69 in *The Darwinian Paradigm: Essays on Its History, Philosophy, and Religious Implications.* London: Routledge, 1989.

Searle, John. *Minds, Brains, and Science.* Cambridge, MA: Harvard Univ. Press, 1984.

Sellars, Wilfred. *Science, Perception, and Reality.* London: Routledge & Kegan Paul, 1963.

CHAPTER 3: THE POSTMODERN PERSPECTIVE
Beginner

Beckwith, Francis J., and Gregory Koukl. *Feet Firmly Planted in Mid-Air.* Grand Rapids: Baker, 1998. A popular, accessible, but thorough critique of prorelativism arguments.

Horowitz, David. *The Professors: The 101 Most Dangerous Academics in America.* Washington, D.C.: Regnery, 2006. Horowitz gets the sociological analyses right, but his analysis does not go far enough. For example, Horowitz does not mention the shift in epistemology (the emergence of scientism that eliminates ethical, religious, and political knowledge) that greased the skids for the radicals in the first place. Rather, he seems to accept this shift himself.

McLaren, Brian. "Emergent Evangelism." *Christianity Today* (November 2004), 42–43. McLaren is generally recognized as one of the prominent so-called emergent church pastor-leaders. To be sure, McLaren is not a philosopher, but I believe that his statements represent crucial data that should be taken into account by any Christian—scholar or otherwise—before they climb into bed with postmodern thought.

Intermediate

Carson, D. A. *Becoming Conversant with the Emerging Church*. Grand Rapids: Zondervan, 2005. An excellent and fair-minded evaluation of the Emergent Church Movement.

Groothuis, Douglas. *Truth Decay*. Downers Grove, IL: InterVarsity Press, 2000. This is the best, most accessible treatment of postmodernism available.

Meek, Ester Lightcap. *Longing to Know*. Grand Rapids: Brazos, 2003. A provocative text that underscores the moral responsibility that all knowers have to reality.

Natoli, Joseph P. *A Primer to Postmodernity*. Oxford: Blackwell, 1997.

Smith, R. Scott. *Truth and the New Kind of Christian: The Emerging Effects of Postmodernism in the Church*. Wheaton, IL: Crossway, 2005. Philosophically astute, gracious but discerning in its assessment. Furthermore, this critique, unlike Carson's, has been respected by Emergent leaders like Tony Jones.

Advanced

Husserl, Edmund. *The Crisis of European Sciences*. Evanston, IL: Northwest Univ. Press, 1970. Husserl ponders the question of just how it happened that arguably the most educated society in history (Germany) could have so easily been led by powerful leaders into some of the most barbarous actions and values the world has ever seen.

Kenneson, Philip D. "There's No Such Thing as Objective Truth, and It's a Good Thing, Too." Pages 155–71 in *Christian Apologetics in a Postmodern World*, ed. by Timothy Phillips and Dennis Okholm. Downers Grove, IL: InterVarsity Press, 1995.

Moreland, J. P. "Postmodernism and the Intelligent Design Movement." *Philosophia Christi* NS 1 (Winter 1999): 97–101.

Putnam, Hilary. "Beyond the Fact-Value Dichotomy." Published in an internal Harvard University faculty newsletter (March 1982). Putnam is an emeritus professor of philosophy at Harvard University. His views are further expounded in *The Collapse of the Fact/Value Dichotomy and Other Essays* (Cambridge, MA: Harvard Univ. Press, 2002).

_____. *Reason, Truth, and History*. Cambridge: Cambridge Univ. Press, 1981, especially chapters 6 and 9.

Reuben, Julie A. *The Making of the Modern University: Intellectual Transformation and the Marginalization of Morality*. Chicago: Univ. of Chicago Press, 1996. An authoritative work from a Harvard history scholar, which painstakingly details the transition from the American liberal arts college to the modern research university from 1880–1930.

Rorty, Richard. *Contingency, Irony and Solidarity*. New York: Cambridge Univ. Press, 1989.

Wells, David F. *All Earthly Powers: Christ in a Postmodern World*. Grand Rapids: Eerdmans, 2005.

CHAPTER 4: FROM DRAMA TO DEADNESS IN FIVE STEPS

Beginner

Levine, Michael. "Why I Hate Beauty." *Psychology Today* 34, 4 (July/August 2001): 38–44. As a Hollywood publicist, Levine argues that constant exposure to physically beautiful women has made single men less interested in dating and married men less interested in their wives.

Seligman, Martin E. P. *Authentic Happiness: Using the New Positive Psychology to Realize Your Potential for Lasting Fulfillment*. New York: Free Press, 2002. As a professor of psychology at the University of Pennsylvania, Seligman has spent his career studying psychological and sociological notions of happiness. With the Baby Boom generation, Americans experienced a tenfold increase in depression compared to earlier generations. The cause of this epidemic is the fact that Baby Boomers stopped imitating their ancestors, who sought to live for a cause bigger than themselves.

_____. "Boomer Blues." *Psychology Today* 18, 3 (October 1988): 50–55.

Intermediate

Budziszewski, J. *True Tolerance: Liberalism and the Necessity of Judgment*. London: Transaction, 2002. A thorough critique of the contemporary notion of "tolerance" and how this contrasts with the classical notion.

_____. *The Revenge of Conscience: Politics and the Fall of Man*. Dallas: Spence, 2000. Provides a thorough theological and philosophical critique of contemporary political forms.

George, Robert P. *Clash of Orthodoxies: Law, Morality and Religion in Crisis*. Wilmington, DE: ISI Books, 2001. An accessible text that refutes secularism and shows that religious reasons are warranted in a contemporary, American democratic context.

McMahon, Darrin M. *Happiness: A History*. New York: Atlantic Monthly, 2005. This book offers an intellectual history that emphasizes how happiness has been viewed as a "natural right" and as an "entitlement."

Novak, Michael. "The Judeo-Christian Foundation of Human Dignity, Personal Liberty, and the Concept of the Person." *Journal of Markets & Morality* 1, 2 (October 1998): 107–21.

Ringenberg, William C. *The Christian College: A History of Protestant Higher Education in America*. 2nd ed. Grand Rapids: Baker, 2006.

Schoch, Richard W. *The Secret of Happiness: Three Thousand Years of Searching for the Good Life*. New York: Scribner, 2006. Provides a comparative religion approach to the "good life." Schoch argues that every strategy for happiness can be placed in one of four categories: "living for pleasure," "conquering desire," "transcending reason," and "enduring suffering." (The book is divided into these four parts.)

White, Nicholas. *A Brief History of Happiness*. Malden, MA: Blackwell, 2006. Provides a philosophical compare/contrast of the ancient and modern notion of happiness.

Advanced

Annas, Julia. *The Morality of Happiness*. New York: Oxford Univ. Press, 2004. Annas' text is perhaps the premier work on the ancient conception of *eudaimonia* as advanced in primary sources from Aristotle, Plato, the Stoics, and many other Greek philosophers.

Beauchamp, Tom L. *Philosophical Ethics*. New York: McGraw-Hill, 1982. Beauchamp considers and rejects an objective theory of value because, among other things, it seems to be futile and presumptuous to attempt to develop such a general theory. As a replacement, Beauchamp proffers subjective preference utilitarianism, according to which the value of an act lies in its maximization of the satisfaction of desires and wants that express individual preferences.

Elkins, Richard. "Secular Fundamentalism and Democracy." *Journal of Markets & Morality* 8, 1 (Spring 2005): 81–93. Critiques the view that democracy requires religious arguments and religious believers to be excluded from political discourse and then offers an alternative to the inadequacy of "secular fundamentalism."

Gregg, Samuel. *On Ordered Liberty: A Treatise on the Free Society*. Lanham, MD: Lexington, 2003. Reviewer Daniel J. Mahoney (Assumption College) writes that "this concise introduction to the principles of the free society provides a welcome antidote to the unreflective relativism that dominates important currents of contemporary academic moral and political philosophy."

Hick, John H. *Death and Eternal Life*. San Francisco: Harper & Row, 1980.

Noll, Mark A. *The Scandal of the Evangelical Mind*. Grand Rapids: Eerdmans, 1994. The "scandal" that Noll outlines "is that there is not much of an evangelical mind."

Smith, R. Scott. *Virtue Ethics and Moral Knowledge: Philosophy of Language after MacIntyre and Hauerwas*. Aldershot, UK: Ashgate, 2003. Offers a thorough critique of Alasdair MacIntyre and Stanley Hauerwas' "linguistic virtue ethics" by showing its failure as a form of moral knowledge and its implications for any further theory of moral knowledge.

Wells, David F. *No Place for Truth*. Grand Rapids: Eerdmans, 1993.

Yu, Jiyuan, and Jorge J. E. Gracia. *Rationality and Happiness: From the Ancients to the Early Medievals.* Rochester, NY: Univ. of Rochester Press, 2003. A multiauthored volume that provides contemporary ancient and medieval scholarship on the conceptual development of *eudaimonia*.

Chapter 5: The Recovery of Knowledge

Beginner

Strobel, Lee. *The Case for Christ: A Journalist's Personal Investigation of the Evidence for Jesus.* Grand Rapids: Zondervan, 1998. Regarding the Kingdom Triangle, if I had to pick one book to encourage and equip believers to recapture knowledge and the life of the mind, it would be this book.

Virkler, Mark and Patti. *Dialogue with God.* Gainsville, FL: Bridge-Logos, 1986.

Intermediate

Beckwith, Francis J., William Lane Craig, and J. P. Moreland. *To Everyone an Answer: A Case for the Christian Worldview.* Downers Grove, IL: InterVarsity Press, 2004. Perhaps the best multiauthored, single volume on Christian apologetics to date. Topics covered in this book include the relationship between faith and reason, arguments for the existence of God, the case for Christ's resurrection, the postmodern challenge to Christianity, Islam, Mormonism, the problem of evil, the existence of the soul, and Eastern thought.

Budziszewski, J. *What We Can't Not Know: A Guide.* Dallas: Spence, 2003. A thorough case for natural law and its formative role in the recovery of moral knowledge. It expands what Budziszewski previously wrote in his 1986 book, *The Resurrection of Nature: Political Theory and the Human Character* (Ithaca, NY: Cornell Univ. Press, 1986).

Richardson, Cyril C. *Early Christian Fathers.* New York: Macmillan, 1970. This text, coupled with the exemplary insights of Michael Green's *Evangelism in the Early Church*, demonstrates that the early church's kingdom priorities included apologetic defenses, demonstration of the kingdom's miraculous power, and compassion for the poor. For example, consider the following citations: Eusebius, *Ecclesiastical History* 4.3 (LCL 1.309); Justin Martyr, *First Apology* 1; Tertullian, *Apology* 37 (LCL 173); idem, *To Scapula* 4 (FC 10.173).

Advanced

Audi, Robert. *Epistemology: A Contemporary Introduction to the Theory of Knowledge.* 2nd ed. New York: Routledge, 2003. A helpful, thorough introduction that admirably distinguishes the central problems, questions, issues, and definitions of contemporary, analytic epistemology. A helpful supplement is

Michael Huemer's *Epistemology: Contemporary Readings* (London: Routledge, 2002).

Chisholm, Roderick. *The Problem of the Criterion*. Milwaukee: Marquette Univ. Press, 1973. An advocate of epistemological "particularism" and refutes "methodism." See also Robert P. Amico, *The Problem of the Criterion* (Lanham, MD: Rowman & Littlefield, 1993).

Henson, Herbert. *Christian Morality*. Oxford: Clarendon, 1936 (esp. pp. 212–13).

Smith, R. Scott. "Post-Conservatives, Foundationalism, and Theological Truth: A Critical Evaluation." *JETS* 48 (June 2005): 351–63. Argues, with wonderful illustration, that knowledge by acquaintance gives us direct access to reality as it is in itself and that we actually know this to be the case in our daily lives.

Chapter 6: Renovation of the Soul
Beginner

Foster, Richard J. *Celebration of Discipline: The Path to Spiritual Growth*. 25th anniv. ed. New York: HarperCollins, 2003. This book has rightly earned the title of a contemporary classic. For more recent work by Foster, see his *Freedom of Simplicity: Finding Harmony in a Complex World* (San Francisco: HarperSanFrancisco, 2005). For a history of various spiritual formation traditions, see his accessible *Streams of Living Water: Celebrating the Great Traditions of Christian Faith* (Trowbridge: Eagle, 2005).

Jones, Timothy K. *A Place for God: A Guide to Spiritual Retreats and Retreat Centers*. New York: Doubleday, 2000. A helpful guide to retreat centers in the United States.

Kendall, R. T. *Total Forgiveness*. Lake Mary, FL: Charisma House, 2002. An exceptional resource for learning to experience and give forgiveness.

Manning, Brennan. *Abba's Child: The Cry of the Heart for Intimate Belonging*. Expanded ed. Colorado Springs, CO: NavPress, 2002. Manning is one of the few contemporary authors who actually gets right what it means to receive and extend the Father's love. See also his *Wisdom of Tenderness: What Happens When God's Fierce Mercy Transforms Our Lives* (San Francisco: HarperSanFrancisco, 2004).

Moreland, J. P., and Klaus Issler. *The Lost Virtue of Happiness*. Colorado Springs, CO: NavPress, 2006. This provides a detailed examination of contemporary and classical understandings of happiness, along with guidance for a life of human flourishing. It offers fresh insight for working through anxiety and depression, along with a rich discussion of the importance of friendship and how it is best cultivated.

Moreland, J. P. *Love Your God with All Your Mind: The Role of Reason in the Life of the Soul*. Colorado Springs, CO: NavPress, 1997 (esp. ch. 4).

Nouwen, Henri. *In the Name of Jesus*. New York: Crossroad, 1989. When you read this or any other Nouwen book, the important thing is to read not simply the content presented, but the feel, the texture, the tone of Nouwen's writings. Nouwen must be read slowly and with the heart if one is to gain from his writings.

_____. *Reaching Out*. New York: Doubleday, 1986.

_____. *The Way of the Heart: Connecting with God through Prayer, Wisdom, and Silence*. New York: Ballentine, 2003.

Willard, Dallas. *The Spirit of the Disciplines: Understanding How God Changes Lives*. San Francisco: Harper & Row, 1988 (esp. pp. 154–92). Provides a careful distinction between "disciplines of engagement" and "disciplines of abstinence."

Intermediate

Gardner, John W. *Excellence: Can We Be Equal and Excellent Too?* Rev. ed. New York: Norton, 1984. Of course, Gardner is confused about to whom we owe our dedication, and he fails to note that one needs to give oneself to a true and important cause. A life aim of being a good Nazi or the best checker player would, obviously, be a life wasted.

Hart, Archibald. *The Anxiety Cure: You Can Find Emotional Tranquility and Wholeness*. Nashville: W. Publishing, 1999. This book should be on the shelf of everyone engaged in pastoral counseling. A must-read about the relationship among adrenaline, stress, anxiety, and depression.

Issler, Klaus. *Wasting Time with God: A Christian Spirituality of Friendship with God*. Downers Grove, IL: InterVarsity Press, 2001.

Lasch, Christopher. *The Culture of Narcissism: American Life in an Age of Diminishing Expectations*. New York: Warner, 1979 (esp. ch. 2). Sociologically and historically demonstrates how the "empty self" is infectiously narcissistic.

Wells, David F. *Losing Our Virtue: Why the Church Must Recover Its Moral Vision*. Grand Rapids: Eerdmans, 1998.

Willard, Dallas. *The Renovation of the Heart: Putting on the Character of Christ*. Colorado Springs, CO: NavPress, 2002. Unquestionably, my first choice for additional insight on spiritual formation is Willard's work, especially this book. For a great introduction (if not a synthesis of sorts) on Willard's conception of discipleship and spiritual formation, see *The Great Omission: Rediscovering Jesus' Essential Teachings on Discipleship* (San Francisco: HarperSanFrancisco, 2006).

Advanced

Childre, Doc, and Howard Martin. *The HeartMath Solution*. San Francisco: HarperSanFrancisco, 1999. More research and scientific studies can be found at their website: http://www.heartmath.org/research/research-publications. html.

Dysinger, Luke. *Psalmody and Prayer in the Writings of Evagrius Ponticus.* Oxford: Oxford Univ. Press, 2005 (esp. p. 104).

Russell, Walter. *The Flesh/Spirit Controversy in Galatians.* Lanham, MD: Univ. Press of America, 1997.

Chapter 7: Restoring the Kingdom's Miraculous Power

Beginner

Barna, George. *Revolution.* Carol Stream, IL: Tyndale, 2005. Based on his polling research, Barna warns that there is a growing sense of boredom with playing church, with the encrusted practices of the traditional church whose only rationale is that they are how we have always done church.

Best, Gary. *Naturally Supernatural.* Cape Town, South Africa: Vineyard International, 2005. This helpful Third Wave text provides biblical insight and personal stories administered by pastoral wisdom regarding what it means to be "naturally supernatural."

Casdorph, Richard. *Real Miracles: Indisputable Evidence That God Heals.* Gainesville, FL: Bridge-Logos, 2003. Casdorph's, Chavda's, and Cherry's books are helpful texts that document that there is medical evidence for healing.

Chavda, Mahesh. *Only Love Can Make a Miracle.* Charlotte, NC: Mahesh Chavda, 1990.

Cherry, Reginal. *Healing Prayer: God's Divine Intervention in Medicine, Faith, and Prayer.* Nashville: Nelson, 1999.

Jackson, Bill. *The Quest for the Radical Middle: A History of the Vineyard.* Cape Town, South Africa: Vineyard International, 1999. A revised edition of this will be available in 2007 or 2008.

Johnson, Steve and Pam. *Theresa: How God Orchestrated a Miracle.* Mukilteo, WA: WinePress, 1998.

Kraft, Charles. *Defeating Dark Angels: Breaking Demonic Oppression in the Believer's Life.* Ann Arbor, MI: Vine, 1992.

————. *Christianity with Power: Your Worldview and Your Experience of the Supernatural.* Ann Arbor, MI: Vine, 1989. These two Kraft books have profoundly helped me in my ministry. I also recommend Clinton Arnold, *Three Crucial Questions about Spiritual Warfare* (Grand Rapids: Baker, 1997).

MacNutt, Francis. *Healing.* Rev. ed. Notre Dame, IN: Ave Maria, 1999. This and Wimber's *Power Healing* provide, in my estimation, the best practical advice on learning how to pray effectively for the sick.

Otis, George Jr. *The Twilight Labyrinth*. Grand Rapids: Baker, 1997. For moving documentary evidence of conversions, see the transformation DVDs done by researcher George Otis Jr. and the Sentinel Group at http://www.sentinelgroup .org/ or by calling (800) 668–5657.

Reid, Dan. "Interview with Graham Twelftree." *Academic Alert: IVP Book Bulletin for Professors* 8, 2 (Downers Grove, IL: Intervarsity Press, 1999): 1–2, 4. Twelftree calls for a revolution in our understanding of contemporary ministry: "Christian ministry that is faithful to the perspective of Jesus and the gospels will be a show and tell activity that ... God [is] powerfully present to forgive, heal, win over the demonic and deliver from danger so that he can have an intimate and whole relationship with his people."

Friday Fax #11, 1997. This is a publication recommended by Jim Rutz that seeks to document credible, miraculous happenings around the globe. These "faxes" are mostly edited by Steve Bufton. *Friday Fax* ended December 2005, but it is continued with *Joel News* (http://www.joelnews.org/frontpage.htm) and *Friday Fax 2* (http://www.english.ffax2.com/).

Rumph, Jane. *Signs and Wonders in America Today*. Ann Arbor, MI: Vine, 2003. Provides examples of credible eyewitness testimony to contemporary miracles.

Rutz, James. *MegaShift: Igniting Spiritual Power*. Colorado Springs, CO: Empowerment, 2005 (esp. pp. 1–55). For up-to-date statistics on this subject, check out "World Christian Database" on-line: http://worldchristiandatabase.org. Rutz has also reported on miraculous happenings in "The Good News about Islam," *WorldNetDaily* (Feb. 21, 2006), 1–2.

Storms, Sam. *Convergence: Spiritual Journeys of a Charismatic Calvinist*. Kansas City, MO: Enjoying God Ministries, 2005. See Storms' website (http://www. enjoyinggodministries.com/samstorms.asp) for further articles.

_____. *The Beginner's Guide to Spiritual Gifts*. Ann Arbor, MI: Servant, 2002.

Wimber, John, and Kevin Springer. *Power Healing*. San Francisco: Harper & Row, 1987.

Intermediate

Arnold, Clinton E. *Three Crucial Questions about Spiritual Warfare*. Grand Rapids: Baker, 1997. More advanced readers will appreciate *Power and Magic: The Concept of Power in Ephesians*. 2nd ed. Eugene, OR: Wipf & Stock, 2000.

Deere, Jack. *Surprised by the Power of the Spirit: Discovering How God Speaks and Hears Today*. Grand Rapids: Zondervan, 1996. Deere has had a profound impact on the Christian community as a proponent of the Spirit's work to heal and provide prophetic ministry. His two books provide theological understanding and pastoral reflection touched by autobiographical insights. To explore prophetic ministry, see Deere's *The Beginner's Guide to the Gift of Prophecy* (Ventura, CA: Regal, 2004).

_____. *Surprised by the Voice of God: How God Speaks Today through Prophecies, Dreams, and Visions.* Grand Rapids: Zondervan, 1996.

Grudem, Wayne A., ed. *Are Miraculous Gifts for Today? Four Views.* Grand Rapids: Zondervan, 1996. Grudem identifies four positions regarding miraculous gifts and, in my judgment, this identification is both accurate and extremely helpful for facilitating understanding and unity among Jesus' apprentices. The four positions are "cessationist," "open but cautious," "Third Wave," and "Pentecostal/charismatic." Sam Storms argues for the "Third Wave" perspective.

Jenkins, Philip. *The Next Christendom: The Coming of Global Christianity.* New York: Oxford Univ. Press, 2002. A distinguished professor of history at Penn State, Jenkins notes that the most significant changes in the world during the last portion of the twentieth century are "precisely religious changes." According to Jenkins, the church is exploding at unprecedented rates in the so-called Third World.

Morphey, Derek. *Breakthrough: Discovering the Kingdom.* Cape Town, South Africa: Vineyard International, 1991. This is the best book that I have read on the Kingdom. Morphey's book is scholarly, exegetical, readable, and practical.

Nathan, Rich, and Ken Wilson. *Empowered Evangelicals: Bringing Together the Best of the Evangelical and Charismatic Worlds.* Ann Arbor, MI: Vine, 1995. The best single volume synthesis of the Third Wave perspective.

Sanneh, Lamin O., and Joel A. Carpenter. *The Changing Face of Christianity: Africa, the West, and the World.* New York: Oxford Univ. Press, 2005.

Tucker, Ruth A. *God Talk: Caution for Those Who Hear God's Voice.* Downers Grove, IL: InterVarsity Press, 2006. If you are in the Third Wave or Pentecostal/charismatic camp, you should read this book. There's much in Tucker's book with which I disagree, but Tucker's book expresses genuine concern about glibness regarding the supernatural. It would mature the so-called "Spirit-oriented" side of the continuum if they would read more books like Tucker's.

Willard, Dallas. *Hearing God: Developing a Conversational Relationship with God.* Downer's Grove, IL: InterVarsity Press, 1999. This book and Deere's books I would wholeheartedly recommend when it concerns learning to hear God's voice.

Advanced

Bradley, James E. "Miracles and Martyrdom in the Early Church: Some Theological and Ethical Implications." *Pneuma* 13 (Spring 1991): 65–81. An informative and insightful article that "focuses upon the beliefs, presuppositions, and attitudes of the fathers toward supernatural phenomena in a setting of persecution."

Fee, Gordon D. *God's Empowering Presence: The Holy Spirit in Letters of Paul.* Peabody, MA: Hendrickson, 1994. Written by a premier New Testament exegete, this 900-page tome is the indispensable contemporary text on Pauline pneumatology in the English-speaking world. In abbreviated form, Fee's scholarship is presented in his *Paul, the Spirit and People of God* (Peabody, MA: Hendrickson, 1996).

Glasser, Arthur F., and Charles E. Van Engen. *Announcing the Kingdom: The Story of God's Mission in the Bible*. Grand Rapids: Baker, 2003. Provides a thorough Kingdom of God missiology, which will benefit missiologists and biblical theologians alike.

Green, Michael. *Evangelism and the Early Church*. Rev. ed. Grand Rapids: Eerdmans, 2003. Highlights three factors that were central to the church's explosive success in her first four centuries: (1) the church's ability to engage in persuasive apologetics and outthink her critics; (2) the transformed character and biblical compassion of believers; and (3) the manifest power of the Kingdom of God by the Spirit through healings, demonic deliverance, and prophetic ability clearly from another realm.

Grudem, Wayne A. *The Gift of Prophecy in the New Testament and Today*. Rev. ed. Wheaton, IL: Crossway, 2000. A thorough treatment of the subject written with the skill of a scholar but with the heart of a pastor desirous to see Jesus' disciples flourish in the prophetic work of the Spirit. Advanced readers will appreciate Grudem's 1982 doctoral thesis, *The Gift of Prophecy in 1 Corinthians* (Eugene, OR: Wipf & Stock, 1999).

Hawthorne, Gerald. *The Presence and the Power: The Significance of the Holy Spirit in the Life and Ministry of Jesus*. Dallas: Word, 1991. This work expands Hawthorne's 1954 M.A. Thesis from Wheaton College, entitled, "The Significance of the Holy Spirit in the Life of Christ."

Kaiser, Christopher B. *Creational Theology and the History of Physical Science: The Creationist Tradition from Basil to Bohr*. Leiden: Brill, 1997. A profound work of primary source, historical scholarship. The last section of chapter 1 seeks to demonstrate that the early church's view of medical knowledge and advancement was rooted in a theology of supernatural healing.

Keener, Craig S. *Gift Giver: The Holy Spirit for Today*. Grand Rapids: Baker, 2001. Provides both biblical and systematic New Testament pneumatology from more or less a Third Wave perspective. This provides a synthesis of sorts from Keener's other works, including *The Spirit in the Gospels and Acts* (Peabody, MA: Hendrickson, 1997) and *3 Crucial Questions about the Holy Spirit* (Grand Rapids: Baker, 1996). Advanced readers may find his Ph.D. thesis intriguing: "The Function of Johannine Pneumatology in the Context of Late First-Century Judaism" (Duke University, 1991).

Ladd, George E. *The Gospel of the Kingdom*. Grand Rapids: Eerdmans, 1959. Argues that the Kingdom of God is primarily the reign, rule, or authority of God himself; secondarily, it is the realm in which that rule is directly exercised, namely, the laws governing the natural world and especially the individual and collective hearts of those who have bowed to God's rule.

Oden, Thomas C. *Life in the Spirit*. Systematic Theology 3. San Francisco: HarperSanFrancisco, 1992. Oden stresses that "as a man, Jesus walked day by day in radical dependence upon God the Spirit, prayed, and spoke by the power of the Spirit."

Rhee, Helen. *Early Christian Literature: Christ and Culture in the Second and Third Centuries*. London: Routledge, 2005. An important work that puts the literature of this era in its historical context and surveys the diversity of apologetic work from some of the prominent patristics.

Twelftree, Graham H. *Jesus the Miracle Worker: A Historical and Theological Study*. Downers Grove, IL: InterVarsity Press, 1999. A tremendous contribution to Jesus studies, since it argues that Jesus performed miracles because he was filled with the Spirit of God. See also Twelftree's *Jesus the Exorcist: A Contribution to the Study of the Historical Jesus* (Peabody, MA: Hendrickson, 1993), which was adapted from the author's Ph.D. thesis.

Wallace, Daniel B., and M. James Sawyer, eds. *Who's Afraid of the Holy Spirit?* Dallas: Biblical Studies Press, 2005. A ground-breaking book in which cessationist scholars rethink the role of the Holy Spirit within that tradition. Wallace and Sawyer identify their view as "pneumatic Christianity" and argue that traditional cessationism is reductionistic and reactionary regarding Pentecostal, charismatic, and Third Wave excesses with respect to the Spirit, and that cessationism is too often rooted in a desire to be controlling. Their book is an encouraging sign that even among cessationists, there is much room for growth in Spirit-empowered Kingdom works.

ENDNOTES

CHAPTER 1: THE HUNGER FOR DRAMA IN A THIN WORLD

1. Helen Roseveare, *Living Faith* (Minneapolis, MN: Bethany, 1980), 44–45. Used by permission.
2. Cited in Mark Hartwig and P. A. Nelson, *Invitation to Conflict* (Colorado Springs, CO: Access Research Network, 1992), 20.
3. For a helpful introduction to postmodernism, see Joseph Natoli, *A Primer to Postmodernity* (Oxford: Blackwell, 1997).
4. Philip Cushman, "Why the Self Is Empty," *American Psychologist* 45 (May 1990): 600.
5. See Martin Seligman, *Authentic Happiness* (New York: Free Press, 2002).
6. Martin Seligman, "Boomer Blues," *Psychology Today* 18, 3 (October 1988): 50–55.
7. For a delightful discussion of what I am calling "thin" and "thick" worlds, see George Mavrodes, "Religion and the Queerness of Morality," in *Rationality, Religious Belief, and Moral Commitment*, ed. by Robert Audi and William Wainwright (Ithaca, NY: Cornell Univ. Press, 1986), 213–26.
8. Bertrand Russell, "A Free Man's Worship," in *Why I Am Not a Christian*, ed. Paul Edwards (New York: Simon & Schuster, 1957), 107.
9. Laura Vanderkam, "Hookups Starve the Soul," *USA Today* (July 26, 2001), cited in Ben Shapiro, *Porn Generation* (Washington, D.C.: Regnery, 2005), 9.
10. See James Rachels, *The End of Life* (Oxford: Oxford Univ. Press, 1986).
11. See Stephen L. Carter, *The Culture of Disbelief* (New York: Basic Books, 1993), 29, 51, 54, 84.
12. For a powerful analysis of the current conflict of worldviews in Western culture, see Nancy Pearcey, *Total Truth* (Wheaton, IL: Crossway, 2004).

CHAPTER 2: THE NATURALIST STORY

1. Address delivered on September 20, 1912, at the opening of the 101st session of Princeton Theological Seminary. Reprinted in J. Gresham Machen, *What is Christianity?* (Grand Rapids: Eerdmans, 1951), 162.
2. David Papineau, *Philosophical Naturalism* (Oxford: Blackwell, 1993), 1.
3. John Post, *Metaphysics: A Contemporary Introduction* (New York: Paragon, 1991), 11.
4. Wilfred Sellars, *Science, Perception, and Reality* (London: Routledge & Kegan Paul, 1963), 173.

5. Michael Kinsley, "If You Believe Embryos Are Humans…," *Time* (June 25, 2001), 80.
6. Dallas Willard, *The Divine Conspiracy* (San Francisco: HarperSanFrancisco, 1998), 92 (cf. 75, 79, 134, 184–85).
7. Phillip Johnson, *The Right Questions* (Downers Grove, IL: InterVarsity Press, 2002), 62–63.
8. Richard N. Ostling, "Intelligent Design Debate Heats Up," *The Orange County Register* (Saturday, Aug. 20, 2005), 14–15.
9. Paul Churchland, *Matter and Consciousness* (Cambridge, MA: MIT Press, 1984), 21.
10. Margaret Carlin, "The Meaning of Life," *The Rocky Mountain News*, Lifestyles section (Wednesday, March 28, 1989), 50.
11. John Searle, *Minds, Brains, and Science* (Cambridge, MA: Harvard Univ. Press, 1984), 98.
12. John Bishop, *Natural Agency* (Cambridge: Cambridge Univ. Press, 1989), 1.
13. Cited in Phillip Johnson, *Darwin on Trial* (Downers Grove, IL: InterVarsity Press, 1991), 127.
14. Daniel Dennett, *Elbow Room* (Cambridge, MA: MIT Press, 1984), 156–65.
15. J. L. Mackie, *The Miracle of Theism* (Oxford: Clarendon, 1982), 115. Cf. J. P. Moreland and Kai Nielsen, *Does God Exist?* (Buffalo, NY: Prometheus, 1993), chs. 8–10.
16. J. L. Mackie, *Ethics: Inventing Right and Wrong* (New York: Penguin, 1977). Cf. Louis Pojman, *Ethics: Discovering Right and Wrong* (Belmont, CA: Wadsworth, 1990).
17. Michael Ruse, "Evolutionary Theory and Christian Ethics," in *The Darwinian Paradigm* (London: Routledge, 1989), 262–69.
18. See Callahan's statement and critique of this position in "Minimalist Ethics," *The Hastings Center Report* 11 (October 1981): 19–25.
19. Alasdair MacIntryre, *After Virtue*, 2nd ed. (Notre Dame, IN: Univ. of Notre Dame Press, 1984).
20. Cited in *The Autobiography of Charles Darwin*, ed. N. Barlow (New York: Harcourt Brace, 1959), 92.
21. Helga Kuhse and Peter Singer, *Should the Baby Live?* (Oxford: Oxford Univ. Press, 1985), 118–39.
22. John Barrow and Frank Tipler, *The Anthropic Cosmological Principle* (Oxford: Clarendon, 1986), 658–77.
23. Joshua Hoffman and Gary S. Rosenkrantz, *Substance: Its Nature and Existence* (London: Routledge, 1997), 98–99.
24. Stephen Jay Gould in "The Meaning of Life," *Life* (December 1988), 84.
25. See J. P. Moreland, *Scaling the Secular City* (Grand Rapids: Baker, 1987); idem, ed., *The Creation Hypothesis: Scientific Evidence for a Designer*

(Downers Grove, IL: InterVarsity Press, 1994); J. P. Moreland and William Lane Craig, eds., *Naturalism: A Critical Analysis* (London: Routledge, 2000).

Chapter 3: The Postmodern Story

1. Cf. Edmund Husserl, *The Crisis of European Sciences* (Evanston, IL: Northwest Univ. Press, 1970), 3–65 and Appendix III.
2. For an excellent and fair-minded evaluation of the emerging church, see D. A. Carson, *Becoming Conversant with the Emerging Church* (Grand Rapids: Zondervan, 2005).
3. See J. P. Moreland, "Postmodernism and the Intelligent Design Movement," *Philosophia Christi* NS 1 (Winter 1999): 97–101.
4. Hilary Putnam, "Beyond the Fact-Value Dichotomy," published in an internal Harvard University faculty newsletter, March 1982.
5. Hilary Putnam, *Reason, Truth, and History* (Cambridge: Cambridge Univ. Press, 1981), esp. chs. 6, 9.
6. Francis Bacon and René Descartes argued centuries ago that the goal of scientific exploration should be power over nature and not truth about the underlying, unseen causes for observable phenomena.
7. Nat Hentoff, "Ideas: The Other Campus Diversity," *Orange County Register* (Aug. 16, 2005), Opinion section, 7.
8. Julie A. Reuben, *The Making of the Modern University* (Chicago: Univ. of Chicago Press, 1996).
9. Ben Shapiro, *Porn Generation* (Washington, D.C.: Regnery, 2005), esp. ch. 3.
10. Ibid., 2.
11. David Horowitz, *The Professors: The 101 Most Dangerous Academics in America* (Washington, D.C.: Regnery, 2006).
12. Ibid., xxvi.
13. Ibid., xlv.
14. C. John Sommerville, *The Decline of the Secular University* (New York: Oxford, 2006).
15. See http://www.oup.com/us/catalog/general/subject/ReligionTheology/American/?view=usa&ci=9780195306958.
16. For a helpful introduction to postmodernism, see Natoli, *A Primer to Postmodernity*. A substantial portion of this section is taken from my invited plenary address at the annual meeting of the Evangelical Theological Society in San Antonio, Texas (delivered Nov. 18, 2004), entitled "Truth, Contemporary Philosophy, and the Postmodern Turn." The address was subsequently published as "Truth, Contemporary Philosophy and the Postmodern Turn," *JETS* 48 (March 2005): 77–88.
17. Brian McLaren, "Emergent Evangelism," *Christianity Today* (November 2004), 42–43.

18. Stanley Grenz, *Revisioning Evangelical Theology* (Downers Grove, IL: Inter-Varsity Press, 1993), 15.
19. Philip D. Kenneson, "There's No Such Thing as Objective Truth, and It's a Good Thing, Too," in *Christian Apologetics in a Postmodern World*, ed. Timothy Phillips and Dennis Okholm (Downers Grove, IL: InterVarsity Press, 1995), 156.
20. Ibid., 157.
21. Natoli, *A Primer to Postmodernity*, 18.
22. Richard Rorty, *Contingency, Irony and Solidarity* (Cambridge: Cambridge Univ. Press, 1989), 4–5.
23. Esther Lightcap Meek, *Longing to Know* (Grand Rapids: Brazos, 2003), 146–47.
24. Ibid., 148.
25. Ibid., 179.
26. Ibid., 182.
27. Ibid., 167. For the best, most accessible treatment of postmodernism available, see Douglas Groothuis, *Truth Decay* (Downers Grove, IL: InterVarsity Press, 2000).

Chapter 4: From Drama to Deadness in Five Steps

1. Joel Kitkin, "A Nation Divided," *The Seattle Times* (May 9, 2004), C1.
2. Mark A. Noll, *The Scandal of the Evangelical Mind* (Grand Rapids: Eerdmans, 1994), 3–4.
3. John H. Hick, *Death and Eternal Life* (San Francisco: Harper & Row, 1980), 92.
4. For more on the contrast between the two senses of happiness, see J. P. Moreland and Klaus Issler, *The Lost Virtue of Happiness* (Colorado Springs, CO: NavPress, 2006), chs. 1–2.
5. Daniel Callahan, "Minimalist Ethics," *The Hastings Center Report* 11 (October 1981): 19–25.
6. Ibid., 24.
7. Ibid., 25.
8. Tom L. Beauchamp, *Philosophical Ethics* (New York: McGraw-Hill, 1982), 83–86.
9. See ch. 1.
10. Michael Levine, "Why I Hate Beauty," *Psychology Today* 34, 4 (July/August 2001): 38–44.

Chapter 5: The Recovery of Knowledge

1. Justin Martyr, *First Apology* 1, cited in Cyril C. Richardson, *Early Christian Fathers* (New York: Macmillan, 1970), 242–43.

2. Herbert Henson, *Christian Morality* (Oxford: Clarendon, 1936), 212–13.
3. See Eusebius, *Ecclesiastical History* 4.3 (LCL 1:309).
4. Tertullian, *Apology* 37 (LCL 173).
5. Tertullian, *To Scapula* 4 (FC 10.173).
6. A longer list was first called to my attention by D. A. Carson; see his *Becoming Conversant with the Emergent Church* (Grand Rapids: Zondervan, 2005), 193–99. In the Scripture quotes that follow, all the italics have been added and any italics in NASB omitted.
7. See Roderick Chisholm, *The Problem of the Criterion* (Milwaukee: Marquette Univ. Press, 1973); Robert P. Amico, *The Problem of the Criterion* (Lanham, MD: Rowman & Littlefield, 1993).
8. R. Scott Smith, "Post-Conservatives, Foundationalism, and Theological Truth: A Critical Evaluation," *JETS* 48 (June 2005): 359–61.
9. Three key books on this subject are Jack Deere, *Surprised by the Voice of God* (Grand Rapids: Zondervan, 1996); Dallas Willard, *Hearing God* (Downers Grove, IL: InterVarsity Press, 1999); Mark and Patti Virkler, *Dialogue with God* (Gainsville, FL: Bridge-Logos, 1986).
10. For more on the content, strength, and centrality of a belief, see J. P. Moreland, *Love Your God with All Your Mind* (Colorado Springs, CO: NavPress, 1997), 73–75.

Chapter 6: Renovation of the Soul

1. Cushman, "Why the Self Is Empty," 600.
2. For more on the empty self, see Moreland, *Love Your God with All Your Mind*, ch. 4.
3. See Christopher Lasch, *The Culture of Narcissism* (New York: Warner, 1979), esp. ch. 2.
4. For a detailed examination of contemporary and classical understandings of happiness, along with guidance for a life of human flourishing, see Moreland and Issler, *The Lost Virtue of Happiness*.
5. A must-read about the relationship among adrenaline, stress, anxiety, and depression is Archibald Hart, *The Anxiety Cure* (Nashville: W. Publishing, 1999). This book should be on the shelf of everyone engaged in pastoral counseling.
6. John W. Gardner, *Excellence: Can We Be Equal and Excellent Too?* rev. ed. (New York: Norton, 1984), 149. Of course, Gardner is confused about to whom we owe our dedication, and he fails to note that one needs to give oneself to a true and important cause. A life aim of being a good Nazi or the best checker player would, obviously, be a life wasted.
7. Dallas Willard, *The Spirit of the Disciplines* (San Francisco: Harper & Row, 1988), 154–92.

8. Luke Dysinger, *Psalmody and Prayer in the Writings of Evagrius Ponticus* (Oxford: Oxford Univ. Press, 2005), 104.

9. Dallas Willard, *The Renovation of the Heart* (Colorado Springs, CO: NavPress, 2002), 117.

10. Richard Foster, *Celebration of Discipline* (New York: Harper & Row, 1978).

11. Henri Nouwen, *The Way of the Heart* (Minneapolis: Seabury, 1981).

12. See www.renovare.org for more information.

13. See Doc Childre and Howard Martin, *The HeartMath Solution* (San Francisco: HarperSanFrancisco, 1999), ch. 1.

14. Ibid., 71.

15. For a fuller treatment of this meditative technique, see Moreland and Issler, *The Lost Virtue of Happiness*, ch. 7. The material here on the heart and meditation has been taken with minor adjustments from this work.

16. An exceptional resource for learning to experience and give forgiveness is R. T. Kendall, *Total Forgiveness* (Lake Mary, FL: Charisma House, 2002).

CHAPTER 7: RESTORATION OF THE KINGDOM'S MIRACULOUS POWER

1. Philip Jenkins, *The Next Christendom: The Coming of Global Christianity* (New York: Oxford Univ. Press, 2002), 1–3.

2. Ibid., 1.

3. See James Rutz, *MegaShift* (Colorado Springs, CO: Empowerment, 2005), 1–55. For up-to-date statistics on this subject, check out "World Christian Database" online: http://worldchristiandatabase.org.

4. For moving documentary evidence of this, see the transformation videos done by researcher George Otis Jr. and the Sentinel Group at www.TransformNations.com. See also, George Otis Jr., *The Twilight Labyrinth* (Grand Rapids: Baker, 1997).

5. Jenkins, *The Next Christendom*, 124.

6. Ibid., 77; cf. 124–27.

7. Richard Spencer, "Millions All over China Convert to Christianity," *The Washington Times* (Aug. 3, 2005), A1, A11.

8. Reported in *Friday Fax* #11, 1997.

9. See Rutz, *MegaShift*, 46 n. 20. The following story is cited in ibid., 21.

10. Charles Kraft, *Christianity with Power* (Ann Arbor, MI: Vine, 1989), 27.

11. 41.

12. Rutz, *Megashift*, 4.

13. Jenkins, *The Next Christendom*, 217.

14. Green, *Evangelism and the Early Church*, 26–27.

15. See George E. Ladd, *The Gospel of the Kingdom* (Grand Rapids: Eerdmans, 1959), 18–22.

16. The best book I have read on the Kingdom of God is Derek Morphey, *Breakthrough: Discovering the Kingdom* (Cape Town, South Africa: Vineyard International, 1991). Morphey's book is scholarly, exegetical, readable, and practical.

17. Thomas C. Oden, *Life in the Spirit* (Systematic Theology 3; San Francisco: HarperSanFrancisco, 1992), 47.

18. Gerald Hawthorne, *The Presence and The Power: The Significance of the Holy Spirit in the Life and Ministry of Jesus* (Dallas: Word, 1991), 234.

19. Dan Reid, "Interview with Graham Twelftree," *Academic Alert: IVP Book Bulletin for Professors* 8, 2 (Downers Grove, IL: InterVarsity Press, 1999): 1–2, 4.

20. Daniel B. Wallace and M. James Sawyer, eds., *Who's Afraid of the Holy Spirit?* (Dallas: Biblical Studies Press, 2005).

21. Wayne Grudem, ed., *Are Miraculous Gifts for Today? Four Views* (Grand Rapids: Zondervan, 1996).

22. Ibid., 341–49.

23. I omit other areas of disagreement because they are less relevant for the purposes of my discussion to follow. For full treatment of these matters, I encourage you to read Grudem's excellent work. Also, consult Rich Nathan and Ken Wilson, *Empowered Evangelicals* (Ann Arbor, MI: Vine, 1995).

24. Sam Storms, *Convergence: Spiritual Journeys of a Charismatic Calvinist* (Kansas City, MO: Enjoying God Ministries, 2005).

25. Rick Nañez, *Full Gospel, Fractured Minds?* (Grand Rapids: Zondervan, 2005).

26. Third Wave and Pentecostal/charismatic believers need to read books written by folks who disagree with them. For example, if you are in this camp, you should read Ruth A. Tucker, *God Talk* (Downers Grove, IL: InterVarsity Press, 2006). There's much in Tucker's book with which I disagree, but her book expresses genuine concern about glibness regarding the supernatural. It would mature the so-called "Spirit-oriented" side of the continuum if they would read more books like Tucker's. I don't suggest this so people will become cynical and overly skeptical of answers to prayer, healings, and hearing God speak. Indeed, I am at pains to say that the Western church needs to lean more on the side of trusting these things than on becoming skeptical. One wants to be wise without being overly skeptical or gullible. But Spirit-oriented churches need to learn from their critics.

27. Charles Kraft, *Defeating Dark Angels* (Ann Arbor, MI: Vine, 1992).

28. Clinton Arnold, *Three Crucial Questions about Spiritual Warfare* (Grand Rapids: Baker, 1997).

29. Jack Deere, *Surprised by the Power of the Spirit* (Grand Rapids: Zondervan, 1996).

30. John Wimber with Kevin Springer, *Power Healing* (San Francisco: Harper & Row, 1987); Francis MacNutt, *Healing*, rev. ed. (Notre Dame, IN: Ave Maria, 1999).

31. See also Sam Storms, *The Beginner's Guide to Spiritual Gifts* (Ann Arbor, MI: Servant, 2002).

32. See Richard Casdorph, *Real Miracles* (Gainsville, FL: Bridge-Logos, 2003); Mahesh Chavda, *Only Love Can Make a Miracle* (Charlotte, NC: Mahesh Chavda, 1990); Reginal Cherry, *Healing Prayer* (Nashville: Nelson, 1999); Steve and Pam Johnson, *Theresa* (Mukilteo, WA: WinePress, 1998).

33. For examples of credible eyewitness testimony to contemporary miracles, besides the sources cited in earlier notes, I suggest Jane Rumph, *Signs and Wonders in America Today* (Ann Arbor, MI: Vine, 2003). Jim Rutz's *Megashift* is a must read in this regard as well.

34. Dallas Willard, as quoted in Bill Jackson, *The Quest for the Radical Middle* (Cape Town, South Africa: Vineyard International, 1999), 380–81.

CONCLUSION: CONFRONTING THE CRISIS OF OUR AGE

1. Jim Rutz, "The Good News about Islam," *WorldNetDaily* (Feb. 21, 2006), 1–2.

2. Carey Goldberg, "The Pursuit of Happiness," *The Orange County Register* (March 11, 2006), 25, 28.

3. Nicholas White, *A Brief History of Happiness* (Malden, MA: Blackwell, 2006).

4. Ibid., vi–vii.

5. Ibid., 173.

6. Paul Campos, "We're Healthy and Wealthy, But Not Happy," *The Orange County Register* (July 10, 2005), 1.

7. George F. Will, "Happiness through Pessimism," *The Orange County Register* (Feb. 23, 2006), local, p. 15.

8. George Barna, *Revolution* (Carol Stream, IL: Tyndale, 2005).

9. Kraft, *Christianity with Power*, 72–75.

10. See his *The Twilight Labyrinth* (Grand Rapids: Baker, 1997); must viewing are Otis' transformation videos available at www.sentinelgroup.org or at (800) 668–5657.

Scripture Index

Genesis
12:11 114
15:8–9 114

Exodus
18:11 114
33:12 115

Numbers
16:28–30 115

Deuteronomy
4:39 115

Joshua
4:21–22 115
23:13 115

1 Samuel
20:3 115

2 Samuel
14:20 115
19:20 115

1 Kings
2:37 115

2 Kings
5:8 115

2 Chronicles
13:5 115

Psalms
4:3 115

Proverbs
10:32 116

Isaiah
49:26 116
65:24 19

Jeremiah
26:15 116

Ezekiel
5:13 116
14:23 116
17:21 116

Daniel
2:45 116
7:19 116
9:25 116

Hosea
4:6 113

Zechariah
2:11; cf. 4:9 116

Matthew
4:23 . . . . 116, 173
13:11 116
16:24–27 . . . 146, 162
22:16 116
22:29 116
24:14 173
24:43 117
28:18–20 173

Luke
1:3–4 117
1:18 117
4:14 174
9:23 146

John
3:2 117
4:25 117
7:17 117
7:27 117
8:28 117
9:20–21 117
9:29 117
10:38 117
14:6 194
14:12 174
21:24 117

Acts
2:22 117
8:12 173
15:7 118
19:8 173
20:18 118
20:25 173
22:30 118
28:22 118
28:30–31 173

Romans
3:19 118
6:11–13 . .150, 152, 163
6:19 . . . .150, 152, 163
7:14 118
8:22 118
8:28 118
12:1 . . . 150, 152, 162

1 Corinthians
4:20 173
8:1 118

8:2 118
8:4 118
11:3 118
12:8–10 175
13:9 118
14:39 182
15:58 118

2 Corinthians
5:1 119
10:3–5 . . . . 32, 37, 46
11:23 13

Galatians
3:7 119

Ephesians
5:5 . . . . 119, 121

Philippians
1:25 119

4:6–7 160

Colossians
3:5 . . . . 150, 152, 163

1 Thessalonians
1:5 119
2:2 119

1 Timothy
1:8 119
4:3 119
4:7–8 . . 150, 152, 163

2 Timothy
3:1 119

Hebrews
2:14–17 174
12:17 119

James
5:20 119

1 Peter
1:18–19 119

1 John
2:3 119
2:18 119
3:2 120
5:2 120
5:13 120
5:15 120

Jude
10 120

Revelation
2:23 120

Subject Index

abortion, 31, 97, 112, 130
Aristotle, 54, 63, 73, 144, 208, *see also* "happiness"
atheists, 23, 26, 27, 28, 37, 46, 48, 77, 154, *see also* "naturalism"

Baby Boomers, 25, 207, *see also* "culture"
belief, *see also* "faith," "knowledge," "truth," and "worldview"
  background, 34
  basic, 33
  behavior and, 131
  central vs. nonbasic, 33, 132–33
  confidence and, 122, 131, 139
  content of, 131–32
  growth of, 133–37, 139–40, 188
  habit-forming, 34
  justified true, 98, 120, 121, 122, 123, 125, 126, 129–30, 132, 186
  moral/religious, 21, 22, 75, 94, 103
  philosophical, 21
  privitized, 22, 31, 36, 45, 52, 53, 130
  reasons/evidence and, 80, 185
  relative, 100
  skeptical, 122
  strength of, 132, 183
  unbelief and, 198
  unjustified false, 123, 126
  will and, 183
Bible, 8, 32, 33, 93, 114–20, 128–29, 130, 131, 150, 155, 159, 169, 175, 178–79, 180, 181, 182, 183, *see also* the Scripture Index

Brazil, 170
Buddhist, 68, 146, 168, 170
Bush, George W., 30–31, 64

China, 168, 222
church, 8, 9, 13, 60, 69, 71, 77, 87, 111, 114, 122, 137, 141, 156, 174, 175, 177, 178, 195, *see also* "Jesus Christi," "Kingdom of God" and "spiritual formation"
cessationism, 175–77, 178, 180, 182, 188, 189, 214, 215
charismatics/pentecostals, 155, 172, 177, 178, 180–81, 188, 189, 201, 213, 214
church (local), 24, 33, 36, 101, 130, 132, 136, 140, 143, 148, 153, 155, 157, 158, 163, 164, 178, 179, 180, 181, 186, 189, 195, 196, 212
church growth, 166–72, 173, 214
early, 111–13, 196, 209, 214, 215
Eastern Orthodox, 14
Evangelical Protestantism, 12, 13, 14, 91, 92, 93, 155, 158, 176, 180, 182, 187
parachurch, 14, 157
playing church, 145, 195
Roman Catholic, 14, 64, 155, 158–59
Third Wave, 177, 178, 180, 182, 187, 188, 189, 212, 214, 215, 216, 223
Third World, 17–19, 32, 167, 169, 175, 191

underground, 168
Western, 111, 166, 167, 169, 172,
    175, 223
Columbine High School, 43
Congo, 170
consciousness, 46–47, 61, 127,
    see also "knowledge,"
    "naturalism" and "value"
culture, *see also* "education,"
    "naturalism" and
    "postmodernism" and
    "worldview."
    addicted, 28, 73, 202
    borrowed capital, 12, 38
    contemporary, 21, 22, 24–25, 35,
        36, 42, 46, 67, 69, 95, 96, 104,
        111, 130, 143, 146
    cult of celebrity, 21, 27–28, 147
    empty self and, 24–26, 37, 95,
        141–43, 147, 162
    Christians and, 13, 76, 83, 88
    high, 94
    ideational, 21, 36, 203
    Kingdom and, 46, 192
    needs, 199
    political correctness and, 9, 12,
        65–66, 73
    sensate, 21, 23, 28, 36, 43, 46, 94,
        203
    secularized, 38, 195
    tolerance and, 65, 70, 71, 72, 73,
        99–104, 107, 207
    void, 12, 21, 30, 195
    Western, 21–24, 30, 38, 66, 89,
        106, 111, 130, 141, 162, 202
    worldview and, 38, 40, 68, 76

Dahmer, Jeffrey, 27, 52
Dawkins, Richard, 55
democracy, 30–31 106, 107, 207, 208,
    see also "culture" and "power"

Descartes, Rene, 67, 77, 83, 123, 124,
    219
Desert Fathers, 155
Derrida, Jacques, 78
determinism, 49–50, *see also*
    "freedom"
    parts-to-whole, 44
    social, 96
    temporal, 44
discipleship, *see* "spiritual formation"
drama, 17–37, 48, 56, 145, 147, 162,
    192, 199, *see also* "Kingdom of
    God"

education, 8, 9, 12, 68–77, 89
    Christian, 9
    decline of, 68–77
    faith vs. learning, 93, 106
    naturalism and, 43, 44
    political correctness, 12, 28, 65,
        73–75
    purposes of, 69, 71–77
    spirituality, 71
    teaching, 34–35, 69, 71, 87–88,
        122, 138
    uni-versity vs. plural-versities, 70,
        74, 194
Emerging church, 67, 68, 78,
        82–83, 205, 206, 219, *see also*
    "postmodernism"
Eshleman, Paul, 168–69
evil, 50–53, 62, 184, 209
    suffering, 28, 52–53, 61, 68, 94,
        208
evolution, *see* "naturalism"

faith, *see also* "belief" and
    "knowledge"
    faith in vs. faith that, 130–31,
        186, 187, 197
    grasp of, 131–33

knowledge tradition and, 8–9,
    76–77, 89, 106, 131, 133, 134,
    137, 138
nature of, 92, 130–33
noncognitive view of, 92–94
risk, 134–35, 140, 180, 182, 183,
    188, 198, 199
flourishing, see "happiness"
Foucault, Michael, 78,
freedom, see also, "moral"
    academic, 70, 71, 72
    cause, 49, 54–55, 63
    classical vs. contemporary,
        98–99, 106, 107, 145
    of will, 49–50, 57, 62, 87
    sexual, 98–99
Freud, Sigmund, 54, 143

Gore, Al, 64–65
Graham, Billy, 135

happiness, 21–26, 36–37, 94–96,
    104, 105, 106, 207, 208, 217,
    220, 224, see also "Kingdom
    of God," "moral," "spiritual
    formation," and "value"
    boredom, 8, 28, 36, 142, 146, 181
    classic, 143–47, 162, 193, 208,
        209, 210
    contemporary, 23, 24, 25, 36, 95,
        106, 144, 145–46, 147, 162,
        193, 194, 195, 224
    depression, 23, 25–26, 104, 157,
        158, 207, 210, 211, 221
    eternal life, 144, 149
    flourishing, 21, 26, 54, 59, 62, 65,
        75, 86, 89, 94–96, 106, 143–49,
        156, 192–93, 210
    paradox of hedonism, 24, 36
    suffering, 28, 50–53, 68, 94, 208
    telos, 21, 22, 23, 24, 26–27, 29, 48,

    54–56, 63, 104, 145, 149, 192,
    194
Heidegger, Martin, 78
Hume, David, 77

image of God, 27, 53–54
Intelligent Design, 13, 44–46, 55, 62,
    94, 160, 176, 204, 206, see also
    "naturalism."
    teleology, 54–56, 63
Islam, 29, 192
    secularism and, 30–31
    terrorists and, 12, 31, 37, 91–92, 107

Jesus Christ, 13, 38, 60, see also
    "Church," "Kingdom of God,"
    "spiritual formation"
    authority of, 77, 101, 143–44,
        145–49, 162, 173, 192
    culture and, 38
    ministry of, 113, 170, 174–75, 188
    Holy Spirit, 174–75, 188, 199
    identity of, 33, 43, 174
    religion of, 92
    teaching, 73, 76, 143–49, 173, 193
    Trinity, 59, 148, 166, 192, 195
    worldview of, 32, 59, 192
Jesus film, 168–69

Kant, Immanuel, 77
King, Rodney, 51
Kingdom of God, 8, 9–10, 13, 14,
    22, 23, 24, 32, 43, 86, 111, 114,
    133, 173, see also "church" and
    "Jesus Christ" and "spiritual
    formation"
    deliverance (demonized), 112, 113,
        135, 168, 170, 171, 172, 173, 175,
        178, 179, 180, 182, 183–84, 188,
        189, 190, 196, 197, 209, 212, 213,
        215

description of, 9, 59, 135, 144, 145,
   146, 148, 149, 151, 155, 162,
   173, 174, 188
drama of, 24, 32, 38, 40, 91, 132,
   135, 140, 145, 146, 148
gospel of, 92, 173–74, 188
growth of, 166–72, 180, 192, 198,
   209
healing, 135, 168, 169, 171, 172,
   173, 175, 177, 178, 179, 180,
   182, 184, 186
naturally supernatural, 135,
   182–87, 188, 189, 196, 199, 212
Spirit empowerment, 112,
   113, 138, 186, 168, 170, 172,
   174–75, 177, 180, 182, 183,
   184, 186, 196, 199, 201, 215,
   216
words of knowledge, 196
Kingdom Triangle, 9, 11, 13, 161, 187,
   195, 199, 200, 209, see also "J.P.
   Moreland"
knowledge, 41–43, 61, 68–88,
   89–90, 91–94, 105–6,
   111–40 see also "belief,"
   "truth," and "naturalism" and
   "postmodernism"
acquaintance, 120, 126–29, 139,
   210
bias, 53, 57, 78, 79, 80
certainty, 44, 61, 74, 83, 115, 119,
   121, 126, 130, 138, 176
Christian, 8–9, 39, 114, 120, 129,
   131
criteria, 53, 102, 122–26
definition of, 114
ethical/moral/religious/spiritual,
   50, 59, 68–71, 72, 76, 77, 86,
   87, 94, 95, 97, 124, 130, 203,
   204, 208, 209
experiential, 79, 116, 119

extent of, 34, 37, 40, 41, 59, 66, 76,
   77, 83, 90, 122–23, 127, 130
know-how, 120–21, 126, 130, 139
nonempirical (nonscientific), 22,
   46, 65, 68, 70–71, 75, 76, 88,
   91–92, 95, 96, 97, 98–99, 106,
   203, 204, 205
of God, 9, 32–33, 46, 70, 114, 121,
   130, 133, 137, 183
propositional, 81, 84, 90, 116, 119,
   120, 126, 129–30, 139
rational awareness, 126
responsibility, 66, 77, 87–88
scriptural importance, 114–20
thought, 8, 9, 10, 81–82, 84, 114,
   127, 129
Kuhn, Thomas, 78

language, see "truth"
Leibniz, Gottfried, 77
Lewis, C. S., 73, 134, 159
Locke, John, 47, 77, 123, 124
Loyola, Ignatius, 156
Luther, Martin, 76
Lyotard, Jean-Francois, 78

Marxism, 23, 77, 96
media, see also "culture"
   Brokaw, Tom, 43
   CNN, 30, 112
   Donaldson, Sam, 65
   Fox News, 73
   Jennings, Peter, 43
   Letterman, David, 65
   Leno, Jay, 65
   MSNBC, 112
   Newsweek, 43
   People magazine, 28
   Rather, Dan, 43,
   Roberts, Cokie, 65
   Time magazine, 42

Turner, Ted, 32
Vargas, Elizabeth, 39
meditation, 159–61, 164, 183, 222,
    see also "spiritual formation"
Mill, John Stuart, 97
Moore, G. E., 124
moral, *see also* "knowledge" "truth,"
    and "value"
  absolutes, 22, 99
  action, 56, 98, 101, 102, 107
  authority vs. power, 102
  blame, 49, 102
  conviction vs. opinion, 97
  duty, 96–98, 103, 104, 106, 142
  egoism, 58
  intuition, 107
  judgment 57, 99, 101, 104
  minimalistic, 96–98
  motives vs. reasons, 57, 58, 63
  normativity, 47, 56–59, 61, 63, 69
  point of view, 28–29, 56–58, 63,
    72, 96, 103, 106
  principles, 100, 102
  properties, 51
  public vs. private, 21, 52, 97
  rational, 58
  realism, 55
  rules, 27, 58, 96, 100, 104
  values, 29, 72, 100–101, 127
  virtue, 52, 65, 69, 79, 94, 96–98,
    106, 107, 114, 142, 144, 145,
    193, 208
Moreland, J.P.
  acquaintances, 11, 170, 174,
    176–77, 198
  Anaheim Vineyard, 11, 165, 170,
    180, 184
  Biola University, 11, 54, 170, 174
  Campus Crusade, 13, 136, 168–69
  church-planting, 13, 180
  conversion, 12, 174, 182

Daniel Pipes, 30–31, 37
deliverance, 184
education, 13, 20, 175, 180, 182
evangelism, 154
healings, 165–66, 198
Kai Nielsen, 154
Kaylon Carr, 136
praying, 136–37, 184, 196, 197, 198
public speaking, 13, 42, 91, 93,
    135, 154, 180, 184, 185, 198
revolution, 14, 196, 199, 200
self-reflection, 134, 135, 169–70
teaching, 165, 170–71
Talbot School of Theology, 184,
    189
therapy, 14
Third Wave, 180, 182, 196, 198
wife, 13, 142, 165, 181, 184

naturalism, 17, 19, 22–23, 26, 30,
    31, 32, 36, 39, 40–63, 66, 67,
    68, 91, 193, 194, 202, 205, *see*
    also "knowledge," "Intelligent
    Design," "postmodernism,"
    and "worldview"
  evolution and, 21–22, 39, 44–46,
    51, 52, 53–56, 61, 63, 93, 98,
    176, 203, 204, 205, 218
  epistemology of, 21, 22, 40,
    41–43, 44, 45, 46, 59, 61, 65,
    66, 68, 69, 70, 72, 73, 74, 87, 88,
    95, 104, 122, 193, 205, 217, 219
  metanarrative of, 40, 41, 44–46,
    59
  metaphysics of, 40, 46–47, 48, 49,
    52, 53, 54–56, 59, 62
  physicalism and, 46, 62
  properties and, 47, 51, 53, 55, 61
  qualities and, 47, 61
  questions and, 59–60
Nazism, 52, 86, 211, 221

Nepal, 170
Newton, Isaac, 54
Nietzsche, Friedrich, 66, 78

Peck, Scott, 28
pluralism, 64, 65, 92, *see also*
    "postmodernism" and
    "relativism"
Poobuanak, Lun, 168
possible worlds, 26, 37, 98
postmodernism, 9, 19, 23, 26, 36,
    64–90, 105, 122, 139, 191,
    205, *see also* "knowledge,"
    "relativism," "truth," and
    "value"
    epistemology of, 23, 77–78, 85,
        86, 104
    modernity vs., 77
    objectivity, 26, 67, 76, 78–80, 89,
        90
    questions, 85–88
Powell, Colin, 30
power, 30, 89, 95, 98, 102
    authority and, 65–66
    Baconian/Cartesian, 67
    politics and, 9, 65, 87
    postmodernism and, 67, 85, 86
pro-life, 96, 97, 98

Reid, Thomas, 77, 124
relativism, 100–104, 107, *see also*
    "postmodernism," "truth" and
    "value"
    combinatorial, 104
    conventionalism, 27, 100, 101, 107
    cultural, 52, 67, 86, 100–101
    ethical or moral, 100
    normative, 103
    Reformer's Dilemma, 101–2
    subjectivism, 100

Renovare, 158, 222, *see also*
    "spiritual formation" and
    "Dallas Willard"

secularism, 9, 21, 30, 31, 43, 65–66,
    68, 75, 91, 99, 193, 195, 200,
    207, *see also*, "democracy,"
    "naturalism," and
    "postmodernism"
Schaeffer, Francis, 76
skepticism, 122–26, *see also* "belief,"
    "knowledge," and "truth"
Skinner, B.F. 54, 55
spiritual formation, 11, 13, 114,
    139, 141–64, 181, 187, 189,
    196, 200, 210, 211, *see also*
    "Church" and "Kingdom of
    God"
    character, 12, 21, 25, 65, 72, 94,
        95, 106, 111, 131, 138, 144, 145,
        148, 150–53, 154, 156, 163
    christlikeness, 9, 153, 214
    direction, 9, 152, 158
    disciplines, 95, 149–55, 162, 163,
        211, 221
    discipleship, 8, 10, 25, 37, 38, 60,
        69, 76, 88, 120, 132, 134, 140,
        141, 144, 178, 180, 181, 182,
        183, 187, 189, 196, 211, 211.
    examples, 112–13
    flesh, 150–53, 156, 163, 179
    friendships, 147, 157, 210
    habit, 34, 146, 149, 150, 154, 155,
        160
    interior 127, 155–61, 163, 164, 196
Stolen Summer, 64, 65
Swinburne, Richard, 81–82

Teresa, Mother, 24, 28, 29

truth, 9, 19, 23, 31, 40, 65, 67, 69, 70,
    71, 72, 74, 75, 77, 92, 97, 98, 100,
    114, 130, 139, *see also* "belief,"
    "knowledge" and "value"
  absolute, 29, 67, 73, 78, 80–85, 87,
    89, 90
  correspondence theory of, 67,
    80–85, 89–90
  language and, 67, 79, 80–86, 90,
    127, 129, 139, 208
  knowledge of, 87–88, 122, 126
  metaphysical vs. epistemic
    notions, 83
  rationality, 67, 78, 89, 98
  truth bearer vs. truth makers,
    80–81, 84, 90

utilitarianism, 50, 97, 208

value, 27, 33, 39, 52, 59, 145
  fact/value, 69–71, 89, 93, 206, 219
  noncognitive, 22, 69, 71

objective, 23, 26, 27, 29, 77, 97, 100,
    208
real intrinsic, 28, 39, 47, 50–51,
    53–54, 55, 62, 63, 68, 202
subjective, 45, 72, 74, 97–98, 155,
    208
Vineyard church, 11, 187, 212

Willard, Dallas, *see* Author Index
Wimber, John, *see* Author Index
Wittgenstein, Ludwig, 78
Womack, Ray, 137
worldview, 33–35, *see also* "belief"
    and "knowledge," "truth," and
    "value"
  belief sets, 33, 132
  function, 34
  narrative, 23, 32, 77–78, 85, 86,
  questions, 8, 34, 48, 56, 57, 58,
    59, 66, 76, 85, 122–23, 125,
    133–34, 135, 144, 151, 186, 198
  set of glasses, 33–34

AUTHOR INDEX

Amico, Robert P., 210, 221
Annas, Julia, 208
Arnold, Clinton E., 184, 212, 213, 223
Audi, Robert, 203, 209, 217

Barna, George, 193, 212, 224
Barrow, John, 53, 204, 218
Beauchamp, Tom L., 97, 98, 208, 220
Beckwith, Francis J., 203, 205, 209
Best, Gary, 212
Bishop, John, 49, 204, 218
Bradley, James E., 214
Budziszewski, J., 207, 209
Bufton, Steve, 213

Callahan, Dan 52, 62, 96, 97, 204, 218, 220
Campos, Paul, 194, 224
Carlin, Margaret, 218
Carpenter, Jocl A., 214
Carson, D. A., 206, 219, 221
Carter, Stephen L., 30, 203, 217
Casdorph, Richard, 212, 224
Chavda, Mahesh, 212, 224
Cherry, Reginal, 212, 224
Childre, Doc, 211, 222
Chisholm, Roderick, 124, 210, 221
Churchland, Paul, 46, 204, 218
Craig, William Lane, 11, 205, 209, 219
Cushman, Philip, 25, 141, 203, 217, 221

Darwin, Charles, 52, 53, 54, 55, 56, 203, 204, 205, 218

Deere, Jack, 184, 185, 201, 213, 214, 221, 223
Dembski, William A., 204
Dennett, Daniel, 49, 204, 218
Dysinnger, Luke, 156, 212, 223

Elkins, Richard, 208
Eusebius, 209, 221

Fee, Gordon D., 214–5
Foster, Richard J., 156, 158, 165, 211, 223

Gardner, John W., 149, 211, 221
George, Robert P., 207
Gilford, Peter, 203
Glasser, Arthur F., 215
Goldberg, Carey, 224
Gould, Stephen Jay, 56, 204, 218
Gracia, Jorge J. E., 200
Green, Michael, 111, 138, 171, 188, 209, 215, 222
Gregg, Samuel, 208
Grenz, Stanley, 78, 220
Groothuis, Douglas, 206, 220
Grudem, Wayne A., 178, 214, 215, 223

Hart, Archibald, 211, 221
Hartwig, Mark, 203, 217
Hawthorne, Gerald, 215, 223
Henson, Herbert, 112–13, 210, 221
Hentoff, Nat, 68, 219
Hick, John H., 94, 208, 220
Hoffman, Joshua, 55, 205, 218
Horowitz, David, 73–75, 205, 219

Huemer, Michael, 210
Husserl, Edmund, 66, 206, 219

Issler, Klaus, 157, 200, 210, 211, 220,
    221, 222

Jackson, Bill, 212, 224
Jenkins, Philip, 166–68, 171, 214,
    222
Johnson, Phillip E., 44, 204, 218
Johnson, Steve & Pam, 212, 224
Jones, Timothy K., 210

Kaiser, Christopher B., 215
Keener, Craig S., 215
Kendall, R. T., 210, 222
Kenneson, Philip D., 82, 206, 220
Kinsley, Michael, 204, 218
Kitkin, Joel, 91, 220
Koukl , Gregory, 205
Kraft, Charles, 169, 184, 212, 222,
    223, 224
Kuhse, Helga, 53, 204, 218

Ladd, George E., 215, 222
Lasch, Christopher, 211, 221
Levine, Michael, 104–5, 207, 220

Machen, J. Gresham, 38, 203, 217
MacIntyre, Alasdair, 52, 205, 208,
    218
Mackie, J. L., 51, 205, 218
MacNutt, Francis, 184, 212, 224
Mahoney, Daniel J., 208
Manning, Brennan, 210
Martin, Howard, 211, 222
Martyr, Justin , 112, 209, 220
Mavrodes, George, 203, 217
McLaren, Brian, 78, 82–83, 205, 219
McMahon, Darrin M., 207
Meek, Ester Lightcap, 87, 206, 220

Moreland, J. P., 204, 205, 206, 209,
    210, 211, 218, 219, 220, 221, 222
Morphey, Derek, 214, 223

Nañez, Rick M., 22
Nathan, Rich, 200, 201, 214, 223
Natoli, Joseph P., 85, 206, 217, 219,
    220
Nelson, P. A., 203, 217
Nielsen, Kai, 154, 204, 218
Noll, Mark A., 93, 106, 208, 220
Nouwen, Henri, 155, 157, 164, 211,
    222
Novak, Michael, 207

Oden, Thomas, 174, 216, 223
Ostling, Richard N., 218
Otis, George Jr., 198–99, 213, 223, 224

Papineau, David, 40, 205, 217
Pearcey, Nancy, 200, 202, 217
Pojman, Louis, 204, 218
Post, John, 205, 217
Putnam, Hilary, 68–69, 206, 219

Rachels, James, 28, 203, 217
Reid, Dan, 174, 213, 223
Reuben, Julie A., 69, 206, 219
Rhee, Helen, 216
Richardson, Cyril C., 209, 220
Ringenberg, William C., 207
Rorty, Richard, 85, 206, 220
Rosenkrantz, Gary S., 55, 205, 218
Roseveare, Helen, 17, 19, 32, 36, 191,
    217
Rumph, Jane, 213, 224
Ruse, Michael, 51, 205, 218
Russell, Bertrand, 26–27, 37, 50, 202,
    217
Russell, Walter, 212
Rutz, James, 171, 192, 213, 222, 224

Sanneh, Lamin O., 214
Sawyer, M. James, 177, 188, 216, 223
Schoch, Richard W., 208
Searle, John, 49, 205, 218
Seligman, Martin E. P., 25, 104, 207, 217
Sellars, Wilfred, 41, 205, 217
Shalit, Wendy, 202
Shapiro, Ben, 73, 202, 217, 219
Singer, Peter, 53, 204, 218
Sire, James, 202
Smith, R. Scott, 127–29, 206, 208, 210, 221
Sommerville, C. John, 75, 219
Sorokin, Pitirim, 21, 36, 203
Spencer, Richard, 222
Springer, Kevin, 213, 224
Storms, Sam, 11, 180, 201, 213, 214, 223, 224
Strobel, Lee, 185, 200, 209

Tertullian, 113, 209, 221
Tipler , Frank, 53, 204, 218

Tucker, Ruth A., 214, 224
Twelftree, Graham H., 174–75, 213, 216, 223

Van Engen, Charles Edward, 215
Vanderkam, Laura, 28, 217
Virkler, Mark and Patti, 209, 221

Wallace, Daniel B., 177, 188, 216, 223
Wells, David F., 207, 208, 211
Wells, Jonathan, 204
White, Nicholas, 193–94, 208, 224
Will, George F., 194–95, 224
Willard, Dallas, 8–10, 11, 13, 43, 153, 154, 155–57, 163, 164, 182, 185, 187, 200–201, 204, 211, 214, 218, 221, 222
Wilson, Ken, 200–201, 214, 223
Wimber, John, 134, 184, 187, 212, 213, 224

Yu, Jiyuan, 209

We want to hear from you. Please send your comments about this book to us in care of zreview@zondervan.com. Thank you.

ZONDERVAN.com/
AUTHORTRACKER
follow your favorite authors